I Speak English

5

Ruth Johnson Colvin

New Readers Press
ProLiteracy's publishing division

I SPEAK ENGLISH, 5th Edition
ISBN 978-1-56420-493-6

Copyright © Ruth J. Colvin 2012, 1997; 1986, 1980, 1978 by Literacy Volunteers of America, Inc.
New Readers Press
ProLiteracy's Publishing Division
104 Marcellus Street, Syracuse, New York 13204
www.newreaderspress.com

Printed in the United States of America
9 8 7 6 5 4 3 2

Proceeds from the sale of New Readers Press materials support professional
development, training, and technical assistance programs of ProLiteracy
that benefit local literacy programs in the U.S. and around the globe.

Consultant: JoAnn (Jodi) Crandall, Ph.D.
Editor: Beth Oddy
Design and Production Director: James Wallace
Production Specialist: Maryellen Casey
Senior Designer: Carolyn Wallace

I dedicate this book to all those who
have shared their ideas at conferences,
in training sessions, and in their books,
as well as to the tutors, teachers,
and students who have added to my
knowledge and given me joy and
encouragement.

Ruth Colvin

ABOUT THE AUTHOR

For years, **Ruth Johnson Colvin** was interested in literacy as a global mission. When she learned that there were over 11,000 people functioning at the lowest level of literacy in her own city of Syracuse, New York, she decided to do something about it. So in 1962, she started Literacy Volunteers. That local effort grew into Literacy Volunteers of America, Inc. (LVA), one of ProLiteracy's founding organizations. LVA trained volunteers to teach adult basic literacy and English, one-to-one or in small groups. Colvin stresses the importance of a learner-centered, collaborative approach to teaching.

The recipient of nine honorary doctorates, Colvin was presented with the President's Volunteer Action Award, the highest award for volunteers in the United States, by then-President Ronald Reagan in 1987. In 2006, then-President George W. Bush presented her with the Presidential Medal of Freedom, the highest award given to a civilian. She was inducted into the National Women's Hall of Fame in 1991.

Colvin has traveled widely, visiting 62 countries and giving training in 26 developing countries. In a richly varied and exemplary career, she has found it most meaningful to assist and encourage practical, grassroot efforts. Colvin continues to work with top professionals in the field, putting the latest research into layman's language and providing how-to teaching techniques.

Colvin is also the author of *TUTOR 8: A Collaborative, Learner-Centered Approach to Literacy Instruction for Teens and Adults; Off the Beaten Path: Stories of People Around the World; A Way with Words: The Story of Literacy; In the Beginning Was the Word: Teaching Reading and Writing Through the Bible;* and *Great Traveling After 55,* as well as books on teaching native language literacy and many newspaper and magazine articles. She and her husband, Bob, live in Syracuse, New York.

ABOUT PROLITERACY

ProLiteracy, a nonprofit organization based in Syracuse, New York, champions the power of literacy to improve the lives of adults and their families, communities, and societies. It works with adult new readers and learners and with local and national organizations to help adults gain the reading, writing, math, computer, and English language skills they need to be successful. ProLiteracy advocates on behalf of adult learners and the programs that serve them, provides training and professional development, and publishes materials used in adult literacy and basic education instruction. It has 1,100 member programs in all 50 states and the District of Columbia, and it works with 52 nongovernmental organizations in 30 developing countries. ProLiteracy was created in 2002 through the merger of Laubach Literacy International and Literacy Volunteers of America, Inc. For more information, please visit **www.proliteracy.org.**

ProLiteracy	**New Readers Press**
www.proliteracy.org	www.newreaderspress.com
info@proliteracy.org	nrp@proliteracy.org

ACKNOWLEDGMENTS

We Americans are all immigrants or descendants of immigrants—unless you're one of the indigenous peoples of North America. My grandparents came as teenagers to America from Sweden in the mid-1800s. They spoke only Swedish and had had limited education. Someone taught them to speak, understand, read, and write English. I'm grateful to those who helped them, and I hope that, in some small way, my teaching others "pays back" just a bit.

I gratefully acknowledge the help given to me over the past 40 plus years by tutors, students, professionals, and volunteers in the field of teaching English to speakers of other languages (ESOL). This book blends and incorporates the most practical ideas for effective teaching that I have learned from interviews with practitioners and students; from workshops, training, and classes; from professional journals, reports, and books; and from my own experience.

This book does not claim that the techniques and principles suggested are original. We all stand on the shoulders of those who, over the past many years, have shared their research and experiences with us. I am indebted to a number of authors whose writings have reaffirmed my own convictions or whose creative ideas I have adapted. Thousands of students and tutors who have participated in training events have also contributed to this fifth edition of *I Speak English* by adding their ideas and sharing their experiences. I am grateful for what they have taught me.

Visits to schools where English is taught to speakers of other languages—both in the United States and elsewhere—have sensitized me to other cultures, traditions, and languages, as well as to the desire of so many students to be able to communicate effectively in English.

In this fifth edition, I have drawn extensively from the insights of ESOL specialists to develop an approach that emphasizes practical language use, comprehension, and the integration of all four skills—listening, speaking, reading, and writing. While the book does cover some theory, the emphasis is on practical and effective lessons that work in real-life situations.

I want to thank the many individuals who have helped by sharing their talents and time in the preparation of earlier editions of this book. Thanks also to those who responded to my call for suggestions for this revision: Linda Church, Mary Early, Todd Evans, Jane Greiner, Jane Hugo, Robin Morgan, Corinne Smith, Robyn Smith, Cathy Varney, Lynne Weintraub, Joyce Whidden, and especially Amy Thorna of the Onondaga County Library. In addition, I'd like to thank the ProLiteracy organizational members that responded to my call for suggestions: Laubach Literacy of Ventura County, CA; Literacy Link–Leamos, Leamos, NM; Literacy Nassau, Freeport, NY; Literacy Volunteers of Bangor, ME; Literacy Volunteers of Burlington County, NJ; Literacy Volunteers of Doña Ana County, NM; Literacy Volunteers of Greater Syracuse, NY; Literacy Volunteers of Monmouth County, NJ; Literacy Volunteers of Santa Fe, NM; Literacy Volunteers of the Lowcountry, Beaufort County, SC; Loyola Community Literacy Center, Chicago, IL; LVA Literacy Unlimited, Framingham, MA; New Mexico Coalition for Literacy; and ReadWest, Rio Rancho, NM.

A special thanks to my editor, Beth Oddy, for checking out every detail and giving practical suggestions.

My deepest appreciation and thanks go to JoAnn (Jodi) Crandall, Ph.D., Professor and Director of the Language, Literacy, and Culture Ph.D. Program at the University of Maryland, Baltimore County. As consultant, she not only reviewed earlier drafts but also looked at this fifth edition and gave suggestions to put this book on the "cutting edge" of the most recent theory, practice, and use of technology.

Ruth Colvin
Syracuse, NY
January 2012

CONTENTS

INTRODUCTION

English is becoming an international language. The demand for opportunities to learn English continues to escalate, not only in English-speaking countries but also in many other countries around the world. Being able to understand, speak, read, and write English does not guarantee that a person can *teach* English. However, if a person understands, speaks, reads, and writes English, that person can learn professionally accepted techniques for teaching English.

This book of basic professionally accepted techniques and principles is written for those who wish to help people with limited or no English language skills to communicate in English. Detailed instructions are provided for teaching English one-to-one, in small groups, or in classroom settings. By applying the simplified methods described here, volunteers with no teaching experience will be able to tutor effectively. The book will also be useful to paraprofessionals and professional teachers. It is intended to be a resource to which you will want to refer as you progress as a tutor or teacher.

I Speak English is intended for instructors teaching English anywhere in the world. But because its primary use will be within the United States, I have related discussions about culture essentially to this country. Where I have made reference to the United States, you will need to substitute cultural examples from your area if you are teaching or tutoring English in another country or region of the world. However, the same teaching techniques apply. Just remember, it's easier to teach a second (or third) language to people who are literate in their native language. If your students are not literate in their spoken language, you will need to have much patience and employ frequent repetition as you use the suggested techniques. Or you might want to consider suggesting that they learn to read and write in their native language before learning English. (See Chapter 12.)

I have used the words *tutors* and *teachers* interchangeably. Whether one is teaching in a one-to-one, small group, or classroom situation, the principles of teaching are the same. I have used *he* and *she* for both students and teachers because men and women play both roles. All names of students and tutors or teachers have been changed to protect privacy.

The need for English instruction is significant. The United States is a country inhabited by millions of people who do not speak English. They want to learn English for many reasons: for school, for work, for citizenship, or for more effective interaction in environments that require proficient English communication.

This revision of *I Speak English* was stimulated by research on communicative competence, which focuses language learning on real-life experiences. It can be used independently or with other ESOL training materials.

Interwoven throughout the text and the training are six underlying themes that you can put into practice as you teach:

1. Respect for students as individuals
2. Learning and teaching by both students and teachers
3. Sensitivity to adults' need for immediate relevance
4. View of teaching and learning as collaborative activities
5. Integration of the four language components
6. Respect for individual cultures and a sensitivity to cultural differences

I invite you to join me and thousands of others across the country as we work together with people who have asked for help communicating in English. As you help others, you will also learn about other countries, other customs and traditions, other peoples, other languages. You will make new friends. You will be a part of a world building bridges between individuals, between communities, and between nations. As a multicultural society, the United States is strengthened by its diversity. A truly pluralistic nation like the United States requires a good deal of tolerance and respect among all of its residents in order to flourish as a society. You will be an important link in the chain of mutual understanding between cultures.

CHAPTER

WHY ENGLISH AS A NEW LANGUAGE?

Need and Demand for English

English for Adult Language Learners in the Community

English for Adult Language Learners in the Workplace

English for Adult Language Learners in Health Situations

English for Adult Language Learners in Family Settings

Summary

NEED AND DEMAND FOR ENGLISH

Why English? It certainly is not the easiest language to learn, nor is it the most logical. However, English is the major language of technology transfer, air and space travel, and international business. It is an important medium of instruction in many countries. There is a growing trend around the world to introduce English to children at earlier and earlier grades.

Often called a "link language," English is the most widely used second language in the world. People from different countries and language communities choose English more than any other language as their common medium of expression. Of the 7 billion people in the world, approximately one in four uses English in some context (Mydans, 2007).

According to a 2011 brief from the Migration Policy Institute (Migration Policy Institute, 2011), in 2010, 9 percent of the U.S. population over age five (25,200,000 people) had limited English proficiency. That group grew by 80 percent from 1990 to 2010 and became both more linguistically diverse and more geographically dispersed.

ENGLISH FOR ADULT LANGUAGE LEARNERS IN THE COMMUNITY

English is an important basic tool for people from other language backgrounds who want to live or study in the United States, Canada, England, or other English-speaking countries. People need to understand and speak English in order to earn a living, to have access to better jobs, to use health facilities, to be able to enroll in training or institutions of higher education, or to interact with people outside their immediate communities. To thrive usually requires the additional ability to read and write English.

According to the U.S. Department of Education, nearly one-half of those enrolled in federally funded adult education programs each year are students in English as a second language (ESL) classes (U.S. Government Accountability Office, 2009). In the United States, ESL is the fastest-growing instructional area in adult education, even at community colleges. However, there are long waiting lists for entry into many of these programs, partly because adult English language learners (ELLs) are highly persistent. And many adult ELLs work at one or more jobs and cannot attend a more typical class or cannot find an available class. So there is a need for alternative approaches. Thousands of people who want to learn English approach organizations like ProLiteracy looking for tutors.

Although many newcomers to America lead rich and rewarding lives in communities where they can rely upon their native language, most also want to learn English. They want to communicate beyond their own cultural and language groups, to make friends in and outside their neighborhoods, to help their children with schoolwork, to participate in community events, to get better jobs, or to enroll in institutions of higher education.

ENGLISH FOR ADULT LANGUAGE LEARNERS IN THE WORKPLACE

Many technical books are written in English, and because much trade and industrial terminology is in English, the demand for it is worldwide. Many adults want to learn English for their own job advancement, whether they reside in the United States or not.

Persons with limited English language skills are finding it harder and harder to find jobs in the United States, and the jobs that are available do not pay well. Employers are insisting that workers have English language, literacy, and math skills. The need for English in business and industry in the United States has been growing steadily in recent years. In resettlement and vocational training programs, the need for English is paramount.

Communication within the workplace is essential. Companies and service industries have recognized the serious communication problems that have surfaced as they have hired more non-English-speaking employees at all levels—technical, business, and professional. Many employers hold free ESL classes on-site to give their employees needed ESL instruction; others refer employees to local ESL classes or tutors. Not only must employees be able to understand and talk to each other, but employers must know that the workers understand oral as well as written instructions. Lives can be in danger when workers cannot understand safety procedures or directions on the job.

> *A local furniture-making company hired many immigrants, giving them opportunities to use and be paid for the carpentry skills they had perfected in their native countries. These workers were diligent, efficient, and willing to adapt to modern tools and machinery.*
>
> *When a fire broke out in accumulated sawdust, the owners instructed employees over the loudspeaker to leave their posts immediately and evacuate the building. One man from Vietnam, an excellent worker, understood little English. He didn't realize the building was on fire. He paid no attention to the loud voices and confusion, continuing to do his work at his station. The owner had to send another Vietnamese worker back into the burning building to tell him in his own language to leave.*
>
> *After that, the owners set up English classes, stressing not only emergency and survival words but also vocabulary related to shop activities.*

This may be an extreme example, but it dramatizes the importance of effective and timely communication in the workplace.

More and more non-English speakers are being employed in technical and professional fields. Conversely, many highly skilled professionals are working in unskilled jobs because they have serious problems communicating in English.

A majority of maids and service workers in tourist areas like Florida do not understand or speak English. They generally do their work quietly without needing to interact with the hotel guests. However, to get higher-paying jobs, they must communicate with guests and must speak and understand English.

In addition to years of hospital experience, Boris had a degree in nursing from a teaching hospital in Moscow. He read and wrote English well, but his listening and speaking skills were very limited. Though he had hoped to earn money to bring his family to the States, no hospital would hire him with his very limited ability to understand or speak English. He washed dishes at a diner while going to school to learn English.

In a large hotel, a guest was confined to her bed. When the maid entered her room to clean, there was confusion. The guest insisted that the maid come in and clean, but the maid couldn't understand and left. The manager was called, and the matter was settled. But the manager shook his head, thinking more and more about English classes for his cleaning staff.

Many Chinese scholars come to the United States for advanced degrees, having passed English tests at an advanced level in reading and writing English. Their major problem is their inability to understand spoken American English—making sense of lectures, understanding clerks in stores or waiters in restaurants, grasping what doctors or nurses say when they have health problems. Also, because they have had few opportunities to actually speak English, their speaking skills are poor, and Americans have difficulty understanding them. Although they have good reading and writing skills, they find it hard to live in America with such limited listening and speaking skills.

Even those who are professionally licensed and are able to read and write English at a professional level may not be able to advance because of limited oral skills.

Work-oriented ESL training can take place through one-to-one, small group, or class instruction in the community or at a work site, often as the result of a contract between a provider agency and an employer. In a community setting, it is usually best to integrate work-related topics with the students' other major areas of interest and need. In a work setting, instruction will usually focus more on work-related vocabulary, specific work procedures, job skills, and company goals. Even in the workplace, it is best—from both the employees' and employers' perspectives—to individualize instruction to the specific needs and interests of students and to broaden the content while still focusing on workplace needs and issues.

ENGLISH FOR ADULT LANGUAGE LEARNERS IN HEALTH SITUATIONS

Communication with doctors, nurses, health aides, and medical office staff is most frustrating for those with limited oral skills in English. Health issues so often arise in emergencies when lives may be at stake. Interpreters may not be available. English listening, understanding, and speaking skills can be critical in such situations.

> *Gregor was in the car with his friend when they were hit by a large truck. His friend was unconscious. Although people passing by tried to help, Gregor couldn't explain what had happened, for he understood and spoke no English. The ambulance came, and Gregor tried to tell them that he wanted to go with his friend, but the driver didn't understand. Gregor was left standing next to the damaged car with tears in his eyes. He had no idea what to do.*

While reading and writing English are important, understanding and speaking English are often survival skills.

ENGLISH FOR ADULT LANGUAGE LEARNERS IN FAMILY SETTINGS

The children of parents who are not native English speakers usually learn English more quickly and easily than their parents do. In a reversal of traditional roles, children often interpret and solve problems for their parents, which sometimes creates stress in a family. This tension is common in the immigrant experience.

Learning a new language does not require abandoning use of the first language at home or ignoring a family's cultural heritage. Some parents will not need, want, or be able to learn English. Yet for many families, when parents learn English, a mutual understanding between the generations is strengthened. Such a family will adjust more easily to the new culture while preserving the authenticity of its heritage as it stresses the importance of drawing on family strengths and life experiences (Auerbach, 1995). Although tensions will remain in many families, learning English can be a tool for uniting rather than dividing generations.

If one of the goals of family and intergenerational programs is to improve the scholastic achievement of children, then providing parental instruction in ESOL is a high priority. Without English, for example, parents are less able to communicate with teachers and officials in the American school system. Similarly, school personnel find it difficult to understand the concerns of parents who have trouble expressing themselves in English. Children whose parents speak, understand, read, and write English and can help their children academically will in all probability do better themselves in school. Parents who know English find it much easier to participate in their children's education.

- They can read their children's report cards and other correspondence from schools.
- They can talk with their children's teachers.
- They can help their children with homework.
- They can communicate effectively with school health workers and other school personnel.

SUMMARY

The need for teaching English to speakers of other languages is rising as the world community becomes smaller. Communication remains a key goal as people strive to coexist peacefully in communities, in the workplace, in health situations, and in family settings. A common language can serve as an important tool in the development of effective communication among diverse groups of people within the United States.

LANGUAGE AS COMMUNICATION

2

Nonverbal Communication

Oral Communication: Listening/Understanding and Speaking

Written Communication: Reading and Writing

Relationships Among the Language Skills

Trends in Teaching English to Adult Language Learners

Summary

The primary purpose of language is communication. Communication—the exchange of information and thoughts through verbal and nonverbal channels—is accomplished in various ways, using the four specific skills of listening, speaking, reading, and writing. Just how much of our time is spent this way? Researchers estimate that we spend about 70 percent of waking time communicating. Of this, an average person spends 45 percent listening, 30 percent speaking, 16 percent reading, and 9 percent writing. Of course, these percentages vary depending on the person and may change as we adapt to new technologies, but unless we are sleeping, we are probably communicating.

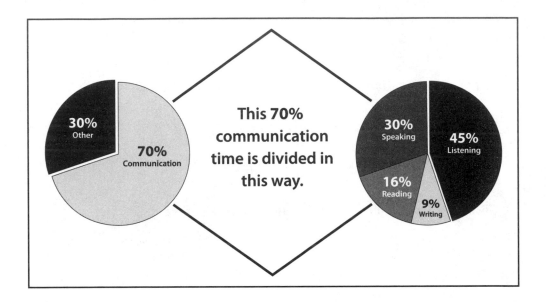

NONVERBAL COMMUNICATION

People who don't speak or understand the same language are still able to communicate.

> When we were in Swaziland, I wanted to visit rural areas to observe their literacy programs and see how I could help. The leaders were hesitant. I convinced them that I could handle any physical hardships, but they countered with my inability to understand or speak their native language, siSwati. I reminded them that there are many ways to communicate—with the eyes, with touch, with sensitivity to mutual concerns and problems. They agreed to take me to rural areas where I sat on the floor in rondevals (mud huts with thatched roofs) with native Swazi women who wanted to learn to read and write. The women accepted me. Smiling as I shook their hands, they looked directly into my eyes and smiled back. We communicated at a deep and inner level, and through an interpreter I was able to work closely with them.

Since nonverbal messages differ across cultures, one needs to pay close attention to what messages students are actually sending through their body language and other signs by listening to and watching them. For example, eyes can convey friendliness or anger. Touch can show sensitivity—it often conveys comfort and support. Showing an open hand or clasping another's hand can show friendships just as a rigid fist can show enmity or anger. Touching another's head often indicates disrespect. A smile or a scowl can reveal inner feelings. Positive or negative feelings and attitudes do show, and the meanings of actions vary across cultures. So as you work with students, be sensitive to people's feelings and learn about and respect cultural differences.

We communicate nonverbally with our body movements—with our eyes or hands or through a look or a pat on the back. For example, imagine I am in a restaurant. I want more coffee and have a hard time catching the server's eye. She finally sees me. I lift my empty coffee cup. She nods and then gestures, as though pouring cream, raising her eyebrows, suggesting a question. I shake my head. Without verbal communication, we've communicated. The server brings me coffee without cream. Sometimes we are conscious of the nonverbal communication around us, but often we are not.

Gestures may have different connotations in different cultures. One can be totally unaware of such nonverbal communications as a raised eyebrow or a cocked head. You and your students, consciously and unconsciously, are sending communication signals. As a teacher, you need to become aware of such signals by learning about your students' cultures and by helping them understand some of the cultural patterns they may experience in the United States.

Music is another form of nonverbal communication. Recognition of a melody can bring a light to one's eyes, even though the words may be foreign.

> *In Russia, I was in a church where everything was different from my church at home—the language, the setting, even the service. However, in the middle of the service, the congregation sang a hymn—in Russian, of course, but to a tune I recognized. I sang along in English, feeling we were communicating, certainly not in words, but through music.*

Many students from other countries are vaguely aware of some American customs, such as the handshake as a greeting. Some common American gestures include waving when departing, beckoning with a forefinger, putting a finger to the lips to ask for silence, smiling to show approval, or frowning and shaking the head to show disapproval. These may or may not be known to newcomers. Common gestures in the United States may be misunderstood or ignored by students since they may have different meanings or no meaning at all in other cultures.

In order to test your own observance of nonverbal communication, watch a TV program without the sound. Can you tell what is being said? Or at a social gathering, stand back and observe the gestures people make, without listening to their conversation. Watch how Americans use their hands; notice how close people stand to each other.

In his book *The Hidden Dimension* (1966), Edward Hall says, "We are often unaware that distances between people in the American society are significant." He suggests that Americans create an "intimate zone" or "personal zone" in which people talk together standing approximately 18 inches apart. If one person moves closer, invading this private area, the other tends to back away. This intimate zone may be much closer or much farther apart in other cultures or may not exist at all.

ORAL COMMUNICATION: LISTENING/UNDERSTANDING AND SPEAKING

While still very young, people internalize the systems of their native languages (the forms and arrangements of words, sounds, and meanings and the basic patterns or structures). Virtually all people are able to perform two language skills in their native languages: listening and speaking. However, not all people can read and write in their own language. In fact, many of the 6,000 or so languages in the world have no written system. In mastering a new language, listening and speaking skills are generally learned first. This makes sense if you consider the following:

- Children understand and speak their native language before they learn to read and write it.
- Almost all people speak and understand their native language, even though many cannot read or write it.

For our purposes, let us consider spoken language as the primary language system and written language as the secondary system. Spoken language is then reinforced by written language as some basic oral patterns are mastered. This sequence seems to be more gratifying and gives students more usable skills than the "translation" approach many of us experienced in our school language classes. How soon written language should be emphasized depends on the individual needs of students. When we begin teaching people a new language, we should consider emphasizing the spoken language. After all, in the course of a day, speaking and listening are required more often than reading or writing.

Some people think that one cannot "know" a language if one cannot read or write it. This is not true. Many people understand and speak more than one language even though they cannot read or write a single word. The converse also is true. Even though a person can read and write a language, that person may not be able to speak it or understand others who are speaking it.

WRITTEN COMMUNICATION: READING AND WRITING

We also communicate by reading and writing words and symbols. Emergency or danger signs and labels communicate practical warnings. Signs giving directions help us find our way. Think of how much knowledge you have learned from reading alone—newspapers, textbooks, magazines, novels, biographies, mysteries, poems, history, literature, manuals, letters, signs, emails, Internet— the list is endless. One way to respond is to take notes, which is impossible without the skill of writing.

RELATIONSHIPS AMONG THE LANGUAGE SKILLS

Listening and reading provide input; they are two channels for receiving information. Speaking and writing provide output; they are two channels for expressing information.

Reading and writing are communicated through written symbols, listening and speaking through aural/oral symbols. If we separate reading and writing from listening and speaking, we fragment language. All four skills are needed in the learning of English.

INPUT		OUTPUT
Listening	**SPOKEN LANGUAGE**	Speaking
Reading	**WRITTEN LANGUAGE**	Writing

TRENDS IN TEACHING ENGLISH TO ADULT LANGUAGE LEARNERS

Throughout the past century and into our present time, we have learned a great deal about second (or third) language acquisition and effective teaching methods. There are several approaches to teaching a new language. (A method is a specific set of procedures compatible with a given trend or approach that, in turn, is supported by certain theoretical assumptions.) *I Speak English* focuses mostly on approaches and practical exercises and activities. Some attention is given to theory to help link practice to core principles.

The grammar translation approach focuses on learning grammatical rules, vocabulary, and the literature of the new language. Emphasis is given to written translation rather than speaking or understanding. Little connection is made between language practice and the real-life communication needs and interests of students. Grammar translation is seldom the only method available for adult ESOL classes in the United States or Canada today, but it is still used in many other countries.

The audiolingual approach reflected a much-needed shift in new-language learning theory by emphasizing speaking and listening skills using repetition and oral drills with controlled materials. In audiolingual classes, greater importance is attached to pronunciation than grammatical explanation, and the first language is not used. Vocabulary is also controlled, limited to learning appropriate words in the dialogue and accompanying drills that characterize the usual audiolingual lesson.

The communicative approach emerged when the need for more practical communication became apparent. It is now used extensively in the United States. It emphasizes practical language use and stresses the importance of comprehension and the integration of all four language skills—listening, speaking, reading, and writing—through natural, authentic, real-life activities and experiences. The students take an active role in the learning situation so that the acquisition of English will be a part of their daily lives.

In this book, we suggest a communicative approach as an umbrella covering content-based language instruction and task-based and project-based learning. We focus on language *use* rather than the structure of language. We emphasize real-life situations and authentic materials, and suggest that you teach listening with understanding and speaking, then balance that with reading and writing. We also incorporate techniques, exercises, and activities from other approaches.

SUMMARY

Communication is a vital goal in learning a new language. Communication can be nonverbal, verbal, or written. A communicative approach is emphasized in *I Speak English* because it focuses on real-life situations and provides students with the practical help they need.

IMPORTANCE OF CULTURE

3

Definition of Culture

Culture Shock

Cultural Preconceptions

Sharing Our Culture

Learning About Students' Cultures

Some Cultural Differences

Respect for Other Cultures

Summary

Communication includes both language and culture. Words have meaning only in the context of the culture in which they are used. For example, if you were to take the *lift* in England, you would be taking the elevator in the United States. But if you asked someone to give you a *lift* in the U.S., you would be asking for a ride in that person's car. Both are English words, but because of the different cultural contexts, the words have different meanings. Some languages have many ways of expressing different types of snow or ice because they are essential aspects of their cultures. Even within the regions of the United States, different words are used to mean the same thing—*pail, bucket; skillet, frying pan; soda, pop.*

Learning about a new culture does not mean giving up one's native culture. But as one learns a new language in a community where other people speak that language, one learns about the community's culture as well. For years the United States was considered a "melting pot" where people from different places blended their cultures into a common American identity. More recently, the United States has been seen as a mosaic of cultures where each group of people maintains its distinctive identity while contributing to a richer, more inclusive society and culture. In the United States, the English language is a major cultural bond shared by most of the population, regardless of ethnic background.

DEFINITION OF CULTURE

Culture is a system of behaviors and beliefs. These belief systems make some things permissible under certain circumstances but nearly prohibited in others. These cultural patterns may vary from country to country and even from area to area within a country. What may be normal or acceptable in one part of the world may be frowned upon in another. In many societies, there is a generally accepted dominant culture to which many people subscribe in various ways. Yet there are often various subcultures that reflect behavioral patterns and attitudes that may be significantly different from those of the dominant culture. Culture reaches all aspects of language and communication.

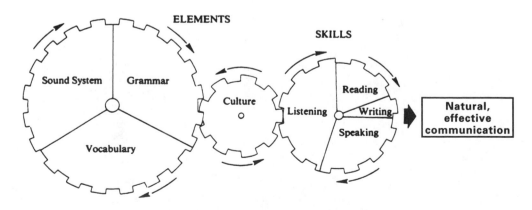

Chart from *Teaching English as a Second Language: A Self-Instructional Course*. Unit I—The Nature of Purpose of Language. Albany, N.Y., State Education Department. 1974.

CULTURE SHOCK

Culture shock is the feeling of disorientation or confusion that occurs when a person leaves a familiar place and moves to a vastly unfamiliar one.

Be aware that ESOL students might be experiencing some degree of culture shock. Outward manifestations may vary. Some people show fatigue and frustration, even hostility; others fear going out alone, depending excessively on fellow nationals for help and companionship. While some adults may feel depressed, others are stimulated. Culture shock affects different people in different ways.

CULTURAL PRECONCEPTIONS

We are products of our culture, and many of our ideas result from cultural bias. Cultural bias often causes stereotyping. For example, we may stereotype the behavior or dress of everyone in a certain group. Stereotypes are too general and too simple. Very few people fall into the "typical" picture. Members of other cultures are as individual as are members of our own culture.

For example, we may imagine all Africans living in tribal villages. However, the fact is that many Africans live in towns and cities very similar to those in the United States and have never lived in a tribal village or heard a tribal drum. Similarly, people from other countries may have preconceived ideas about life in the United States. When they think of the culture of the United States, they may envision gangsters on every street corner and cowboys riding the range and roaming across the American plains.

SHARING OUR CULTURE

People new to the United States often want to know more about the customs, attitudes, and cultural patterns of this country. As teachers, we have a responsibility to help our students learn and understand such information, which should be included in language lesson plans. Like other national groups, Americans vary from individual to individual. However, some attitudes and practices are common among most Americans.

Many Americans like being independent. They see independence as an essential aspect of freedom. Most live and treat each other quite informally with an openness that is sometimes refreshing but occasionally brusque. Americans generally value punctuality—the confusing variations in timing (appointments, plane and bus schedules, etc.) will be discussed later. In America, many women now work outside the home and have much more freedom than in previous times. We teachers may be proud of the United States and its customs, but we must not imply that American customs are the best.

Traditional basic American beliefs, values, and culture are traits that affect all aspects of American life. Stories, lesson plans, and exercises depicting American lives and culture, especially helpful for advanced ESOL students, are included in *American Ways* (Datesman, Crandall, & Kearny, 2005).

LEARNING ABOUT STUDENTS' CULTURES

Many of us know little about the customs, cultures, and even the locations of other countries. As you learn new perspectives and gain more information from your students, you will probably want to learn more about their native lands from them.

Before you start working with a new student, you might want to learn more about that student's country, its customs and traditions, its people, as well as its geography and history. First, find the country or the city on a map. Often it will have a new name or spelling—Zambia (formerly Northern Rhodesia), Myanmar (Burma), Mumbai (Bombay), Beijing (Peking), Kalkata (Calcutta). Then read about its history. Check magazines like *National Geographic* for articles about the country and its people. Finally, read novels that are written by natives of that country or novels that are set there. In addition to seeking out maps, novels, and magazine articles, check with your local librarian and go to the Internet to find other resources on specific peoples and countries. An informative and useful resource for understanding specific cultural and language differences is *CultureGrams,* a collection of information about individual countries and U.S. states published by ProQuest and sold through the Internet (http://www.culturegrams.com).

Learning a new language and trying to adapt to a new culture are difficult tasks, and the process can be frustrating. It is important for ESOL teachers to empathize with students. Becoming acquainted with your students' native countries and cultures can help build the needed rapport between you and them. Such interest on your part is important to building long-term relationships and indicates a sincere interest in your students as individuals. A little knowledge can prevent you from unknowingly offending your students.

Be aware of cultural differences even in learners from the same country. Look at collective as well as individual characteristics. Some cultures have gender issues (female teachers cannot have male students, and male teachers cannot have female students). In many countries, all education is teacher centered. Individual initiative is discouraged. In some cultures, teachers are held in such high esteem that students believe teachers have all the answers, while others are skeptical of anything new.

Consider your students' cultural attitudes toward work, time, family, strangers, experiences, status, problem solving, environment, relationships to others, authority, commitments/appointments, discipline, personal responsibility, and bureaucracy. The more you can learn of your students' culture, the more you will understand the differences as well as the similarities. Remember, both your culture and your students' cultures are equally valid.

SOME CULTURAL DIFFERENCES

It would be impossible to detail all the cultural differences around the world, but you should be sensitive to the fact that differences exist. Greetings, for example, vary from culture to culture. The American *Hi! How are ya?* or a wave of the hand indicates an informal friendliness. In some cultures, it is polite to be more formal and to inquire about the health of each member of the family. Handshaking is common in many cultures, but it is done in different ways— sometimes firm and brisk, other times limp and relaxed. Another approach is to grab the thumb and wrist with a hearty verbal greeting. In some cultures, a kiss on both cheeks is the familiar greeting by both men and women. In some Asian cultures, the custom is to place the palms of one's hands together and give a slight bow. Americans and Asians generally limit touching to a handshake. Latinos tend toward a "touching culture," greeting each other with hugs, kisses, vigorous handshakes, and pats on the back.

When being introduced in America, a woman may offer her hand or may simply nod. She might say, *How do you do?* or just *Hi!* Men more generally greet with a handshake. Teenagers greet each other more casually. Your students will need to know how to recognize the occasion for each behavior. Much will depend on relative social status, age, gender, or perhaps the circumstances of the moment. If your students are newcomers, you may want to try practicing greetings in role-playing situations.

Facial expressions convey various meanings in different cultures. Surprise or shock among people in the United States is often shown by opening the eyes wide and raising the eyebrows. To a Chinese person, this is often a sign of anger, while to a Puerto Rican, it can be a sign of lack of understanding. In Asia, respect for teachers, for the elderly, and for people in high positions is often shown by casting eyes downward. Most adult Americans of any age and status, on the other hand, expect others always to look them in the eye.

The accepted distance between people conversing is influenced by culture. People from some parts of the world, especially Latin America, feel comfortable standing close to one another. In conversation with an American, the Latino may feel snubbed and consider the American aloof because of the American's distance, while an American may feel stifled by the Latino's closeness.

Time is viewed differently in different cultures and countries. In some cultures, a meeting or an appointment at 10 a.m. starts "about 10 a.m."—it is accepted that a meeting will start when everyone gets there. However, in America, time is much more exact. If an appointment is at 10 a.m., it means it'll start at exactly 10 a.m. You're expected to be there 5 to 15 minutes before the designated time.

Some American gestures and body movements may be offensive to people of other cultures. If you're interacting with someone from a specific country, you might want to search for "gestures and body movements" on the Internet to get several websites describing what is acceptable or considered rude in that culture. Here are a few gestures or movements that are not acceptable in some parts of the world:

- Crossing your legs
- Making eye contact
- Touching someone's head
- Sitting so that the sole of your foot is exposed
- Beckoning with your index finger
- Accepting or touching anything with your left hand

Just knowing some of the cultural codes may help you become sensitive to your students' outlooks as you work together.

In many cultures, great emphasis is put on hospitality. Sharing food is an important way of showing friendship and gratitude. In cultures where great importance is put on maintaining a close extended family, any relative, no matter how distant, has the right to ask for hospitality.

In the United States, it is acceptable for dinner guests to arrive five or ten minutes later than the time set, but not an hour late or early. However, job candidates should arrive a little early (e.g., five to ten minutes) for an interview. American time standards vary, depending on the situation.

Teachers are held in high regard in many countries. Sometimes this attitude is so prevalent that students feel the teacher is always right and knows all the answers. Students need to know that this would be impossible for anyone. If you do not know answers to some of their questions, admit it and tell your students that you will attempt to find the answers. Also, students should know that we are all engaged in learning and teaching and that we have much to learn from each other.

Even advanced ESOL students may not understand the cultural differences that they will encounter between their homelands and the United States. These can have an impact on adult language learners in the workplace, in school, and in the community. Your students will appreciate your sensitive help.

RESPECT FOR OTHER CULTURES

It is important never to take lightly another culture's way of doing things. As much as possible, keep an open mind and avoid value judgments when dealing with cultural differences. Instead, show honest interest and learn all you can about your students' backgrounds. It can be fun to taste native dishes from other countries and to learn about their customs and holidays. One culture is not better than another. It's just different.

SUMMARY

If you are conscious of the importance of cultural understanding and if you obtain a basic grasp of effective techniques and approaches for teaching ESOL, you will be on your way to becoming an effective teacher. You will likely become a more sensitive person in your day-to-day life, thereby enriching all of your life experiences.

Getting to know at least one person from another country who speaks a different language helps expand your awareness of the great variety of human experience. Just as the one person you meet represents his or her country and its customs, you may be the only person from your culture with whom your students get well acquainted. Accordingly, you represent a "typical" person from your country or culture to your students—quite a challenge for each of us!

LEARNERS AND TUTORS/TEACHERS

Who Are Those Who Want to Learn English?
Immigration Patterns
International Students/Guests, Migrants, Immigrants, Refugees
Reasons for Learning English
Profiles of Adult English Language Learners
Common Characteristics of ESOL Learners
Summary of Learner Characteristics

Who Are Those Who Want to Teach?
Why People Want to Teach
Is There a Need to Know the Students' Languages?
Profiles of Effective ESOL Tutors and Teachers
Characteristics of ESOL Tutors and Teachers
Summary of ESOL Tutor/Teacher Characteristics

WHO ARE THOSE WHO WANT TO LEARN ENGLISH?

North America is a land of immigrants. Our ancestors came to the United States from other countries and lands. We like to think of them with nostalgia and fond memories. They brought a rich heritage to their new homeland. But if they hadn't learned to communicate in English, they would have had difficulty learning new ideas or sharing much of their traditional life with people from different language groups or communicating outside their communities in the United States. English was and still is the common language for general communication among the diverse groups that make up American society.

Newly arrived foreigners may be viewed with suspicion and mistrust, with pity and compassion, or perhaps with friendliness and generosity. They have been transplanted from a familiar native land to the United States, where they may face a new language, a different lifestyle, strange foods, an unfamiliar government, homesickness for friends and family, and often an immediate need for employment. All of these combine to make life very difficult indeed.

Immigration Patterns

Native American Indians migrated to North America thousands of years ago and Mexicans were living in the Southwest before it became part of the United States. Some groups, such as Africans, were transported and enslaved. Most others came by choice. For a variety of economic, political, or religious reasons, these immigrants saw the New World as a place for a better life.

Spanish, Portuguese, English, and French settlers were followed by Dutch, German, Irish, Swedish, and Scottish groups. Since most of the colonies followed English customs of law and government and the people in power spoke English, English became the dominant language used in America.

Before 1960, the great majority of foreign-born U.S. residents came here from Europe and Canada (92 percent in 1850; 75 percent in 1960). Earlier in that period, most Europeans were from Northern and Western Europe, but from about 1930, the balance shifted toward Eastern and Southern Europe. In addition, many immigrants came from China between 1860 and 1880, and from Mexico between 1850 and 1860 and again from 1920 to 1960. Since 1960, the immigration pattern has shifted. More than half of the 37,606,000 foreign-born residents in the United States in 2010 were from Latin America (54 percent), another 27 percent were from Asia, and only 12 percent were from Europe; 30 percent of this foreign-born population had less than a high school education. One in 10 did not speak English. In 2000, the largest groups in the United States were from Mexico, China, the Philippines, India, Cuba, Vietnam, El Salvador, Korea, and the Dominican Republic (Schmidley, 2001; U.S. Census Bureau, 2011, Tables 3.1 & 3.5).

Often communities developed when immigrants with similar backgrounds lived in the same area. These communities currently exist in all major American and Canadian cities. Historically, Scandinavians and Germans settled in

Minnesota and the Dakotas. Many immigrants stayed near their ports of entry: Cubans in Florida, Asians in California (as well as along the railroad lines across Canada), Mexicans in southern California and Texas. Often, after a family first settled in the United States, family members decided to move to a different state to be closer to a larger, similar ethnic community or to find a climate closer to that of their native country. Immigrants often brought with them a particular skill or trade and traveled to settle in the place where their talents could be utilized and where relatives and friends were already established in similar jobs. It seems to be human nature to want to go where you have friends and relatives, where someone understands your customs and knows your language, or where you can find familiar work.

International Students/Guests, Migrants, Immigrants, and Refugees

People from around the world continue to come to the United States and Canada as well as other English-speaking countries for many reasons. Some come to study and often stay, while others work to get advanced degrees or professional experience but intend to return to their homelands. English is usually mandatory for them, but often their wives or husbands accompany them and know no English. Others come as migrants, immigrants, or refugees—many having no or limited English.

Migrants are persons who move—sometimes seasonally or yearly, sometimes occasionally—within a country or from country to country. We think of migrants who travel from Florida to Maine picking fruits and vegetables, but migrants also move from Mexico or Guatemala to work in the United States.

Immigrants are foreign-born persons coming to live in a new country. Most of our ancestors were immigrants to America or Canada.

Refugees are people who have been or have credible reason to believe that they may be persecuted for their political beliefs, race, nationality, or membership in a social or religious group. Some come because of natural disasters—earthquakes, tsunamis, or such life-threatening situations as famine and drought. Asylum seekers are refugees who come directly to the United States, while refugees typically come from refugee camps or neighboring countries.

If these newcomers to America don't know how to understand and speak English, it is difficult for them to get jobs, to make medical appointments, even to shop or cope with life generally in this new country.

Reasons for Learning English

General needs and demands for English in the community, workplace, health situations, and family were described earlier. But individual students have specific motivations for learning English. For example:

1. They need life skills to be able to survive and function in their new country—to be able to go shopping, find adequate housing, communicate

with medical personnel, answer the telephone, understand the media, and deal with the banking and credit systems of their new country.

Prany and Souk were refugees from Laos, living in a midwestern city. They had two small children and lived in a tiny apartment with only essential furniture and clothing. Prany tried to remember how to get to the local market, but she got lost. Because she knew no English, she couldn't ask directions and found her way home only by chance When she went shopping, she picked out only familiar foods and held out her American money, hoping the cashier wouldn't cheat her.

2. They want to get jobs. For example, a factory worker needs to be able to follow instructions in English. An accountant from one country may find himself working as a maintenance worker in the United States because he cannot transfer his work skills to the English-speaking job market.

Juan Vargas came to the United States from Mexico to get a better job and find more opportunities for his family. He could not understand or speak English. He worried about venturing out on a bus when he could not ask directions or understand anyone. He also thought he could not even apply for a menial job if he could not communicate in English.

3. They need additional academic training. People who are well educated and can read and write English fluently often need help with oral communication skills. Others who have received degrees or certification in their home countries sometimes find that their credentials are not sufficient for employment in the United States. Many bring family members who can speak little or no English.

Shen taught civil engineering at a university in China. He passed the written English tests and was enrolled at an American university to do graduate work. Although Shen could read the required books in English, he could not follow the lectures and was getting further and further behind in class. He could not ask his fellow students for assistance because he could not understand their fast-spoken English.

4. They want to make friends in this new country.

Hidaat was a Fulbright scholar from Eritrea, a small country in northern Africa. She was the only person from her country at her American university. She was the only person who spoke Eritrean, and since she spoke and understood little English, there was no one there with whom she could talk. Because of her halting English and shy nature, she found it difficult to talk with strangers, even students in her classes.

5. They want to become citizens and need help to pass the citizenship test.

Chiang Ping came to the United States from Hong Kong several years ago. He has been working diligently on English. Chiang's job as a checkout clerk in a local supermarket has given him opportunities to practice his listening and speaking skills. He is now studying the history of the United States and learning about the workings of its government as he prepares to take the examination to become an American citizen.

6. They want to be able to speak English with other members of their families.

   Marta came to America to be with her son and his wife and their American-born children. Marta spoke only Spanish. Even though her son and his wife spoke Spanish, their children most often spoke English, and Marta felt left out of most of the family activities.

7. They want to help their children in school.

   Tatiana was a high school teacher from Russia. As she watched her son struggle with his homework, she knew she could help him more if only she knew English. She knew how important it was for parents to communicate with and work closely with their children's teachers. How could she attend a teacher-parent conference without knowing English?

8. They realize how important knowing English can be to their personal safety.

   Rescue workers at a car accident were frustrated because it was difficult to communicate with injured migrant workers to ask where they hurt, to tell them not to move, and to assure them that an ambulance would take them to the hospital. Interpreters were recruited at the hospital, but at the scene of the accident, the injured were frightened because they couldn't understand their rescuers' instructions. They realized that understanding and speaking English in America could be of critical importance.

Bringing real-life needs and experiences from outside the classroom into the lessons makes learning English practical. Students will practice more and will remember better when they can use daily what they learn in class.

Profiles of Adult English Language Learners

There is, of course, no "typical" ESOL student. As a teacher, you should become as informed as possible about your students. They may be male or female, young or old, with no formal education or with advanced degrees. They may come from various ethnic, religious, and economic backgrounds, some knowing much about the United States and its history, others knowing almost nothing. Sometimes they have misinformation and false ideas about Americans that eventually need to be amended.

Common Characteristics of ESOL Learners

Most adult ESOL learners share the following characteristics:

- They need friendship and acceptance.
- They fear embarrassment.
- They experience stress in their new surroundings.
- They have responsibilities in addition to learning English.
- They are highly motivated.

- They have widely varying backgrounds and needs.
- They have difficulty pronouncing certain sounds.
- They have problems understanding English speakers.

They need friendship and acceptance.

Most of us are so involved in our own daily lives that we forget that there are people living in the community who really need to be accepted as neighbors and friends, not just allowed to live nearby. This is illustrated in the following incident:

> *Two American travelers stopped for a sandwich at a small diner in a rural American town. The woman serving them had a heavy foreign accent. Conversation between the Americans and the waitress brought out the fact that she was Greek, had been in the United States for six years, had some family back in Greece, and loved living in America. She had become a citizen and was proud of it, but she couldn't understand many aspects of American life. She wanted and needed someone to explain and discuss American holiday customs, politics, schools, and parent organizations. Almost all of her associations were with other family members, and it was difficult for her to become part of a larger American community. She felt she couldn't take the initiative to meet new people. Invitations to American homes would have been most welcome.*

As Americans, we can and should become sensitive to the need newcomers have for friendship and acceptance. In doing so, we enrich ourselves and our lives.

They fear embarrassment.

Students often hesitate to try to speak English because they fear making mistakes. You can instill confidence in them by making your lessons progress at a pace compatible with their abilities. Small successes in beginning lessons can build to bigger successes as students realize they are communicating in English.

They experience stress in their new surroundings.

Many non-English-speaking persons are scared to try to speak any English. Knowing only a few words, such as *hello* and *thank you*, is not enough to last through a community meeting or a session at the employment agency. When one needs help in an emergency, it can be a frightening experience not to be able to explain what is wrong. On the other hand, some non-English-speaking persons may seem loud and boisterous. Often this is a defense mechanism to cover up a lack of confidence. People react to stress in many different ways.

They have responsibilities in addition to learning English.

Newcomers to America have responsibilities beyond learning English. They are concerned about where to live, how to find jobs, and how to care for their families. Teachers must take these responsibilities seriously. You can do so by integrating your students' concerns about their lives into your lessons, as long as you and the students are comfortable doing so.

They are highly motivated.

Most ESOL students are highly motivated. They realize why they need to learn English. Many know what they want to learn and are persistent about learning it. Their motivation enhances their ability to learn English.

Success in learning a new language depends not only on innate ability, but also to a great extent on whether students want to learn and feel capable of learning. How quickly people learn to understand and speak English will depend on many things, such as how easily they absorb a new language, whether or not they are literate in their first languages, the amount of time they spend with people who speak English, and their personalities and levels of persistence. Some students may feel they are not learning fast enough, and this might make them more driven or in need of extra encouragement.

They have widely varying backgrounds and needs.

Like all others, ESOL students are shaped by their backgrounds. One student may have had extensive education and come from a family of high stature. She may resent her new situation. She may even seem arrogant. Another student may come from very modest means. He may be here without his family. Often an entire family has pooled its resources to send just one member of the family to the United States to work toward a better life. Some come as refugees and bring their whole families. The father will be exposed to some English because of his work. The children will be exposed to English in their schools. But the wives and elders often are stay-at-home mothers or grandparents who have no exposure to English. Each learner brings a different need.

If your student cannot read or write in his or her spoken language, you may want to refer to the section that discusses the advantages of teaching basic first language literacy as a first step to English (Chapter 12). Whatever your students' backgrounds, it is up to you as a teacher to help them set and achieve their own goals of learning English and understanding more about their new culture.

They have difficulty pronouncing certain sounds.

Adults with excellent formal education often have difficulty speaking the English language intelligibly. Producing certain sounds and stress patterns characteristic of spoken English may present a major difficulty for some because these sounds do not even exist in their native languages.

Each language has its own sound system. Some African languages have click sounds. French has some vowel sounds that are difficult for learners. Native English speakers have as much trouble imitating these sounds as speakers of other languages have with some English sounds. Learning to speak another language often requires a whole new set of muscular movements to make the appropriate sounds and involves a new set of stress and intonation patterns.

They have problems understanding English speakers.

Many ESOL students can read and write English and can even repeat English words well, but they cannot understand what is said to them, especially because we Americans usually speak so rapidly. Asking questions that require more than a *yes* or *no* answer can help teachers know if students comprehend. Native English speakers use many contractions, slur words together (*Wha-cha-do-in?* means *What are you doing?*), and use colloquial phrases, idioms, and slang. These language patterns are incomprehensible to ESOL students at first and can be very frustrating. Much empathy is needed.

Summary of Learner Characteristics

Whoever your students are, whatever their backgrounds are, whatever abilities or weaknesses they show, you must be sensitive to each individual's real needs and interests. By using the how-to skills that are taught later in this book and your own insights, you can help someone communicate in English and live a fuller life.

If a student speaks no English and can understand nothing you say at first, be patient. If you start simply and build slowly, little successes will bring flashes of comprehension when understanding does come. You will learn how to begin with students who speak no English. If you are the first person with whom your students can communicate in English, you will have become very important in their lives—a real reward for each of you!

All students have strengths and weaknesses. You'll be working to help them, and you'll note where they need help as you fill out individual Learner Profile Sheets (see page 69), but do also remember to build on individual strengths as you work together. Do your students show strengths like these? Be sure to include them in the student profiles you create. The student:

- is highly motivated
- is self-confident
- has a job (is not in job market)
- seldom misses a lesson
- comes to class on time
- does homework
- has family/friends for support
- is educated in home language
- knows Roman alphabet
- has some education in English
- has good social skills and interacts with people
- has leadership skills
- is willing to try new things
- is willing to listen
- wants a GED/college

Why People Want to Teach

Some people want to travel, to learn about other cultures, and to meet people from other countries but have not had the opportunity. Meeting and working with people from other countries by teaching them English can open up the world without travel. Others plan to travel through the Peace Corps or another humanitarian group. They know that English teaching skills will be useful, and they want to learn those skills now—not only to get valuable experience that fits in with their plans but also to have the chance to help someone immediately.

Some people seem to be born teachers. Some were professional teachers and either want to continue in retirement or want to supplement their teaching of children by teaching adults. Some have had no teaching experience but know they would like to try. Still others have heard the stories of their grandparents who came to America from another country—lonely, frightened, and knowing no English. They feel they are giving back something that was probably given to their ancestors. Teaching ESOL students provides an opportunity for anyone to teach.

Whatever your motives, the desire to help and willingness to give time to teaching, while very important, are not enough. Learning strategies and techniques for teaching English to speakers of other languages; learning how to assess students' strengths, needs, interests, and goals; and learning how to plan lessons are all essential to effective teaching. This book provides many practical tools.

Is There a Need to Know the Students' Languages?

One question continually arises with regard to teaching students who speak little or no English: How important is it for the teacher to speak and understand a student's native language? Most teachers will not know their students' languages. It is not necessary for the teacher to have this knowledge. Knowing some words can be useful for explaining a difficult concept or giving directions, but it can also be a crutch to lean on. When students and the teacher speak the same language, they may revert too often to it instead of stretching to use English. You may also have a group of students who speak different languages. It won't be possible to know all of their languages.

Certainly you should not avoid a student's language completely. There are obvious advantages to knowing it, such as ease in explaining an abstract term or the security of sharing a common language. A bilingual dictionary (English and your student's native language) can be helpful, provided that your student can read his or her native language. It might be too time-consuming to spend 10 minutes attempting to act out the meaning of a difficult word like *develop* or *justice* when you could explain it in the native language or look it up in a bilingual dictionary. Learning some words in your student's language can also help build rapport, especially when your pronunciation is not quite correct.

Another question often arises: Should teachers try to learn students' languages as they teach? Except for learning a few phrases and showing that you, too, experience difficulty in trying to learn another language, we suggest not, at least not from your students. Your students came to the program to learn English, not to participate in language exchange.

Profiles of Effective ESOL Tutors/Teachers

Throughout history, individuals have made a difference—sometimes for good and sometimes for evil. Don't underestimate the extent of your own influence, even on one person. Don't worry if you are not a professional teacher. The quality of the teacher-learner relationship often makes the difference between an effective and a frustrating teaching/learning experience. The basic ingredients of this relationship are good communication skills (particularly active listening), the ability to help your students learn to speak effectively, and—above all—empathy.

Whatever your previous training, some of the skills you already have will help you to learn the new teaching skills you need. Technical skills that encompass practical methods for teaching English are crucial—but equally important are patience, enthusiasm, creativity, adaptability, and respect for your student.

Characteristics of ESOL Tutors/Teachers

Effective tutors/teachers:

- are well trained
- are learner-centered
- plan and keep records
- exhibit the following personal qualities:
  - understanding and respect
  - patience
  - adaptability
  - enthusiasm and encouragement
  - sense of humor
  - cultural sensitivity
  - creativity
  - accountability
  - responsibility
  - realistic expectations
  - commitment

They are well trained.

How can you prepare yourself to teach someone to understand, speak, read, and write English? Just an ability to understand, speak, read, and write English won't suffice. Learning the skills and techniques for teaching ESOL and making well-thought-out lesson plans are essential to becoming an effective tutor or teacher.

Workshops and college courses that prepare tutors and teachers to work with ESOL students are offered in many communities and through ProLiteracy. There may be conferences of ESOL teachers offered by local chapters of Teachers of English to Speakers of Other Languages (TESOL) that you can attend. Your local literacy program may also offer in-service workshops. All such training opportunities increase one's ability to help someone learn to understand, speak, read, and write English. You will get new insights and learn new techniques by continuing to seek out training opportunities.

They are learner-centered.

Learner-centered teaching is directly related to the students' needs and goals. It involves keeping students' needs at the heart of instruction and seeing students as partners in the learning process. Effective teachers must be attuned to their students' goals and immediate needs so that lessons can be designed to address these needs and goals. Students need to gain their own skills, not to see a demonstration of the skills the teacher possesses. Teachers must show how, not show off. Specific techniques for teaching learner-centered communication skills will be discussed in detail later.

They plan and keep records.

As a volunteer tutor or as a professional teacher, you are responsible for planning lessons with input from your students, for teaching, and for keeping records. Your main job is to help your students develop new skills, and each session must be an opportunity to help your students learn more English. Because there never seems to be enough time for all you anticipate doing, plan your lessons carefully. Make the most of your time together. Keep a good mixture of review, new learning, and fun. Stay on task. Do not try to solve all of your students' personal problems. After concentrating on the lesson and meeting some success in learning English, students can often view personal problems with new hope and understanding.

They exhibit the following personal qualities.

Understanding and respect

Your students may have had problems finding a place to live, getting a job, and even functioning in everyday ways. They may have found it hard to use local transportation, to buy food, or to get help in an emergency. Successful tutors and teachers understand that students overcome many obstacles every day, and they respect those efforts and abilities.

Patience

Effective teachers have many virtues, but perhaps the greatest of these is patience. Sometimes learning may seem very slow, but there are times when all the carefully built knowledge seems to come together at once, and the student suddenly says, "Oh, I see!" Eventually, the stepping stones you provide allow students to function independently and use English in new situations. Your patient work becomes worthwhile, and both you and the student experience the joy of learning.

Adaptability

People are infinitely different. Some have phenomenal memories, others have keen intuition, some have a knack for learning through observation, and some are patient plodders who will learn if you are patient enough to allow them time. Your challenge is to adapt your teaching to your students' learning styles. Keep your mind open to new ideas, and plan to use a variety of teaching techniques.

Enthusiasm and encouragement

Keep your enthusiasm high, and give genuine encouragement to your students. Help your students enjoy small successes along the way to the long-term success they seek. However, do not pretend success when both of you know that it has not been achieved. Excessive excitement and urging are not conducive to real learning, but genuine respect for each student's growth can be a source of help and pride.

Teachers often blame themselves if their students are not learning English quickly enough, but there are many reasons why the pace may be slower than you or your students would like. Try not to take this personally, but remind yourself that each student's "one step at a time" often consists of tiny steps. To empathize, advise, and teach without becoming disillusioned presents a delicate balancing act for teachers. You may want to get together with other teachers to share experiences and techniques and to provide support to each other.

Encourage students to use English not only in their lessons but also in their daily lives. Suggest that listening to TV and radio programs can be good practice in hearing and understanding the spoken language as well as an effective way to gather information. Remind your students that participation in other group conversations is helpful and that other classes might be available in their communities for further study and reinforcement.

Sense of humor

A tough task is often made easier by including some light moments. Laughter often reduces tension, and sharing a good joke is a fine way to build a relationship and to add pleasure to some otherwise hard work. A teaching hour with several laughs in it will seem like a much shorter time. When you laugh, be sure your students are laughing with you. Remember, adults can be very sensitive, especially in areas where they feel insecure and inadequate. Try learning—pronouncing and remembering—a few words in the language of one of your students. That should provide a laugh as well as keep you reminded of the difficulties in being the student.

Cultural sensitivity

ESOL tutors and teachers need to be sensitive to what students are facing. If you have traveled or lived in another country without knowing the local language, you know how difficult even everyday activities can be. Some teachers may be immigrants themselves and thus will understand some of the real problems, frustrations, and dreams of newcomers. But most of us have not had this experience and must try to compensate by educating ourselves about our students' cultures and by being aware of both our verbal and nonverbal interactions.

Students may need explanations about some of the cultural systems of their new country. Little things you take for granted should be shared with your students. Students are more likely to feel comfortable and more easily accepted if they know the general cultural patterns of their adopted country. They are then free to choose for themselves how they will respond to them. By the same token, knowing some of the cultural patterns of your students' countries will help you find similarities to and contrasts with American ways. You can learn about these through your reading as well as through discussions with students.

Creativity

This book encourages teacher creativity. Individualized lessons are most effective when you use the basic techniques and exercises as a springboard for your own creative endeavors. Use your own imagination as your confidence in your teaching skills increases. Don't overlook ESOL textbooks. Imaginatively used, they can be an excellent basis for instruction. Once you feel comfortable with the basics, the next step toward creativity becomes easier. Every technique and exercise can be adapted to individual needs.

Accountability

You are accountable to your sponsoring organization or your supervisor for giving reports on the progress of your students. Before you plan a new lesson, it is helpful to write up what happened in the past lesson. These records will give you an ongoing report of your students' progress throughout the year, making yearly reports much easier. Your notes can be kept in individual student folders or portfolios, and you should share these with your students periodically. You are indeed accountable to each other to prepare for lessons and to communicate with each other in a timely way about schedule changes or postponements of teaching sessions.

Responsibility

Success stories are stimulating, but not all students are equally successful at learning English. Some are highly motivated to learn the new language. Others seem less so, for many reasons. Your responsibility is to act as a sounding board for some of the common problems that ESOL students encounter. Respond with timely lessons that, whenever possible, draw upon issues students face. You are not expected to help students solve every problem they confront. Your primary task remains teaching English through relevant content.

Realistic expectations

As a teacher, you have a responsibility to help your students become independent as quickly as possible. Yet you must be realistic. It is not practical to set goals too far above a person's current abilities or to expect endless hours of study when a student has home responsibilities and a full-time job. There are a number of reasons that people learn at different rates. Consider these factors:

- Some adults have never been to school and have little confidence that they can even learn.
- Some students need considerable repetition; others absorb and remember almost everything right away.
- The first language of some students may be much like English; the first language of other students may use a different alphabet and have few words, if any, similar to English.
- Some students have many opportunities to practice their English outside of class; others do not.
- Some students may have prior experience learning other languages.

Whatever the ease or difficulty of learning, treat your students as individuals and allow for differences in rate and style of learning.

You may be easily discouraged if you measure your students' progress by your own standards in learning other things. Remember, language learning is hard work. If you've ever tried to learn a foreign language, think back to your own attempts. Patience and praise for small successes probably did much to encourage you to continue trying. The same principle holds for all learners.

Commitment

An effective tutor or teacher makes a real commitment to the job. Your work will pay off in tangible and intangible ways. A teaching commitment requires:

- training—mastering techniques for teaching ESOL
- planning—setting short- and long-range goals with your students and writing out lesson plans that will work toward meeting those goals
- dedication—teaching one student or small group for at least two hours each week for a minimum of a year, or teaching a class for at least one year
- accountability—keeping progress records and reporting them to your sponsoring organization or supervisor

Summary of ESOL Tutor/Teacher Characteristics

You are not expected to solve every personal problem your students have, but perhaps you can steer your students to someone who can help. You certainly need to respect them as adults who are overcoming real problems as they try to improve their ability to communicate in English. Motivated learners and a creative, trained teacher who is willing to adapt and offer practical instruction make a winning combination. Learning a new language can be an exciting adventure. What is best for one student may not always be right for another. Individualize your teaching by adapting your teaching methods, activities, and materials to meet individual needs.

This can be done even when tutoring several students or teaching a class. You might want to divide even beginning English language learners into those who have minimal education in their native language and those who have had more education. It's embarrassing for those who have had limited education. They need more time and more help, and they may become frustrated when they can't keep up. They often just drop out. It is also frustrating for those with more education to wait for those with less. If you can't divide the class, think about ways in which you can pair learners and let those with more education help you teach.

While many ESOL teachers are native English speakers, it's a real advantage to have learned English as a new language yourself, especially if you've come from the same language community as the students assigned to you. Because you've faced similar struggles, you can offer keen insights into the needs, goals, and problems your students identify and can become a role model for them.

LEARNING AND TEACHING

Nature of Language
Dialects, Accents, and Styles of Speaking
Vocabulary and Sentence Structure
Stress, Rhythm, and Intonation Patterns
Pronunciation

Learning and Teaching Styles

Learning Differences

One-to-One, Small Group, and Classroom Settings
One-to-One Settings
Small Groups
Classroom Settings

Collaborative/Participatory Learning
Group Behavior

Summary

Effective acquisition of a new language is not only a mental process but an emotional and social one as well, since language is a part of culture, and learning involves the whole person in community with others. This chapter considers some of these diverse processes in the following discussion on speech patterns, learning styles, and collaborative learning—whether through one-to-one, small group, or classroom instruction.

The purpose of this book is not to describe fully the components of English grammar but rather to help new tutors/teachers understand some specific aspects of the English language that will aid them in their teaching. Thus, the following discussion of language is geared toward the immediate needs of teachers. We will concentrate on the significance of the following:

- Dialects, accents, and styles of speaking
- Vocabulary and sentence structure
- Stress, rhythm, and intonation patterns
- Pronunciation

Dialects, Accents, and Styles of Speaking

Oral language is a system of meaningful sounds used to communicate. These sounds are meaningful because they are produced in a patterned way that is mutually understood by speakers of the same language.

To get a clearer idea of what it means to say that oral language is a system of meaningful sounds having patterns, think of these three kinds of sounds:

1. Noises heard in traffic or at a construction site. These are a jumble of sounds with no particular pattern or structure.

2. People talking in a foreign tongue. These sounds are understood by some people but probably not by you. The sounds follow a regular pattern and thus have structure. You just don't know the structural pattern or the meanings of the sounds.

3. People talking in English. These sounds are organized into patterns, too. If you know English structure and vocabulary, you can understand the meaning. A person who does not speak or understand English cannot isolate words from among the streams of sound. For communication to take place, both the speaker and the listener must know the subsystems—vocabulary, structure, sounds, stress, rhythm, and intonation patterns—inherent in that language. Each subsystem has its own set of rules. Some of the rules that govern English systems are different from rules that govern other language systems.

English, like other languages, has dialects or variations. Are American and British English different dialects of the same language? What about accents—a Brooklyn accent, a southern accent, a midwestern accent?

Most of us use both formal and informal styles of speaking, depending on the situation. Words that are proper in one situation or setting may not be accepted in another. Speech used in introducing a guest speaker is usually more formal, while speech used during a family outing is more informal. Informal styles often include language with multiple meanings, idioms, even slang. Technical language could be an example of one type of formal language. Every professional group has its own specialty words or jargon. Thus, practical English must be adaptable. It is the responsibility of the teacher to explain the different ways English is used and to work with students to identify the various contexts in which they need to understand and speak English.

Vocabulary and Sentence Structure

The vocabulary of a language is a collection of the words of that language. These words can refer to particular objects, actions, or feelings, or they can be modifiers or connecting words. Vocabulary expansion is an important part of learning a language. As teachers, we must be aware that the vocabulary needs of individual students must be addressed. For example, the vocabulary required by an engineer may be very different from the vocabulary needed by a farmer, a nurse, or a new mother, even though they are all using the same language. There is a list of the most frequently used English words in Appendix L, page 234.

The structure of a language consists of the grammatical rules that govern relationships between words and parts of words. It includes rules for word order. For example, *The dog chased the boy* has meaning for speakers of English partially because of the order of the words. We know who is doing the chasing because the noun *dog* comes before the verb *chased.* Compare that with *The boy chased the dog.* As another example, consider the difference in *He trains seals* and *He seals trains.* Many of us cannot remember the names of the parts of speech, and we may not be able to state the rules that apply to correct usage. However, we understand what is said because we know the vocabulary and recognize the pattern or structure. Because structure is so important in English, you will need to help your students learn it.

Stress, Rhythm, and Intonation Patterns

The way words are pronounced also conveys meaning, as does the way words are stressed in sentences. Depending on which word is stressed, a sentence can take on a different meaning. For example, look at these sentences. *JOE drove the car home* (not Bill or Bob). *Joe DROVE the car home* (he didn't push it or have it towed). *Joe drove the CAR home* (not the jeep or the bike). *Joe drove the car HOME* (not to the garage or to school).

Each language has a rhythm of its own. Some are smoother and more liquid. Others are more abrupt and staccato. Living in an area where the language you are learning is spoken gives opportunities to feel the language's rhythm subconsciously.

Intonation is sometimes called the melody of a language. It refers to the pitch changes used in speaking. These intonation patterns play an important role in conveying meaning. For example, *Joe DROVE the car home?* (After the accident, it wasn't in such bad shape that he couldn't? Unbelievable!) Other languages have pitch assigned to each word. In Chinese, for example, the word *ma* can mean *mom, numbness,* or *horse,* depending on the tone.

Pronunciation

Some students can read, write, and understand English fairly well, but they find that although they *think* they're speaking English, people have trouble understanding them. They need help with pronunciation. There are many ways you can help these students. We'll address this in Chapter 7 when we discuss speaking English.

LEARNING AND TEACHING STYLES

People learn in a variety of ways. Some people are visual learners. Others learn best through listening. Some learn best when they combine actions with speaking. And others learn best through reading and writing. It's important to be sensitive to your students' learning styles and be aware of your own style of learning and teaching.

You may want to look at your own approach to learning. Do you prefer to look at a problem or a lesson as a whole and then examine the parts, or do you prefer to look at the smaller pieces or parts of a problem or lesson before exposing yourself to the bigger picture? You can find out on the Internet. Type "What's your learning style?" into a Google search box, and you'll find a list of sites with questionnaires that assess learning style. Your students will vary in their learning preferences because people do not all learn in the same way.

Alice Omaggio Hadley (2000) suggests that students as well as teachers have differing needs, styles, and preferences. Some people learn best through the senses—the ears, the eyes, touch, and movement. Some people prefer learning with others, interacting in small groups, while others seem to learn best doing individual projects. Some learners thrive on exciting and creative new settings; others prefer structured guidance. Teachers should be sensitive to all of these differences.

Some students are extremely shy, tending not to talk when in a group, especially with members of the opposite sex. Others want to talk continuously, dominating the group. As much as possible, it is up to the teacher to encourage equal participation by directing questions to shy students and gently letting the more vocal students know that all students must be given opportunities to speak.

How a teacher approaches learning situations affects how students learn. Teachers may use a responsive, collaborative learner-directed way of teaching or a more controlling teacher-directed way. Both approaches can be effective, and teachers often practice an eclectic approach, incorporating elements of each.

Some students will expect an exclusively teacher-directed approach, since this is probably the way they were taught as children. However, experience has shown us that the learner-centered approach is usually more effective when you are working with adults. In the beginning, teachers may want to consider adjusting their teaching styles to conform completely to their students' learning styles. Sometimes the students' styles and the teachers' styles are already similar. Sometimes they are exactly opposite. Over time, the teachers and the students will likely adjust to each other's styles.

How can a teacher find the best ways for individual students to learn when they speak and understand only limited English or no English at all? One way is to observe which ways seem most comfortable for the students and in which situations they seem to learn and retain the most. Or you can ask them. Do they seem to learn better by seeing pictures, by experiencing an event (going to a market, walking through a kitchen identifying objects), by hearing (from radio or TV), by memorizing (repeating again and again), or by writing (as a reinforcement to the speaking and hearing)? You will want to concentrate on their best learning styles, but you will also want to introduce different learning styles since students can benefit from using a diversity of approaches to learning.

It is often difficult to pair up teachers and students who have the same teaching and learning styles. To establish an effective learning climate, teachers must learn to blend their own teaching styles with their students' learning styles. Yet students need to stretch a bit, too. Adrianne Bonham (1988) suggests that learners be encouraged "to expand their style range rather than seek only comfortable experiences." Learners as well as teachers benefit from style flexibility.

Whatever the teaching and learning styles of teachers and students, learning is most effective when sensitive and careful planning, a willingness to adapt, and enthusiasm and patience are a part of each session. Your goal is to build success into each lesson. Even small successes give positive reinforcement to your students. You are trying to help them become self-sufficient so they can function more effectively using English in real-life situations outside the tutoring session.

LEARNING DIFFERENCES

Research and experience suggest that a sizable percentage of adults who have reading problems have learning disabilities or at least have learning differences. This means that learning to read is an unusual struggle for these students, in comparison to learning other skills. Most of them have average or above average intelligence. If you suspect that even one of your students might have a learning difference or disability, you might want to refer to *TUTOR 8* (Colvin, 2009), where an entire chapter discusses such problems and suggests solutions.

Many of us have trouble remembering small things—remembering where we put the car keys or where we parked the car, for instance. Setting up a pattern or a simple routine can help us remember.

- To remind yourself not to forget things, put your hand up and touch the exit door panel as you leave a room. This should trigger you to look back and see whether you've forgotten anything.

- Do you have a hook for your car keys but often forget and just lay them down? When you take the keys out of the car, hold them tightly with thumb and forefinger, reminding yourself NOT to lay them down but to immediately put them on the key hook. They'll always be there next time.

- When you park your car, note which column you are in, #7 for instance, or in the row opposite the M in the store's name, 7M. Say it three times, or jot it down on a piece of paper. You'll find your car.

Many students have memory difficulties—they have trouble retaining what they've read or heard. Ask them to put what they read into their own words in smaller and smaller chunks, perhaps sentence by sentence. Putting their thoughts into words that they say aloud often helps cement those thoughts in memory.

Some have trouble focusing on specific assignments. Be careful not to give them more than they can handle. If they can't multitask, break down larger tasks into smaller chunks. It often takes them longer to process new information, so be patient. Give them more time than you'd expect.

Some students have trouble remembering new vocabulary words. You might suggest that they say and write each new word three times, saying it as they are writing it—the first time, writing it and saying it slowly syllable by syllable;

the second time, saying it but a bit more slowly than normal; and the third time, saying it as spoken normally. Repetition in a patterned way usually gives automatic recall.

Encourage your students to write reminders of appointments, classes, and homework assignments in their monthly calendars. And encourage them to set a pattern of looking at their calendars each morning. We all need these daily reminders.

Basically, all the techniques suggested for beginning and low-level learners in this book apply to those with learning differences. The main difference is that such students need much more time for specific tasks, more repetition, and much patience on your part.

You'll find a Learner Profile Sheet on page 69. Use it to identify the strengths and weaknesses of individual students and to locate suggestions for specific help in *I Speak English*.

There is a bright side for learners who have learning problems/differences. Once they've overcome or learned to cope with their problems, they'll be more likely to accept and overcome bigger challenges later in their lives.

ONE-TO-ONE, SMALL GROUP, AND CLASSROOM SETTINGS

ESOL is taught in one-to-one, small group, and classroom settings. Each situation has advantages and disadvantages.

One-to-One Settings

Traditionally, ESOL tutors in volunteer programs have taught on a one-to-one basis. This format has many advantages.

Many new tutors are hesitant to try teaching more than one student. It can be a bit overwhelming, particularly since no two students are at exactly the same level. With only one student, the tutor does not feel restricted to a rigid time schedule because the time and day of the teaching session can be adjusted by a simple phone call.

Many students are more comfortable when they have their own private teacher. They feel their lessons can be more individualized and the pace can be adjusted to their needs and abilities. The time and place of teaching can be adapted to the needs of both tutor and student.

Many ESOL students are so embarrassed by their limited English that they are frightened to enter a class or even a small group. But they are willing to face a teacher in a one-to-one arrangement, knowing that there will be no competition and their lessons will be kept confidential.

If ESOL students understand or speak little or no English, they will probably need individual help. In these cases, a one-to-one match may be best. Two or three one-to-one tutors might want to bring their students together occasionally to form small conversational groups. If program resources are available, many students profit by a combination of one-to-one, small group, and classroom instruction.

Small Groups

Teaching students in a small group—as opposed to one-to-one—can have many advantages. For example, less pressure is put on the individual to perform or respond to every question. Students also learn from each other. Through role playing, teachers can set up more authentic activities that approximate the use of English outside of class. I suggest that a small group consist of four to six students. If the students are from the same country, they can feel the moral support of their compatriots. They can discuss successes or problems in their native language and encourage each other, but they should interact in English in class.

Having students from different countries in the same group can also be an advantage. It would be impossible for them to speak to each other in their native languages in class. Because they must speak English, they tend to progress faster. And they learn that they are not the only ones having problems with pronunciation, comprehension, reading, or writing. The faster ones can help the slower ones. Students are often stimulated as they see learning from several viewpoints.

Tutors who have worked with small groups as opposed to one-to-one often feel it is more rewarding. They can help more learners without much more preparation, and there isn't the same great disappointment when a student doesn't show up—someone is always there. Also, the fun and learning with group activities or games often override any extra work, and grouping students of similar abilities makes lesson planning easier. However, it is important that you keep a separate folder for each student so you can evaluate individual progress. Once a group spirit is attained, the students seem to become independent more quickly. They learn from each other. The teacher is not the only source for learning the new language.

Sometimes the question of adding new members to an established group comes up, especially if some members have dropped out. It could be stimulating, but the group must consider whether or not they want new members. If the group has attained a closeness that has encouraged growth, members might hesitate to invite a new person. Consideration must be given to the level of English (speaking and understanding as well as reading and writing) of the group and of the new student, as well as how the new student's personality would fit with the group. Each group must decide for itself.

In a small group, there will be times when all members will be working together—collaborating on a special project, discussing specific topics, or learning something new. But there should also be times when students are working individually or in pairs. It is up to the teacher to plan lessons that are varied, that ensure rich interaction, and that build in comfort so that every student will be able to work up to capacity.

Experience has shown that having members of the same family in the same group can be problematic. It may be best to place spouses and children in different groups or to match family members with individual tutors.

Classroom Settings

Classrooms just mean more students. There is still the same dynamic between people who want help in learning to understand, speak, read, and write English and someone who has been trained and is willing to teach English.

Most classes include students who are at a similar level—beginning, intermediate, advanced. Teachers can plan their lessons using predetermined goals.

A class can be divided into smaller special study groups where the more advanced students can help those who struggle. Peer teaching is an excellent way to share and learn. Or a class can be divided into groups where previous education is a consideration. Having students with similar previous education has many advantages. Students with strong native education usually learn English at a faster pace, while those with no or minimal education in their native language are generally slower and need more help. If their co-students have had more native language education, they will probably progress faster, leaving the low-level students embarrassed and frustrated.

Classroom teachers have a real challenge but also a wonderful sense of accomplishment as their students form new friendships and become confident in their practical use of English.

COLLABORATIVE/PARTICIPATORY LEARNING

One school of thought contends that we learn from each other in our interactions. We can refine our thinking best by discussing with others, reading what others have written, and listening to what others say. We learn and communicate by sharing as social beings. This is the essence of collaborative/participatory learning.

Collaborative learning can take place with one student and one tutor working together as well as in small groups or in classroom settings where students learn both from each other and from the teacher. The teacher facilitates learning but also learns as part of the group. In all three settings, you will learn to set mutually determined goals, negotiating what happens in lessons. Both students and teachers are participating in the lessons, teaching and learning together during the teaching process. They share not only English but also perceptions as they mutually expand their social worlds.

Collaborative teaching means that you and your student or students are a team working together for a common purpose. Ideally your students have stated their goals and needs, and you have assessed their skills. They will have many things in common, but you will find differences, too—such as backgrounds, interests, abilities, and time available for home assignments. Together, you can work out plans to help your students attain their goals.

Group Behavior

As you work together, you will find that your relationships with your students are changing. You are trying to make your students more independent of you while building bridges to new learning.

Whether you work with 1 student or with 4 or with 25, you are a group. Only when you work independently are you alone. Consider the five stages of group behavior as suggested by Tuckman and Jensen (1977):

1. **Forming** • As the group forms, the students expect the teacher to take the lead in planning lessons, setting goals, and setting up rules for the group.

2. **Storming** • As individuals within the group grow more independent, there might be resistance to the teacher taking total leadership. Students may question the value of some of the techniques and materials. This indicates growth and shows that it is time for students to assume more responsibilities.

3. **Norming** • As group members work closely together, a sense of cooperation and a greater sense of unity usually develop. Individual personalities emerge, and decision making by the students becomes more evident. They become less dependent on the teacher for guidance.

4. **Performing** • Lessons have become more relaxed, with teachers and students accepting each other, working together, and taking responsibility for decision making. There is a sense of accomplishment and satisfaction as skills of listening/understanding, speaking, reading, and writing are integrated into meaningful tasks.

5. **Adjourning** • Eventually the teaching lessons must end. Adjourning should not be done abruptly. Time should be allowed for affirmations, for sadness at parting, and for closure. Perhaps a final celebration session can be planned where certificates are given or students share their best work over the year. Perhaps the students will want to plan a final meeting over lunch or coffee. Parting will be easier for the students if they know they can continue to call their teacher and each other for help or encouragement or just to keep in touch.

It is important to keep in mind that this definition of stages is only a model. Although actual group dynamics are usually more complex than the model suggests, the stages sensitize us to the ideal of a group's evolution, and that can help guide our work.

SUMMARY

Whether you work in a one-to-one, small group, or classroom setting, you will want to be sensitive to your own preferred teaching styles and your students' varied learning styles. Be mindful of differences in dialects and accents as you focus on speech patterns and pronunciation. Use authentic materials whenever possible. All will come together as you continue reading this book and as you learn detailed techniques and lesson planning. Working collaboratively, you will be aware of the growth of your partnership or group as your students progress toward the attainment of their goals.

ASSESSMENT

Background Information
  Profiles of ESOL Students

Assessment Tools

Proficiency Guidelines
  National Reporting System (NRS): Educational Functioning Levels (EFL)
  English as a Second Language Oral Assessment (ESLOA)
  Reading Evaluation—Adult Diagnosis (READ)
  Speech Samples
  Portfolios

Learner Profile Sheet

Summary

Assessment is the process of collecting and reviewing information about individual students to give you and the students a basis on which to evaluate their progress and the quality of their work. To be effective, assessment must be linked to instruction and must measure student progress. It is important to see how your lessons have affected students' lives.

Regardless of what information may be needed for administrative purposes, it is critical that assessment reflect the needs, learning goals, and progress of students. Whatever their backgrounds are, whatever abilities or weaknesses are evident, you must be sensitive to each individual's actual learning needs and development. Effective assessment always enhances and guides a student-centered instruction program.

BACKGROUND INFORMATION

Students and teachers all come with the "baggage" of past lives and experiences. Some of this baggage is beautifully wrapped, while other baggage is worn and broken. All baggage contains dreams and hopes, yet there is often despair and loss of self-worth and self-confidence as well. Remember, this literacy program is learner-centered, and we must build on the dreams and hopes, on the positive aspects of each student's life.

Before you start teaching, you should have information on the background of each of your students—native country and language, length of time spent in the United States, marriage and family status, age, education, work status, level of English, etc. This information is usually collected during an intake interview with the student before he or she is matched with a tutor or before a student is assigned to a specific class. A sample student intake form is included in Appendix D.

Profiles of ESOL Students

People who come for help with learning English can generally be divided into five groups:

GROUP A • Adults who cannot understand, speak, read, or write any English and are not literate in their native languages.

> *Tai Doan and Huong Nguyen came to America as refugees and were sponsored by a local social services agency. They were peasant farmers in Vietnam and had lost their homes during the war. They were taken by relief agencies to refugee camps before coming to America. Neither Tai Doan nor Huong Nguyen had ever been to school, and neither could read or write in Vietnamese. They knew no English.*

Adults in Group A are often the most difficult to teach. Some argue that these students would learn English more quickly if they were taught to read and write in their native languages first, especially if a native language is based on the Roman alphabet. The bonus of learning to read and write in their native languages is obvious—learners can keep their native languages alive, and they can read newspapers and letters from home as well as be literate in their spoken languages. More on the advantages of becoming literate in a native language before trying to learn English is in Chapter 12. But adults must decide for themselves whether they want to learn to read in their own languages before learning to communicate in English. Native language literacy programs may be available, but you must respect the wishes of your students, and they may or may not wish to participate in such programs.

In some cultures, the spoken language may not have a written form, so the students may not have had opportunities to read in their own language. We tend to think of this as a deficiency, but in fact, these students often have excellent oral memories. We can play to that strength.

GROUP B • Adults who cannot understand, speak, read, or write any English but who are literate in their native languages. They may have anywhere from a few to many years of formal education in those languages.

1. Students who speak a language written in the Roman alphabet, such as French, German, Portuguese, or Spanish.

    Ramón is 35 and was born in Saõ Paulo, Brazil. His father was a bricklayer of moderate means, and Ramón attended high school. Although English is completely foreign to him, he speaks, reads, and writes Portuguese, a language that uses the Roman alphabet.

2. Students who are literate in a language that does not use the Roman alphabet, such as Hindi, Arabic, or Chinese.

    Prakash Singh is from Jaipur, India, and cannot understand, speak, or write English. He is not married and was a clerk in a bank in rural India. He came to America to join his two brothers, who have started an Indian restaurant. He graduated from middle school in Jaipur, having had all his education in Hindi. Hindi does not use the Roman alphabet.

Some Group B students may learn rapidly, but many feel they must learn the way they were taught in school. They want to translate, and they often want to take notes in the native language. This might be helpful, but try to ensure that they do not depend entirely on their written notes. It is important that they learn to hear and understand the oral language. Exercises and lessons stressing listening skills can be helpful.

Sabeen came from a small town in Syria to a city in Upstate New York as an 18-year-old bride in an arranged marriage. She graduated from high school and speaks, reads, and writes Arabic. She can communicate with her new husband and his family in Arabic, but she cannot understand or speak English. She wants to be in contact with other young Americans. An early pregnancy has made her more anxious to learn English. Her inclination in her tutoring sessions is to write anything she learns in Arabic. Encouraging her to listen, paraphrase, and later write notes in English helps her with conversational English as well as with writing.

GROUP C • Adults who may read and write English at a high intermediate or advanced level but who have limited ability to speak and understand English. Some of these learners have immediate specific needs (English for specific purposes, or ESP) because they are master craftsmen in their former countries (carpenters, plumbers, electricians) or are doctors, nurses, or specialists in other fields. They need help with listening and speaking in English.

> *Wei Li has advanced degrees in engineering from Heilongjiang University in the People's Republic of China. He studied English for 8 years, and he reads and writes it well enough to pass the necessary tests to be enrolled in an American university. However, he has problems understanding the lectures in class and is hesitant to leave his dormitory for fear of getting lost. He has found that Americans do not understand his English when he asks for directions, and he does not understand their answers.*

Many students have studied English in their own countries for more than 10 years. They may have received good scores on the Test of English as a Foreign Language (TOEFL) or a similar test, been admitted to American universities, and been able to read and write technical materials at the undergraduate or graduate level. However, they still have great difficulty understanding lectures and the speech of the Americans they encounter every day. They feel inadequate when they speak English and are hesitant to try, for they have found that most English speakers cannot understand them. Ask Group C students to listen to English language audio recordings, radio and TV programs, and your own voice; then ask them to paraphrase what they hear. This may be difficult for them, but it helps to address their specific needs.

GROUP D • Adults who are neither first nor second generation—they are Generation 1.5. These learners came to the United States some years ago and attended secondary school or even some elementary grades in the United States. They are very fluent speakers of English but may have problems with reading and writing. Some are studying in our community colleges. Because they are fluent speakers of English, they are offended when asked to attend ESL classes. They don't need help with listening and speaking skills, but they do need help, especially with writing in English.

> *José reads and writes in Spanish and has had 8 years of school in Puerto Rico. He attended high school in the United States but dropped out. He has been working in maintenance at a local hotel and speaks English well. He wants to improve his reading and writing in English so that he can get a better job.*

GROUP E • Adults who can understand, speak, read, and write English reasonably well but with some limited proficiency and who have asked for help to improve their English skills.

> *Ibrahim, 27, is from Somalia. He learned English in the refugee camps in Kenya. Ibrahim can read and write English, and he can understand and speak enough English to get by, but he wants help with pronunciation and idioms.*

Many ESOL students are in Group C or E. They can understand and speak some English, but they have trouble with colloquialisms and idioms. They often have sentence structure and pronunciation problems, making it difficult for others to understand them. Their limited mastery of English often restricts achievement of their goals. Although learners in Group D can often read and write English fairly well, they may say when questioned that they do not understand everything they read.

Comprehension of English is a problem. It is up to you to address your students' needs as you individualize their lessons. Keeping new words, sentences, and concepts in the general sequence of listening/understanding, speaking, reading, and then writing will help many students improve their English. Keep in mind that you will always be mixing and matching the four communication channels—listening, speaking, reading, and writing. Be prepared to stay flexible.

To help students who understand and speak English well but have problems reading and writing it, go directly to the reading and writing instructions in Chapter 8. Much more detailed help in teaching reading and writing in English is given in *TUTOR 8* (Colvin, 2009). Or you can refer such students to tutors specially trained to teach basic literacy or to basic literacy classes.

Whichever group your students fit into, you must always remember to find out about their interests and needs. Tailor your lessons to their goals.

> One Russian carpenter was unable to continue his trade in the United States even though he was in an area where there was much building. He didn't know the names of the tools, he could not describe them in English, and he could not understand the details of a job when they were in English. The English skills he needs would be different, for example, from those needed by a stay-at-home mom.

Many students in Groups C and D need English for occupational or specific purposes (ESP) or what has been called vocational ESL (VESL).

ASSESSMENT TOOLS

If programs are even partially funded by government and other agencies, specific assessment tests are often mandated. Programs need to identify and evaluate instructional practices and measure student achievement. There are several assessment tools to test the listening, speaking, reading, and writing abilities of adult ESOL students including the following:

- CASAS (Comprehensive Adult Student Assessment Systems)
- BEST Literacy (Basic English Skills Test—for reading and writing)
- BEST Plus (Basic English Skills Test—for listening and speaking)
- CELT (Comprehensive English Language Test)
- MTELP (Michigan Test of English Language Proficiency)
- TOEFL (Test of English as a Foreign Language)
- TABE CLAS-E (Tests of Adult Basic Education Complete Language Assessment System—English)

Some tests are administered by institutions at set times, and others may be administered by individuals after they have received special training. Most students take a pre-test when they enter an adult ESL program and a post-test at a later designated time to show whether they have made progress. Be sure to find out whether a particular test is mandated in your program and when a student should be tested.

PROFICIENCY GUIDELINES

As with all teaching, you do not want to start too far above or too far below your students' levels of ability. How do you determine whether individual students speak and understand little English, are fairly independent in the use of English, or are somewhere in between? A first meeting with your students will give you a general impression of their abilities and interests, but as you continue your meetings, you will be able to assess areas of your students' growth that sometimes are not evident using informal observation and analysis. A variety of published instruments are available to help teachers assess their students' needs.

National Reporting System (NRS): Educational Functioning Levels (EFL)

The National Reporting System for Adult Education (NRS) is an outcome-based system used by state-administered, federally funded adult education programs. Within its set of Educational Functioning Levels, it identifies six levels of English as a second language attainment: beginning ESL literacy, low and high beginning ESL, low and high intermediate ESL, and advanced ESL. Approximately 100 hours of study are needed for an adult to move from one level to the next.

At each level, expectations for listening, speaking, basic reading, writing, and functional workplace skills are defined. The skill descriptors illustrate the types of skills students entering a level are likely to have, but they are not a complete or comprehensive delineation of all of the skills at that level. Programs measure level completion and advancement by assessing students with a standardized pre- and post-test. A complete list of ESL levels and descriptors is in Appendix B.

English as a Second Language Oral Assessment (ESLOA)

English as a Second Language Oral Assessment (ESLOA) (Shaffer & McLean, 1996) is another tool to help you develop individual student profiles. This instrument measures the amount of English already known and defines areas where help is needed.

The ESLOA Level Description Grid has three levels—beginning, intermediate, and advanced—and describes the abilities of people at those levels under the following headings: General, Listening, Speaking, Work, Reading, Writing.

Beginning includes work on basic conversational English listening and speaking skills. *Intermediate* extends the work on conversational English (listening and speaking) but also includes reading and writing, starting with words, phrases, and sentences that the students can already understand and repeat. At the *advanced* level, students will probably need help with pronunciation and with understanding everyday, and possibly technical, English (in radio and TV broadcasts, lectures, or meetings where many people are speaking).

Unless your students speak English quite well, you can assume that they will want and need help with understanding and speaking. On the other hand, if their most important need is to improve their English reading and writing skills, you might want to explore the ideas in *TUTOR 8* (Colvin, 2009).

Reading Evaluation—Adult Diagnosis (READ)

READ (Colvin & Root, 1999) was written specially to be an easily administered tool for informal assessment. It is designed to identify and measure adult students' progress with specific reading and/or writing strategies and skills. It tells what students already know in reading and where the gaps are.

READ measures the following competencies:

1. Basic sight word recognition.
2. Specific word analysis skills in relation to:
   Names and sounds of letters (consonants)
   Blends (*bl, br,* etc.)
   Word patterns (*mat, sat, fat; might, sight, fight*)
   Reversals (*was* for *saw*)
   Variant vowels (vowel sounds other than short vowels)
3. Level of reading ability (word recognition in context)
4. Level of reading and listening comprehension

Information from *READ* will help you decide which skills need reinforcement and what portion of your lessons should be devoted to each skill. Since the results give approximate levels of listening and reading comprehension, you could also use them as a general guide in developing lessons and selecting materials.

Speech Samples

Morley (1991b) suggests that three types of pronunciation assessment—diagnostic evaluation, ongoing evaluation, and actual performance—should be included in the complete assessment of ESOL students. Two kinds of speech samples should be recorded early in the teaching sessions:

1. Oral reading. Use a standardized script that incorporates as many features of English pronunciation as possible.
2. Free speech. Encourage free speech by asking open-ended questions.

These samples can then be compared to recent assessment recordings to help students note their progress and to identify areas where more practice is needed.

Portfolios

A good way to provide continuous assessment of your students' needs is to keep a portfolio, or working folder, for each student. You may want to include personal information as well as samples of work, your own notes, the student's progress charts, and your personal assessment after each teaching session. While most portfolios contain written work, we suggest that you also include samples of recorded speech, if possible. Many students want to keep their own portfolios and are willing to make self-evaluations. You may want to make copies of all information so that both of you can have a copy. Be sure that all work done by the student includes his or her name and is dated so that progress can be tracked.

Individual portfolios may include the following:

- Personal information: name, address, telephone number
- Copy of intake form
- Record of student's attendance
- Information from assessment tools
- Learner Profile Sheet (see page 69)
- Teacher's notes about student's needs and interests
- Student's short-term and long-term goals
- Teacher's notes on student's strengths and weaknesses
- Recorded Language Experience stories
- Recordings of speaking exercises
- Checklist of TV shows and movies watched
- List of radio programs listened to
- Checklist of where English was used
- Writing samples
- Student's self-evaluation
- Student's personal word list
- *READ* test scores showing specific needs in reading

Besides showing students' progress, portfolios can also highlight areas that need special attention. For example, some students may be having trouble pronouncing certain sounds in English such as /th/, /ch/, and /sh/. This difficulty may or may not obstruct communication. If you can understand these students, and if others in the group can understand them, it is probably not important at an early stage to address this problem. Make a note of it, and include appropriate pronunciation exercises later on. Other students may bring in idioms that they have heard and don't understand. That should alert you to specific needs and goals. Your notes in individual student portfolios can help you with lesson planning.

You might want to include in your lesson plans a set time, perhaps every two to three months, to review portfolio contents with your students. Together, you can decide which writing and recorded samples to keep and which to remove. These review sessions can be exciting because students often haven't realized what concrete progress they've made.

LEARNER PROFILE SHEET

Everyone has strengths and weaknesses. We suggest that you identify individual strengths and share those strengths with the students, giving them the self-confidence they often need. By analyzing ESL Educational Functioning Levels (see Appendix B) and the results of *READ*, ESLOA, and other assessments; and by observing your students' work, attitudes, and actions at your teaching sessions, you can identify where your students need help. The Learner Profile Sheet can help you locate targeted instructions that address those weaknesses (see page 69). Keep a Learner Profile Sheet in each student's portfolio.

SUMMARY

Because the needs and backgrounds of students are so varied, using a range of assessment and evaluation tools is important. The ESL Educational Functioning Levels grid—with its descriptions of each of the six English levels plus suggestions for lessons—provides baseline data as well as a practical way to show progress. ESLOA and *READ* help you identify needs and give suggestions for teaching. Speech samples and portfolios are specific examples of student work. The Learner Profile Sheet helps you identify the specific needs of individual students and shows you where to target instruction. These tools will help you plan lessons and will give you and your students tangible evidence of their progress.

LEARNER PROFILE SHEET

Creating learner profiles will help you focus on the specific needs of individual students and identify which characteristics apply to each student. By reviewing students' work, observing their actions at your teaching sessions, and noting the results of diagnostic assessment, you can see their specific needs. Mark appropriate characteristics and note the pages for targeted instructions in *I Speak English*.

Student's name _____ Date _____

Visual problems ☐ yes ☐ no If yes, describe _____

Hearing problems ☐ yes ☐ no If yes, describe _____

Diagnostic test reports 118

_____

Identify student's individual "group" ☐ A ☐ B ☐ C ☐ D ☐ E 61

Identify student's skill levels—ESL Educational Functioning Levels 197

Strengths. 41

_____

Interests. 119

_____

Targeted Instructions   Pages

Information processing. 54

    ☐ Difficulty focusing 54

    ☐ Longer time to process information. 54

    ☐ Memory difficulties 54

Listening/understanding 73

    ☐ Hearing individual sounds 85

    ☐ Comprehension 77

    ☐ Idioms 109

    ☐ Dialogues, telephone or free conversations 77, 105, 114

    ☐ Contractions (*will not = won't*) 89

    ☐ Understanding lectures (advanced students) 79, 140

    ☐ Suggestions for exercises/activities/games for beginning students. 245

    ☐ Suggestions for exercises/activities/games for intermediate students. 245

    ☐ Suggestions for exercises/activities/games for advanced students 245

Speaking. 80

    ☐ Saying letters/individual sounds 85

    ☐ Numbers—time, money 151, 152

    ☐ Pronunciation 85

- ☐ Stress, rhythm, intonation 83
- ☐ Making new English sounds (/*r*/, /*th*/, etc.) 85
- ☐ Dialogues, free conversations 105, 114
- ☐ Sentence structure, grammar 110
- ☐ Expanding vocabulary 112
- ☐ Suggested exercises/activities/games for beginning students 245
- ☐ Suggested exercises/activities/games for intermediate students 245
- ☐ Suggested exercises/activities/games for advanced students 245

Reading 117

- ☐ Decoding words 125
- ☐ Sight words 123
- ☐ Language Experience 119
- ☐ Rhyming—patterned words 127
- ☐ Multisyllabic words 97
- ☐ Oral reading (fluency) 130
- ☐ Comprehension in reading 131

Writing 133

- ☐ Handwriting 133
- ☐ Spelling 139
- ☐ Punctuation/grammar 139
- ☐ Composition—process writing 134
- ☐ Journals/Language Experience stories 137

Additional helps 236, 241, 245

- ☐ Suggested lesson plans for beginning students 241
- ☐ Suggested lesson plans for intermediate students 242, 243
- ☐ Suggested lesson plans for advanced students 243
- ☐ Suggested websites for tutors/teachers, learners, and specific subjects 236

Comments:

___

___

___

___

Summary:

___

___

___

___

___

CHAPTER

TECHNIQUES, STRATEGIES, AND ACTIVITIES FOR TEACHING LISTENING AND SPEAKING

A Communicative Approach

Listening and Understanding (Reception)
  Total Physical Response (TPR)
  Colored Paper Exercises
  Telephone
  Comprehension Checks
  Information Gathering
  Summary

Speaking (Production)
  Modeling English
  Stress, Rhythm, and Intonation Patterns
    Stress
    Rhythm
    Intonation
  Pronunciation
    Individual Sounds
    Minimal Pairs
    Linking
    Pausing
    Contractions and Reduced Expressions
    Homographs and Homophones
    Prefixes and Suffixes
  Oral Exercises—Drills
    Simple Substitution Drill
    Complex Substitution Drill
    Response Drill
    Transformation Drill
  Backward Buildup
  Chain Drill
  Creative Oral Exercises
    Sentence Combining
    Restatement
    Sentence Completion
    Continuing Story
  Dialogue
    Memorized Dialogue
    Free Dialogue
  Idioms
  Sentence Structure/Grammar
  Expanding Vocabulary
    New Vocabulary Within Known Structures
    New Vocabulary Within Word Groupings
    Word Cards and Vocabulary Notebooks
  Free Conversation

Importance of Practicing Listening and Speaking Skills

Summary

A COMMUNICATIVE APPROACH

The goal of our English language learners is to be able to communicate in English—to understand what is said and to be understood in real-life situations—as well as to be able to read and write in English. A communicative approach emphasizes comprehension and uses authentic materials in realistic situations in an effective and practical way. This approach focuses on listening and speaking balanced by reading and writing.

Students will be able to understand some words in the new language immediately. They will be able to speak some words and sentences, using practical communication skills within the first few lessons. By reading words they have heard and spoken and by writing those words as well, students can reinforce their oral/aural learning. Separating reading and writing from listening and speaking simply fragments language.

This approach is learner-centered and learner-directed, allowing students to set their own goals. It stresses the language needed and sought by the students and gives opportunities for individualized lessons. Students are encouraged to participate in all aspects of the lessons. Because all four skills are taught (listening, speaking, reading, and writing), students can work from their own learning styles while being exposed to other learning and teaching styles. The goal is communication: Students should be able to understand what they hear, speak so that others understand them, read with comprehension, and express themselves on paper.

The emphasis is on communication in real-life situations. Students often get excited when given opportunities to work on things that happen in their daily lives, for example, deciding whether it's better to buy a secondhand car or commit to a longer credit deal on a new car. Success comes often when lessons focus on students' interests outside the classroom. Let them know that what they learn in class can help them in their daily lives.

Most of the tried-and-true ESOL techniques, strategies, and other activities can be used by adapting the subject matter to the practical vocabulary your students want. When generic vocabulary is used in an example, teachers can use the concept demonstrated and adapt the vocabulary to match the needs of specific students. Start simply, but always adapt each exercise to individual goals. To help you understand suggested techniques and strategies, we will describe them separately. In your lessons, however, you will mix and match them. Be careful not to overuse any one. Rely on your judgment, and concentrate on techniques and strategies that work best for your particular students.

Remember when your mother or grandmother made a cake from scratch? She took things that you wouldn't eat separately (flour, butter, baking powder, water, eggs, vanilla, spices), mixed them together in appropriate proportions, and what came out? A tasty and beautiful cake!

So it is with teaching English. It's not just teaching from a workbook alone; it's not just teaching individual listening and speaking skills; it's not just teaching phonics, sight words, patterns, or comprehension skills alone; it's not just working with individual learning styles. Combine them all in appropriate proportions, and what comes out? A person who can understand, speak, read, and write English.

Although strategies and exercises are important, they should not be used in isolation. As much as possible, draw from real-life contexts for language exercises, and use these as a springboard to stimulate authentic communication. The goal is to transfer knowledge gained from strategies, exercises, and other activities to the students' everyday lives.

LISTENING AND UNDERSTANDING (RECEPTION)

You *listen* when the radio or TV is on. You *listen* when someone calls you on the phone. You *listen* when your child calls. You *listen* when the doctor examines you. You *listen* at the airport or bus station when departure changes are announced. Then you respond. If most people spend an average of 45 percent of their communication time listening and 30 percent of their communication time speaking (see Chapter 2), much teaching time should be given to these two areas.

> We were working in China, trying to learn as much as we could about the people, their customs, and their daily lives. We also had to "survive," that is, go from one place to another, buy supplies from local markets, order in a restaurant, find the ladies' and men's rooms—all the things we take for granted when we can speak a language.

> I cannot write Chinese. I cannot read Chinese. I cannot speak Chinese. I cannot understand Chinese. If I could have only one of these four skills, which would I choose? I would choose to be able to understand what was said around me. Seeing that we were foreigners in distress, some people tried to be helpful, and how I wished I could understand what they were saying! A close second choice would be to be able to speak Chinese so that I could ask questions and respond to instructions. Of course, I wanted to be able to read the Chinese street signs, the billboards, and the bus schedule so that I could be more independent. But I could survive without being able to read and write. It was very difficult even to get by without understanding and speaking any Chinese.

Listening is a primary source of learning for those who want to master a new language, followed closely by speaking. Effective listening will be the basis of communication with your students.

Many ESOL students have said that although they can understand their teacher, they have problems understanding other people.

My husband and I were visiting Turkey. A colleague there who spoke English quite well was impressed that I had learned the greeting and a few words in Turkish. She asked me why I had bothered to learn even a few Turkish words. "Because I'm a guest in your country." She was aghast. Then she asked, "Why are you against my country?" She had heard "against" her country when I said I was "a guest" in her country.

Using slower, more precise English is helpful to beginning and intermediate learners. Because we often slur words, newcomers sometimes don't hear them correctly. They hear *haryu* when we say *How are you?* Let your students know it's polite and OK to ask *Will you repeat that please?* or *Please speak more slowly.*

But remember that our goal is to help students comprehend the English that is spoken by natives—usually fast, full of contractions, and with words running together. Thus, we must be careful not to speak too slowly or enunciate much more clearly than we usually do.

Even beginning ESOL learners profit by listening to a variety of native speakers to get the rhythm of the language. They may not be able to understand all the words, but they'll get the feel of spoken English. Listening activities should be included in each lesson.

More advanced students might enjoy hearing recorded texts. The bonus for new English learners is that they can practice listening to another English-speaking voice, and they can replay the recording whenever they want. Give your students as many tools and options to strengthen their listening skills as possible. Let them choose which best fit their needs.

Total Physical Response (TPR)

Total Physical Response (TPR), developed by James J. Asher, focuses on actions following action verbs or commands. It is an effective way to ensure listening comprehension even for absolute beginners. The teacher gives oral commands and demonstrates physical responses. Then students respond to the commands with the requested actions. No oral responses are expected; the responses are the actions of the students. When students perform appropriately, you know that they understand.

You may want to establish some useful gestures needed for nonverbal communication with your students:

- **Listen**   Often students repeat whatever you say. If you want them only to listen, you can indicate for them to be quiet and listen by cupping your hand next to your ear, putting your finger on your lips, and saying, *Listen!* or *Shh!*

- **Respond**   If you want your students to imitate you or respond or answer a question, open your hand, palm up, toward the students.

- **Repeat** When you want your students to repeat what you said, open your hand, palm up, toward the students, and use the charade gesture meaning *Come on* (hand open, palm up, fingers moving).
- **Teacher responds** When you expect to respond yourself, point to yourself as you start talking.
- **Speak together** When you want your students to say something with you, point one hand at yourself and gesture with the other hand in a circular motion to include all your students, as in charades.

For beginning ESOL students, it's important to start simply. Use a command, directing the students to act. At first, use simple commands, demonstrating as you speak. For example, *Stand up*. Repeat the command, stand up yourself, and gesture to your students to stand up. Then move to *Sit down*. Again, demonstrate and suggest the desired response. Then try *Walk, Stop,* and *Turn around*. As the teacher, you walk, stop, and turn around to demonstrate. You can add more vocabulary when you feel it is appropriate (e.g., *Take one step. Take two steps. Open the door. Close the door.*).

In a Total Physical Response activity, be sure that the action corresponds to the sentence. Be sure that both you and your students are seated as you say, *I'm sitting*. Stand up and gesture for the students to stand as you say, *I'm standing*. Start walking and encourage the students to walk as you say, *I'm walking*.

When your students understand as demonstrated by their actions, you can give the appropriate gesture for them to repeat the commands. They can take turns telling you or other members of a small group what they want you or others to do. They are already in the leadership role, deciding what they want done. Even at this beginning stage, collaborative teaching is taking place—the teacher is not the only one giving directions.

After the students have understood and have said the words, the teacher can write them on a piece of paper or a board. The teacher reads the words first and then asks the students to read and then write them.

Continue with some more commands, giving the appropriate demonstrations, expecting only a physical response, no words. Commands such as *Point to* _____, *Touch* _____, or *Pick up* _____ could be combined with *the door, the table, the book, your head,* or even *the red book*. As students master commands, add other verbs, such as *open, close, give, take*. Only after the students have demonstrated that they understand the words by appropriate actions will you ask them to repeat the words, then read them, and finally write them. You might want to include other commands and questions that the students can use in their daily lives: e.g., *Where is the* _____*? Show me the* _____. *How much* _____*? May I have* _____*?*

TOTAL PHYSICAL RESPONSE

Teacher gives/demonstrates direction.
Students respond with action.

Stand up.
Sit down.
Walk.
Turn around.
Stop.

Point to the door.	Touch your nose.	Pick up the book.
the table.	your finger.	the red book.
the window.	your hand.	the black book.
the floor.	your head.	the green book.
the book.		
the pen.		

The substituted words should keep to the same pattern, with only one word or phrase changing at a time.

Point to the door.
Point to the table.
Point to the pencil.

Vary the commands along with the vocabulary only when your students are more advanced.

Pick up the yellow pencil.
Stand by the window.
Turn off the lights.

When your students understand and can repeat these commands, give them opportunities to read and write those same words. You might want to label the items or the pictures.

This same exercise can incorporate vocabulary specifically needed for individual students. If a student is a hairdresser, you might have him bring in objects used in the beauty salon: comb, brush, hair dryer. If a student is a carpenter, appropriate objects might be a screwdriver, a wrench, a saw, and a hammer. If possible, create a picture file of objects that are important to your students. You can use these in TPR and other activities as well.

Colored Paper Exercises

A practical and easy method of teaching listening skills is to use pieces of colored paper as props for following directions. This is an excellent exercise for students who understand or speak little or no English. It is fun and relaxing for beginning students, but it can also incorporate more difficult concepts and new vocabulary as learners' skills increase. Detailed instructions are in Appendix F (page 209).

Telephone

Telephone conversations call for advanced listening skills. Gestures and visual contact cannot help communication. The ears alone must do the work. Practice at making telephone calls gives excellent training in both listening and speaking. Enunciating clearly on the phone is especially important. One Spanish-speaking student kept hearing *all of you* as *I love you* during a phone conversation. You can imagine the complications this might create!

One way to help your students learn to listen and speak via telephone is to have two people sit back-to-back, simulating a situation where there is no eye contact. The two people could be you and a student or two students. Have similar objects available to both (e.g., several books, pens, and other objects). Have one student give directions. For example, *Open the red book to page 68, and put a marker on top of the page number. With the black pen, draw a circle and a square at the bottom of the page.* Check to see that the listener has understood enough to do what the speaker asked. Then switch roles.

A next step could be asking your students whom they need or want to call. You can then practice realistic telephone conversations with them. The students can suggest the situations—a call to make a doctor's appointment, to get a bus schedule, or to speak to a child's teacher. Learners may require detailed scripts at first, then scripts with open-ended sections for them to fill in. Finally, ad-lib conversations can provide follow-up and model the real event. You and a student or two students could role-play.

Secretary: Dr. Brown's office. May I help you?

Patient: This is Mr. Malipo. I need to make an appointment for Tony, my three-year-old son. He has a bad earache.

Secretary: Can you bring him in this afternoon at three?

Patient: Yes, thank you. We'll be there at three.

Comprehension Checks

Some people can pronounce words in English that they do not understand. Be careful not to assume comprehension simply because the words are said correctly. During a teaching session, you can often sense that your students do not understand a word you have said—sometimes by a quizzical look, a cock of the head, or raised eyebrows.

An important part of your job in teaching language skills is to ensure comprehension of what you say. If you ask, *Do you understand?* a nod or even a response of *Yes* does not guarantee comprehension. ESOL students are often embarrassed that they do not understand or may want to please you by saying that they do. You can do a real service to your students by suggesting that it is proper and polite to say *I don't understand. Would you please repeat that?* or *Would you please speak more slowly?* In any case, we do need to find other ways to determine to what extent they understand.

Give your students oral directions. Action following direction shows comprehension. More advanced students can not only follow directions but can also tell you what they did.

Please open the window, and tell me what you did.

If your student opens the window and then says, *I opened the window,* you know the student understood. If the response is, *I open. . .* , you model the correct response, *I opened the window,* gesturing for the student to repeat the entire sentence.

COMPREHENSION CHECKS

- **Action to follow directions**

- **Questions**

- **Paraphrase**

- **Back-to-back session with common directions**

How you state a question often determines what kind of a response you will get. There are questions where a *yes* or *no* response is appropriate.

> *Is the door closed?*
> *Is the book blue?*

Although *yes* or *no* questions elicit simple responses, students must understand the whole question in order to answer correctly.

Questions can be phrased to allow for alternate answers. For example:

> *Is the door open or closed?*
> *Is the book red or blue?*

With these questions, the right answer is contained in the question. In a way, either/or questions both teach and check comprehension at the same time. For example, comparatives can be reviewed using either/or questions:

> *Is it hotter here or in your country?*
> *Does it rain more here or in your country?*

Still other questions demand more language in the answer, for example, Wh-questions *(who, which, where, what, when, and why).*

> *Who is president of the United States?*
> *When was the Constitution of the United States written?*
> *Why do you want to work at that company?*

Open-ended questions are appropriate for advanced students because they require longer answers. Closed questions can be answered with *yes* or *no. How* questions usually require that students state a fact or explain a process. For example:

> *How do you register your children for school?*
> *How do you get to work?*
> *How is the climate in your country different from the climate here?*

Pictures, actions, and basic question patterns can help ascertain whether or not your students really understand the meaning of both spoken and written language.

Information Gathering

Advanced students can be asked more problem-solving and information-gathering open-ended questions. These demand greater knowledge and require more inference. For example:

> *If you needed a plumber, how would you find one, and how would you determine whether he or she was qualified?*

The teacher must vary the level of difficulty of questions in accordance with the abilities of individual students and the nature of the tasks.

Some students who read in their own languages may resist practicing listening skills because they are attuned to written messages. But such students may not be able to understand a conversation or a radio broadcast in English. They know more at eye level than at ear level and often insist on seeing the words in print. This may defeat the very purpose of their work with you. Encourage them to listen for comprehension of a word, phrase, or sentence, and then to repeat it, assuring them that you will give them the written version later. Then suggest that they try to write the words if that will help them remember, without worrying about spelling them correctly. Then they can compare your words with theirs to see if they heard right and to check their spelling, which they can correct if they wish.

Suggest that difficult lectures or broadcasts be recorded by you or by the students so that they can listen as often as necessary. You could suggest that both you and your students listen to the same radio or TV news broadcast and discuss it at a lesson together. By giving your students an opportunity to review what they heard, you will help them develop the thinking skills needed for effective listening as well as for effective reading. You might suggest that intermediate or advanced students focus on one news commentator at a time in order to get used to that person's pronunciation. In this case, it's helpful to have the students read the news headlines in the newspaper or online *before* they listen to the commentator. This gives them an opportunity to predict the main stories.

Summary

You can practice listening skills in your lessons by keeping the focus on your students and their concerns. Here are some important listening skills:

- **Listening reflectively** Responding to a person by giving back both the message and the feelings behind it in a tentative manner.
  - ° **Parroting:** Repeating exactly, word for word, what the other person has said.
  - ° **Paraphrasing:** Giving back the speaker's idea in your own words, rather than repeating the speaker's words.
  - ° **Focus questioning:** Helping the speaker keep to the point he or she is making, asking questions like *Just what is it that you don't understand?*
- **Encouraging** Letting the speaker know he or she is being heard.
  - ° **Maintaining interested silence:** Helping the speaker talk about a difficult problem because you give him or her space to think before you react.
  - ° **Opening doors:** Issuing an invitation to the other to speak through cues—silence, or words that indicate you are willing and have the time to listen. Use phrases such as *You seem troubled, You sure look excited, How did it go?*
  - ° **Asking open-ended questions:** Encouraging the speaker to elaborate by bringing ideas to mind that the person isn't aware of. For example, ask *What do you want to do now?* instead of suggesting a course of action.
- **Summarizing** Stating the main points of the other's conversation in two or three sentences.

SPEAKING (PRODUCTION)

Speaking follows listening so closely, you can hardly separate them. You've seen examples in the listening section where students are given opportunities to speak as soon as listening comprehension is ensured.

Language is for communication. The type of language you focus on with your students should be authentic and relevant. It should be authentic in the sense that it is the type of language people actually speak, not textbook English. It should be relevant in that the language relates to your students' needs and interests. It should focus on the things they want and need to communicate. Work with the vocabulary and objects your students know or want to know and those in which they've shown an interest. Keep in mind, though, that your goal is to help your students expand their English communication skills rather than simply to learn isolated vocabulary or decontextualized grammatical rules. Consider the following anecdote:

> *One teacher said that she worked with two people from Peru. They had lived in New York City in a Spanish-speaking community for seven years. They understood English well. They could even read and write English. They tried to speak English, but they told the teacher that people almost never understood them. Their teacher agreed—it was nearly*

impossible to understand their English. They needed help with stress, rhythm, and intonation patterns as well as with individual sounds.

Many of our ESOL students are looking for accent-free English, but while accents are appealing, the important aspect of learning English is to be understood. Accents that do not interfere with listeners' understanding need not be a problem. Pronunciation differences are only important when they make communication difficult or impossible. Don't expect your adult students to overcome a foreign accent easily or completely. Accent elimination in another language is difficult for most adults. However, it is important for them to hear and be able to reproduce sounds effectively if that is their goal. *I spik Inglis* can become *I speak English* with practice.

New teachers of oral language skills are often overly concerned about correcting students' pronunciation of English words. Unless pronunciation interferes with communication, you should not correct it in the early lessons, perhaps noting the difficulties so that you can work on them later. Of course mistakes will be made, and they are often embarrassing to new language learners. Errors are evidence of learning. Don't focus on them; instead, model the correct sounds, words, or sentences. You might want to note student errors that you want to correct later by jotting them down on your Specific Help Needs Chart (Chapter 10, page 180).

A child learning to talk is constantly imitating, improvising, and practicing. However, the adult who is learning a new language has one difficulty that the child does not have. The child has no inhibitions about practicing, whereas many adults, fearful of sounding foolish by mispronouncing words, are much more reticent. But even for a child, learning a new language takes time.

Many of us have studied a foreign language at one time or another, but we may not be comfortable speaking with a native speaker of that language. We may become self-conscious and tongue-tied, even though we might be able to read the language quite well. It is up to you as a teacher to establish a comfort level for your students so that they are relaxed enough to try the new sounds and the new words.

In a misguided effort to be understood by newcomers who understand and speak little English, we sometimes chop our sentences short. It's OK to use short sentences, but they should be grammatically correct. Sometimes a longer sentence, spoken slowly, is more comprehensible.

> *A woman, trying to be helpful to her Laotian friend who didn't speak English very well, said,* "You here stay. I take baby. I put her down for nap." *The woman believed that she was making it easier for her friend to understand. If she had said,* "You stay here. I'll take the baby and put her in her bed for a nap," *the words would have been just as easy to understand if spoken a bit more slowly than normal but with proper stress and intonation.*

Modeling English

Much of learning a language is a matter of imitation and practice. Your students must hear and understand what is said in a normal tone and at normal speed. What is said can then be repeated and become a regular part of a new English speaker's discourse.

While nouns and verbs communicate a lot, the major units of meaning in English are phrases and sentences, not individual words. Therefore, use phrases and sentences as the basis for instruction. Because your students need to understand English as it is spoken in America, your speech becomes an important model they follow. It's often helpful to speak slowly and distinctly to beginning students, but generally speak naturally, repeating if necessary to give the students a second or third chance to catch the sounds and intonation. Here are a few do's and don'ts, using the sentence *The woman is walking down the street* as an example:

1. Don't overarticulate. Words can become distorted if you overemphasize certain sounds (e.g., *waa-lking* for *walking, streee-et* for *street*). It is important that when you speak English to your students, it is not distorted but represents the language they will hear in normal conversation, unless you are trying to help focus attention on a particular sound. Most people your students hear will not overarticulate except for emphasis (e.g., *I'm sta-arved!* or *Watch out!*).

2. Don't speak too slowly. Students who become accustomed to a speaking rate geared to the lowest level will find it difficult to converse or to understand normal speech. (*The woo-man izzz waah-king dow-en the street.*)

3. Don't speak too loudly. Speaking loudly does not facilitate understanding. Your students don't have trouble communicating in English because they are hard of hearing. (*THE WOMAN IS WALKING DOWN THE STREET!*)

4. Do be aware of correct intonation. The meaning can be changed, for example, if the voice rises at the end of a sentence. This rise indicates that a question is being asked. (*The woman is walking down the street?*)

5. Do be aware of correct stress. Avoid the use of unnatural emphasis on certain words. (*The woman is **walking** down the **street**.*) She is not running and is not on the sidewalk.

6. Do be natural. Use phrases and contractions as you normally would. (*The woman is walking down the street* or *The woman's walking down the street.*)

While they expect students to repeat what they say with similar speed, stress, and intonation through modeling, many teachers forget to use repetition for more complex activities—to develop grammar structures and expand vocabulary and meaning. We're all natural mimics, so use repetition throughout your lessons, always checking for comprehension. If you model a sentence or a structure and if your students show comprehension of what you have said and repeat it, they will be using listening and speaking skills.

Stress, Rhythm, and Intonation Patterns

In learning a new language, stress, rhythm, and intonation patterns are as important as vocabulary and comprehension.

Stress

Without being conscious of it, native speakers naturally stress some syllables in a word and some words in a phrase or sentence. Stressed syllables or words are usually louder, more clearly enunciated, and longer. Unstressed syllables or words are generally reduced, shorter, and weaker.

> *am* **bi** *tious*
> *de* **vel** *op ment*

Changing the stress on individual words within a sentence can alter the emphasis of meaning. For example:

> *Roberto is sitting on the CHAIR (not on the sofa or on the floor).*
> *ROBERTO (not Luis or Maria) is sitting on the chair.*

Sometimes words with the same spellings are pronounced slightly differently with the stress on different syllables. The content will give the clue for pronunciation. For example:

> *The court clerk made a* **<u>record</u>** *of all the testimony.*
> The first syllable is stressed when the word is used as a noun.

> *She was asked to* **<u>record</u>** *all the testimony.*
> The second syllable is stressed when the word is used as a verb.

Rhythm

Every language has a rhythm of its own. Hearing English every day in real-life settings or on the radio, TV, or audio recordings helps learners become familiar with the rhythm of the language.

Here is one way you can help your students hear the rhythm of the English language. Read a sentence, and have the students tap out the syllables with a pen on a table or clap out the rhythm with their hands. After they have tapped through a sentence and repeated it several times, ask them how many taps they made. The students may not agree on the number of taps in the sentence. That is OK at the beginning of the lesson. Native English speakers tend to run words together, but the rhythm of the language is based on the sound of the sentence, not necessarily on the actual syllables in the sentence. If the students are having trouble agreeing on the number of syllables in your sentence, slow down a bit so as not to run the words together. This may change the number of syllables they identify at first, but after they have repeated the sentence several times, encourage them to practice natural speaking. Start simply and go to more complex sentences.

My name is Alphonse. I'm from Mexico. (10 taps)
I got a telephone call from home; I'm so happy. (13 taps)
Let's go to the supermarket and get some food for dinner. (15 taps)

Rhythm can be also taught through songs, poems, and choral readings.

Intonation

Intonation refers to pitch changes, often called the melody of a language. Unnatural pitch may interfere with communication. Without correct intonation, a person can't always be understood, no matter how perfect the utterance.

As she describes in *New Lives in the New World* (1975), Nila Magidoff discovered that it takes more than word knowledge to communicate effectively.

> *Nila arrived in the United States from Russia and was asked to give a speech for the Russian War Relief Organization. Her English was limited, but she optimistically said she would do it if they would give her two weeks. Two weeks? To Nila, even two weeks seemed impossible—but she decided she could do it by writing down 50 words every day and learning them phonetically. Every day she learned 50 more words, and every night she prepared a new list of 50 words. To help her pronunciation, she went to the movies and listened to poetry on audiotapes. She had not sought out a tutor because she felt she could move ahead faster on her own. She felt that if she knew the words, people would understand what she said, even though she was sure her speech would have grammatical errors. The big day arrived, and she gave the speech. She felt certain that her efforts had proven effective. What a disappointment it was when one man took her hand and said, "Thank you so much. I didn't understand a word you said, but it was all so beautiful."*

Nila Magidoff learned that the meanings one wishes to communicate require not only knowledge of specific words and correct word order but appropriate intonation patterns as well.

A world of meaning is expressed through intonation patterns that we most often learn by listening and repeating, not by memorizing rules or specific instructions.

One way to help your students understand and hear the changes in pitch is to say a sentence and convert its intonation pattern into a singsong pattern. For instance, even a simple question like *Where are you going?* could be converted into *la la la **la** la?* with the emphasis on the fourth syllable. Even though your students don't understand the meaning of the sentence, they can hear the rise and fall of the pitch pattern.

Would you please tell me where Highway 80 is?
*la la laaa la la la la la **lala** la?*

In this sentence, *please* is naturally extended, so *laaa* is extended; *80* is naturally emphasized, so *lala* is emphasized. The question mark indicates a rise in pitch. For this exercise, suggest that your students concentrate on the intonation patterns rather than on the words.

The pitch of the native English speaker's voice naturally rises slightly at the end of questions that require a *yes* or *no* answer (*Will you go to the library with me?*) instead of dropping as it does in a statement. The rise in pitch provides an important cue that you are seeking an answer. If you slow down your speech and overemphasize stress and intonation, natural intonation patterns can become distorted, leaving meaning unclear.

Pronunciation

Pronunciation is most important. You might have good grammar and a sizeable vocabulary, but if your pronunciation isn't good, you probably won't be understood; you will not communicate.

Traditionally, teaching of pronunciation has focused on the practice of isolated sounds or words without regard for the context in which those sounds or words occur. In a communicative approach, stress, rhythm, intonation, as well as individual sounds for understandable pronunciation must be learned, since adequate mastery of real-life speech is what is needed to be understood. Phrases and complete sentences, therefore, provide better contexts than isolated words or sounds when you are helping students learn pronunciation, although sometimes—as in minimal pairs work—isolated words are the key.

Individual Sounds

Before students can approximate a sound not found in their native languages, they must hear and recognize that sound when it is contrasted with similar sounds. Can they hear the difference between *lice* and *rice,* between *led* and *red*? Have your students point to *l* or *r* as you say each word. The sequence of learning requires that the sound be *heard* distinctly and then *identified* so that attention can be focused on it. Don't be discouraged if your students can't hear or produce all English sounds. Remember—understanding their speech is the objective, not perfect diction.

Many students can hear certain words or sounds, and they can repeat the words or sounds, even correcting their own mispronunciations. But for others, hearing and correcting can be very difficult, especially if that particular English sound does not exist in their native language. It is helpful to show your students how to form the sound. For example, if your student has trouble with the /th/ sound, tending to substitute /t/, /d/, /s/, or /z/ (depending on his native language), you can help him correct the sound by contrasting two words with those sounds:

> *thank – tank*
> *though – dough*
> *think – sink*
> *thing – zing*

You might suggest that they put their tongues between their teeth and breathe out. Demonstrate by making the sound yourself, or give your students a mirror so the students can see the mouth's shape and the tongue's position.

Some students can't *hear* the ending consonants in words and thus don't say these final consonants. They hear only *"ca"* when *can* or *cat* is spoken.

She hears: *Ca you go with me?* or *The ca is under the table.*

You might want to stress the last consonant when this is the problem. Say *cannn* or *cattt* and have your student stress the *n* or the *t* as well as final consonants in other words.

Many words have an entirely different meaning when only one sound is changed. *Sin* is much different in meaning from *seen, tin* from *teen, fill* from *feel*. Make sure your students understand that when communication is distorted by mispronunciation, the resulting meaning is often radically changed.

While some feel that individual sounds should be isolated, others believe that sounds can be heard and corrected better by hearing the sounds in words and sentences.

Minimal Pairs

Spanish-speaking students often have difficulty with the English /v/. Students from other language backgrounds typically have trouble with the /th/ sound. Many Asians confuse /l/ and /r/. Others have trouble distinguishing /v/ and /b/, /i/ and /ee/, /m/ and /n/, /oo/ and /o/, /eh/ and /ah/. As a result, certain words will confuse your students because they sound alike to them: *vest* and *best, thin* and *tin, read* and *lead, moon* and *noon, soup* and *soap, letter* and *ladder*. It is your task to help them hear the differences.

You might use minimal pairs, two words that differ in only one sound (e.g., *set* and *sat, bet* and *bat*), to focus on the differences. Select a group of word pairs that provide examples of the same contrast (e.g., the /p/ and /b/). Use a regular dictionary or a rhyming dictionary if you need help.

pill – bill	*pair – bear*
pail – bail	*pest – best*
pie – buy	*pull – bull*

Try to use familiar words to keep the exercise short yet meaningful. At first, use words that represent concrete items (*pear/bear, pill/bill*). Occasionally they will not be spelled similarly (*pair, bear*), but spelling is immaterial for this exercise. It is the sound similarity you are looking for. Keep sets of minimal pairs together at first (*pear/bear, pill/bill*). Later, mix them up and see if your students can hear the differences (*pear, pill, pull*).

1. First, you will want your students to hear the difference between /p/ and /b/. Ask your students to listen as you say each word in each pair. Have them raise one finger when they hear the /p/ sound and two fingers when

they hear the /b/ sound. Or you might have them write /p/ and /b/ signs and have the students hold up the appropriate card.

2. Next, you will want your students to produce just one of those two sounds in different words, then words using the second sound. They will say the words by repeating them after you.

Teacher: *pill*   **Teacher:** *bill*
Student: *pill*   **Student:** *bill*

Teacher: *pair*   **Teacher:** *bear*
Student: *pair*   **Student:** *bear*

3. To help your students understand that these small sound differences are important, put the words with contrasting sounds into different sentences and contexts.

Where's the pill? I have to take it now.
Where's the bill? I have to pay it now.

Repeat the first question in each pair above, letting the students give the appropriate follow-up sentence:

Teacher: *Where's the pill?*
Student: *I have to take the pill now.*

Teacher: *Where's the bill?*
Student: *I have to pay the bill now.*

A correct response indicates that the student can now hear the difference between /p/ and /b/.

4. Next, reverse the roles. Let the students ask the questions, and you respond. If you give the responses they expect, they will know that they are pronouncing the sounds correctly.

For home practice, you could write the pairs of words and suggest that your students practice repeating both words until they can say and hear the differences clearly. But it would be even more helpful to record the sounds. You say the paired words, leaving a space so that your students can repeat the words.

Pronunciation Contrasts in English (Nilsen & Nilsen, 2010) gives detailed instructions on how to form all the sounds of English and suggests minimal sentences that contrast two confusing sounds; it also lists the languages of students who may have difficulty with those sounds.

Please SIT in this SEAT. These shoes should FIT your FEET.

Linking

We often link ending consonant words with words beginning with a vowel. Native speakers of many languages link words all the time. When the last consonant of a word is the same as the first consonant of the following word, we usually pronounce that sound only once, linking the two words.

Call the main number. We often say: *Call the mai-number.*

Often words that begin with a vowel are linked to a preceding consonant.

I'm eating an apple. We often say: *I'm eating a-napple.*

Alert your students to the speech patterns, and give them exercises so that they can hear and say linked words correctly.

Pausing

Native English speakers speak in "chunks" or thought groupings. In writing, this is often shown with punctuation. Where we pause often determines whether our spoken language is comprehensible or incomprehensible. Note the difference in meaning when pauses fall between different words.

Martin said (pause), *The grocer gave incorrect change.*
Martin (pause), said the grocer (pause), *gave incorrect change.*

One exercise to help your students pause at meaningful times is to write out sentences and put a slash mark (/) where you suggest pausing or taking a breath. You can use slash marks to show pause breaks in simple substitution drills and in dialogues or wherever they would be helpful. Start with short phrases; then group them together for longer chunks.

Let's walk / to the market / to get vegetables. /
Let's walk / to the library / to get books. /
Let's walk to the market / to get vegetables and fruit. /

You can also use dialogues:

- *Where are you going?/*
- *I'm going / to the garage / to have my car fixed. /*
- *How long / will you be gone? /*
- *About two hours, /so don't wait for me. /*

Another exercise to help students practice pausing is to have them repeat telephone numbers, pausing after the area code and again at the dash:

622 / 495 / 3027

Contractions and Reduced Expressions

Most English speakers use contractions in place of full pronouns and verbs (e.g., *isn't* for *is not, he's* for *he is*) and reduced expressions that blend two or more words into one (e.g., *helpim* for *help him, wanna* for *want to*).

Iz'ee working? in place of *Is he working?*
Do you wanna come along? in place of *Do you want to come along?*

We sometimes insert a *y* or a *w.*

I am a student. We say: *I yam a student.*
Who is that? We say: *Who wiz that?*

It would be a mistake for the teachers, in an effort to teach "correct" English, to avoid the use of contractions, or reduced expressions, or to try to pronounce each word individually and distinctly. In everyday English, your students are more likely to hear *I won't, She's goin,* or *Where d'ya work?* than *I will not, She is going,* or *Where do you work?* Students will need to know that *I'm* means *I am,* but specific knowledge of contractions can be emphasized later. The shorter version may be more immediately useful in speaking, depending on the people the student speaks with most often.

It's important for students to know contractions, and three general verbs that are helpful are *be, have, will.* They are used all the time and are well worth teaching.

> *I'm, you're, she's, he's, it's, we're, they're, aren't, isn't, wasn't, weren't*
> *I've, you've, she's, he's, it's, we've, they've*
> *I'll, you'll, she'll, he'll, it'll, we'll, they'll*

Homographs and Homophones

Some words are spelled the same but have different meanings and pronunciations—these are called *homographs.*

> Can you *read* this story?
> I *read* it yesterday.

> *Live* your life well.
> There is a *live* fly buzzing around.

Other words—*homophones*—sound the same but have different meanings and often different spellings.

> She was home sick with the *flu.*
> The bird *flew* out of the cage.

> I just *knew* he was in the room.
> I bought a *new* dress.

> Every *week* I go to see my mother.
> After the exercise class, I felt *weak.*

Prefixes and Suffixes

Prefixes and suffixes are excellent ways to add new vocabulary words, and they're usually the same sounds. Once students learn base words, you can explain how specific prefixes change the meaning of those words. *Non-* changes a word to the negative (*stop* becomes *nonstop,* meaning never stopping), while *re-* means *again* (*call* becomes *recall,* meaning to call again or remember).

One of the most disturbing is the ending for past tense: "*-ed.*" It has three distinctly different sounds, three ways to pronounce the final "*-ed*":

1. "*-ed*" pronounced as an added syllable "*-id*"
2. "*-ed*" pronounced as "*t*"

3. *"-ed"* pronounced as *"d"*

Native English speakers don't even think of the different sounds of *"-ed"* at the ends of specific words. They just "sound right." But there are rules:

1. If the base of the verb ends with a *"t"* (*want*) or a *"d"* (*add*), the *"-ed"* is pronounced *"-id"* (as in *did*) as an extra syllable (*wanted, added*).

2. If the base of the verb ends with a voiced *"p"* (*help*), *"f"* (*laugh*), *"s"* (*miss*), or an unvoiced *"sh"* (*wash*), *"ch"* (*march*), or *"k"* (*look*), the *"-ed"* is pronounced */t/* (*helped, laughed, missed, washed, marched, looked*).

3. If the base of the verb ends with all other sounds (*play, allow, grab*), the *"-ed"* is pronounced */d/* (*played, allowed, grabbed*).

Remember, we are talking of *sounds,* not letters or spelling.

As with all rules, there are exceptions: When some *"-ed"* words are used as adjectives, the *"-ed"* is pronounced (*aged, blessed, crooked, dogged, learned, needed, ragged, wicked, wretched*).

Oral Exercises—Drills

Drills are extremely important in facilitating new language acquisition. They provide a structure to reinforce patterns of learning and at the same time allow for improvisation. As the following discussion will demonstrate, drills range from the simple to the complex. In a communicative approach, drills should be created from real-life situations so that they can ultimately be used in authentic English-speaking settings.

Simple Substitution Drill

Substitution drills are very useful because they give students a model of correct sentence structure. In a simple substitution drill, you merely substitute one word, leaving the rest of the sentence the same. Be sure your students understand each sentence you say. Use vocabulary that is familiar to them. The point of this exercise is to practice putting words into the correct sentence structure. You might start with sentences about objects in the room, pictures in a magazine, or sentences with action verbs that can be demonstrated. As always, substitute the vocabulary in this exercise with words related to your students' interests. To begin, point to an object and say (gesturing for the students first to listen, then repeat):

> *It's a chair.*
> *It's a pencil.*
> *It's a book.*
>
> *Point to the motor.*
> *Point to the tire.*
> *Point to the fender.*

Put the baby's diaper in the drawer.
Put the baby's blanket in the drawer.
Put the baby's clothes in the drawer.

Names of objects from students' personal word lists (words they've identified as important) can be used in this drill.

Using this drill, your students can get intensive practice with a single grammatical structure. However, don't be misled into thinking your students can say these sentences independently just because they can repeat them easily. Repeat the same sentences several times. Repetition helps build confidence by providing practice of learned material that can then be used in varied contexts.

A word of caution when using the substitution drill: When a new word is substituted in a sentence, it is common to overemphasize that word. If you do this, your students, using you as a model, will do the same thing. For example, using pictures to demonstrate what you are saying, you might unintentionally say:

The MAN is running.
The WOMAN is running.

In a normal conversation, you probably would not stress *man* or *woman* unless you were comparing the man and the woman. You might stress the word *running*. Therefore, generally, as you substitute words in a structure, be careful to talk with natural stress and intonation:

The man is running.
The woman is running.

Once the students have learned even a simple speech pattern, show how it can be used again and again by changing just one word, adapting to vocabulary your students want and need. You can make this simple substitution drill more challenging by changing two words instead of one, keeping the structure the same. For example:

It's a green pencil. It's a striped shirt.
It's a red book. It's a leather belt.

SUBSTITUTION DRILL

I'm	eating.	
	reading.	
	carrying.	
You're	carrying	the book.
They're	carrying	the books.
He's	reading	a newspaper.
She's	reading	a recipe.
I'm	eating	my lunch.
We're	eating	our dinner.

This same substitution drill can be made more challenging by showing a picture and giving the sentence structure, having the students listen, and then asking them to repeat. For example:

The family is going to the clinic.

Then give only the word to be substituted, perhaps showing appropriate pictures: *supermarket, library, school.*

Teacher: *The family is going to the clinic.*
Student: *The family is going to the clinic.*

Teacher: *supermarket*
Student: *The family is going to the supermarket.*

Teacher: *library*
Student: *The family is going to the library.*

Teacher: *school*
Student: *The family is going to the school.*

SIMPLE SUBSTITUTION DRILL

Substitute one word in a sentence.
Use an appropriate action or picture for comprehension.

It's a book.	I'm sitting.	Joe is reading.
It's a chair.	You're sitting.	Joe is working.
It's a pencil.	We're sitting.	Joe is playing.

Give one cue word. The student substitutes it into the pattern.

Teacher: *The children are playing in the yard.*
Student: *The children are playing in the yard.*

Teacher: *garden*
Student: *The children are playing in the garden.*

Teacher: *field*
Student: *The children are playing in the field.*

Complex Substitution Drill

More complex substitution drills can be used for more advanced students. They are called complex drills when the substituted words go into different slots in the sentence. Students have to think about the meaning of each word as they decide where the word must go:

Teacher: *The family is going to the clinic.*
Student: *The family is going to the clinic.*

Teacher: *Girl.*
Student: *The girl is going to the clinic.*

Teacher: *Walking.*
Student: *The girl is walking to the clinic.*

Teacher: *Library.*
Student: *The girl is walking to the library.*

After the students have heard, understood, and spoken the words in the substitution drills, write those same words on paper or on the board so that the students can read and write them.

COMPLEX SUBSTITUTION DRILL

After giving a basic sentence, give only the cue word for substitution.

Teacher: *Mary is walking to school.*
Student: *Mary is walking to school.*

Teacher: *running*
Student: *Mary is running to school.*

Teacher: *work*
Student: *Mary is running to work.*

Teacher: *John*
Student: *John is running to work.*

Response Drill

An early step toward getting your students to be independent is to work on response drills. Through the previous substitution drill, you have already taught the students statements that could be answers to questions. Through repetition, the students will begin to sense an answer pattern that will help them use what they've been practicing in other settings. You can start by having students make statements and ask questions about activities in each other's daily lives using the drills they have been practicing.

For beginning-level students, actions and pictures will be necessary to supplement the drill. Of course, before you ask the question, you must be certain that your students have the information and language practice needed for the appropriate answer. You are not quizzing for facts. You are giving repeated practice in understanding and responding to common questions. Thus, at the beginning levels, your procedure should be to model and teach the answer first, have the students repeat, and then ask the question. Your first activities will be obvious and simple, using any available pictures or props (e.g., opening a door, walking around a table). Afterward, let students suggest activities.

Teacher: *I'm eating dinner.*
Student: *I'm eating dinner.*

Teacher: *What are you doing?*
Student: *I'm eating dinner.*

After several repetitions, reverse the procedure. Suggest that the students ask you or each other the questions.

Be careful not to ask questions beyond your students' comprehension. Build on words the students already know, and help them learn to say words and sentences commonly used in ordinary conversation.

Teacher: *I'm studying English.*
Student: *I'm studying English.*

Teacher: *What are you studying?*
Student: *I'm studying English.*

When you have taught a basic structure, such as *I'm going to the library. Where are you going?*, you can suggest putting different words in the same slot by showing different pictures.

Teacher: *I'm going to the library.*
Student: *I'm going to the library.*

Teacher: (shows picture of a post office) *Where are you going?*
Student: *I'm going to the post office.*

Teacher: (shows picture of a supermarket) *Where are you going?*
Student: *I'm going to the supermarket.*

Variations of the response drill are endless. You could include a real or imaginary visit (using pictures) to the local grocery store to shop for food and teach the students the various ways items are sold (e.g., by the pound, by the loaf, by the dozen).

Teacher: *I'd like a dozen rolls.*
Student: *I'd like a dozen rolls.*

Teacher: *I'd like a loaf of bread.*
Student: *I'd like a loaf of bread.*

Teacher: *I'd like a pound of cheese.*
Student: *I'd like a pound of cheese.*

Using appropriate pictures, the question and answer would be:

Teacher: *What would you like?*
Student: *I'd like a dozen rolls, a loaf of bread, and a pound of cheese.*

Notice that you are actually combining the response drill with a substitution drill.

Early in the teaching sequence, you might want to help students become familiar with the names of various types of appliances or pieces of furniture in the home. You can draw stick figures or cut out pictures from magazines to help as you use the response and substitution drills.

Use pictures to elicit a variety of responses. Eventually you won't have to model the response; it will come naturally. The length of time this will take will depend on the picture, the vocabulary, and the student. When you show pictures to your students, this question could be answered simply or with a detailed reply:

Teacher: *What's this man doing?*
Student: *He's fishing.*
Or *He's trying to catch fish, but he'll have a hard time because he doesn't have a net.*

Teacher: *What's this man doing?*
Student: *He's walking.*
Or *He's walking to work, carrying a newspaper.*

Questions about pictures often give your students a chance to provide a wide range of responses. As you ask the question *What's the girl doing?* you might expect the answer *The girl is sitting,* but one student may say, *The girl is smiling,* and another may say, *The girl's playing.* You have helped them use acquired vocabulary independently. Encourage creativity. Creativity fosters learning and is fun.

Creating their own questions is an important milestone for students. They need to learn to ask questions for which they need the answers. They will want to be able to understand practical responses as well. You can ask what language needs your students had that week and incorporate them into the lesson.

Student: *Where do I get the bus for Main Street?*
Teacher: *Go to the next corner. The bus comes every 10 minutes.*

You can always end each exercise by writing the words and sentences used, giving the students the opportunity to read and write the words and sentences. As your students advance, start asking questions for which you haven't already given the answers. This exercise requires real thought and leads to authentic communication.

RESPONSE DRILL

The teacher holds a picture of a woman in a supermarket.

Teacher: *The woman is in the supermarket.*
Student: *The woman is in the supermarket.*

Teacher: *Where is the woman?*
Student: *The woman is in the supermarket.*

Transformation Drill

In the transformation drill, students:

- change positive statements to negative statements and, conversely, negative statements to positive statements

- change statements to questions and questions to statements

Prepare the students for changing a positive statement into a negative one by having them repeat both the positive and negative sentences after you. Pictures or quickly drawn stick figures may help with comprehension.

Teacher: *The man is happy.*
Student: *The man is happy.*

Shake your head as you say:

Teacher: *The man is not happy.*
Student: *The man is not happy.*

After your students have had sufficient practice with both positive and negative sentences and understand the pattern, continue with a more complex transformation drill, supplying the cue word *not*.

Teacher: *The man is happy. Or The man's happy.*
Student: *The man is happy. Or The man's happy.*

Teacher: *Not.*
Student: *The man is not happy. Or The man isn't happy.*

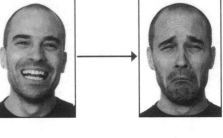

As your students understand the positive/negative transformation, you might want to teach how some negatives do not merely add the word *not* but actually change the wording a bit. As you show a picture of a boy holding a dog, you could say:

Teacher: *Jimmy has a dog.*
Student: *Jimmy has a dog.*

Teacher (cover dog with your hand): *Not.*
Student: *Jimmy does not have a dog. Or Jimmy doesn't have a dog.*

Or

Teacher (holding picture of a motorcycle): *Is this a bus?*
Student: *No, it's not a bus. It's a motorcycle.*

TRANSFORMATION DRILL
Positive to Negative

Teacher (pointing to pen): *This is a pen.*
Student: *This is a pen.*

Teacher (pointing to book and shaking head): *This is not a pen.*
Student: *This is not a pen.*

For more advanced students:

Teacher (showing picture of a bus): *This is a bus.*
Student: *This is a bus.*

Teacher (showing picture of a motorcycle): *not*
Student: *This is not a bus. This is a motorcycle.*

Question patterns may be more difficult. When changing statements to questions, you can cue the students by holding up a card with a question mark on it. You may have to teach the symbol for question mark.

Model the sentence, and have the students repeat it. Then restate it in question form as you hold up a card showing a question mark.

Teacher: *Harry is going to work. Or Harry's going to work.*
Student: *Harry is going to work. Or Harry's going to work.*
Teacher (holding ? card): *Is Harry going to work?*
Student: *Is Harry going to work?*

Model several sentences in this way. Then try giving a statement, holding the ? cue card.

Teacher: *Marie is reading a book. Or Marie's reading a book.*
  (Hold ? card as cue.)
Student: *Is Marie reading a book?*

As students start to understand changing statements to questions, you might say:

Teacher: *Ask me if I'm going home after class.*
Student: *Are you going home after class?*

Teacher: *Ask Mary where you can find the bus schedule.*
Student: *Mary, where can I find the bus schedule?*

TRANSFORMATION DRILL
Statement to Question

Teacher: *José is going to the library.*
Student: *José is going to the library.*
Teacher (holding ? cue card): *José is going to the library.*
Student: *Is José going to the library?*

Transformation drills can also be useful when teaching harder concepts, such as irregular past tense verbs (*see/saw, come/came, go/went, am/was, think/thought*). These exercises, too, can be reinforced by having the students read and then write the words they have been practicing orally.

Backward Buildup

Often a sentence, or even a word, is just too long for students to repeat it correctly the first time. They may have no problem at the beginning but have trouble near the end. Backward buildup provides practice in repeating long words or sentences with more practice at the end where the problems are. If you maintain the same intonation patterns and repeat each syllable or phrase, your students will be consistently hearing those same patterns.

If your students have problems saying a long word such as *inexplicable*, divide it into parts (*in-ex-plic-able*) and say the last part, *-able,* gesturing for the students to repeat. Then say and ask students to repeat *-plicable, -explicable,* and finally *inexplicable.*

In the following sentence, *We're going to the supermarket to buy meat and vege-tables for dinner*, students can often repeat the first two phrases correctly, but they frequently stumble on the third and usually can't remember the fourth.

First, divide the sentence into phrases:

We're going / to the supermarket / to buy meat and vegetables / for dinner.

1	2	3	4
OK	OK	problem	problem

Say the sentence as a whole. Then begin the backward buildup. Start on the last phrase, proceeding forward from there. Use a natural stress and intonation pattern for each fragment.

Teacher: *For dinner.*
Student: *For dinner.*

Teacher: *To buy meat and vegetables for dinner.*
Student: *To buy meat and vegetables for dinner.*

Teacher: *To the supermarket to buy meat and vegetables for dinner.*
Student: *To the supermarket to buy meat and vegetables for dinner.*

Teacher: *We're going to the supermarket to buy meat and vegetables for dinner.*
Student: *We're going to the supermarket to buy meat and vegetables for dinner.*

Thus, there is more repetition of the phrases that cause the most difficulty. As usual, follow up the oral practice by allowing the students to read and then write these same sentences.

Because you can speak and understand English, these sentences give you no trouble. If you were trying to say them in a foreign language, however, you'd probably struggle, too. To empathize with the difficulty your students experience, try the following technique with a friend, using telephone numbers. Have your friend say the entire sentence (three sets of number phrases) at a normal speed.

Friend: *425-346-2917*
You: *425-346* (probably)

If this is too easy, try it with four or more sets of numbers. No matter how many sets of numbers are used, this exercise illustrates the difficulty that students have when learning a new language.

The backward buildup technique helps students remember phrases or numbers long enough to put them all together. To remember 378-541-1623, try this.

Friend, then you:	*1623*
Friend, then you:	*541-1623*
Friend, then you:	*378-541-1623*

This technique can be used with lower-level students who have trouble with shorter sentences, but it is particularly helpful as your students are expected to repeat longer and longer sentences.

BACKWARD BUILDUP

If conversational English students have trouble repeating a complete sentence as modeled by the teacher, start the drill by using the last phrase of the sentence.

He went / to work / at six o'clock / on Tuesday morning.

Teacher: ...on Tuesday morning.
Student: ...on Tuesday morning.

Teacher: ...at six o'clock on Tuesday morning.
Student: ...at six o'clock on Tuesday morning.

Teacher: ...to work at six o'clock on Tuesday morning.
Student: ...to work at six o'clock on Tuesday morning.

Teacher: He went to work at six o'clock on Tuesday morning.
Student: He went to work at six o'clock on Tuesday morning.

Chain Drill

A chain drill is a good way to have people in a small group or in a class introduce themselves. It's easy yet informative. To begin, sit with your students around a table, or arrange your chairs in a circle. You could start by saying:

My name is. . .

Turn to your neighbor at your right or left and say:

What's your name?

That person responds with his or her name and asks the same question of the next person. This continues around the circle.

The repetition is simple enough so that even a shy beginning-level student can participate and gain confidence. The chain drill can be expanded to other statements and questions. Always give your statement first as a model and then ask a question:

I'm from New York State. Where are you from?
I'm from Puerto Rico. Where are you from?

If your students are from different countries, you might have a globe or a large map available, giving students an opportunity to pinpoint their countries.

You can add other questions, each time varying the chain drill a bit:

I've lived in Middletown for 20 years. How long have you lived in Middletown?

I drove my car to school. How did you get here?

I have two children and six grandchildren. Do you have a family?

I like to play golf and ski. What do you like to do?

I took a walk last night. What did you do last night?

Another chain drill activity is for the students to make up a narrative based on a picture, an activity, or an experience. Each student adds one phrase or one sentence to the story and must repeat all the preceding phrases or sentences. Exactly the same wording is not necessary; paraphrasing is perfectly acceptable.

For example:

Teacher: *When Maria first came to America, she. . .*
First Student: *When Maria first came to America, she didn't have a friend.*
Second Student: *When Maria came to America at first, she didn't have friends or a teacher.*

One variation would be to have each student add a sentence or short paragraph that continues a story without repeating the parts that came before. Such improvisation is especially useful with advanced students in helping them to discover and expand the range of their mastery of English.

Teacher: *The Gómez family decided to go on a picnic.*
First Student: *They wanted to see the big lake they had heard about.*
Second Student: *But first they had to get food to bring.*

Even with beginning students, you can use chain drills to give practice in understanding and saying confusing individual sounds. Have pictures available of objects whose names begin with the confusing sounds. For example, if the confusing sounds are /d/ and /b/, have pictures of foods whose names start with *d*—*doughnuts, dates*—and pictures of foods whose names start with *b*—*bananas, beans*. Have the students choose pictures and substitute the words shown in their pictures in the appropriate place, adding more words.

We went to the market and got doughnuts and bananas.
We went to the market and got dates and beans.

Chain drills help students relax and have fun at the beginning of lessons while also giving practice in listening and speaking.

CHAIN DRILL

Students respond and continue.

Teacher: *I'm from New York State. Where are you from?*
First Student: *I'm from Poland. Where are you from?*
Second Student: *I'm from Vietnam. Where are you from?*

Creative Oral Exercises

There are an infinite number of exercises that allow students to use language creatively. A few of these exercises follow.

Sentence Combining

Giving your students an opportunity to create more complex sentence structures from simple sentences can help students with independent speaking.

Teacher: *This coffee is hot. This coffee is strong.*
Student: *This coffee is hot. This coffee is strong.*

Gesture by bringing two hands together to suggest combining the sentences as you say:

Teacher: *This coffee is hot and strong.*
Student: *This coffee is hot and strong.*

Your students will get the idea and respond with new examples.

Teacher: *The truck is large. The truck is expensive.*

If you gesture to combine those sentences, students will probably say:

Student: *The truck is large and expensive.*

Teach additional connecting words such as *but, so, when, before, after, then,* and *because.* Write each word on an index card. Let the students choose a card. Say two sentences that can be combined with the connecting word they picked.

Teacher: *The building is five stories high. It is difficult to walk to the top floor.*
Student: *The building is five stories high, so it is difficult to walk to the top floor.*

Teacher: *I burned my tongue. I drank hot coffee.*
Student: *I burned my tongue because I drank hot coffee.*

SENTENCE COMBINING

1. Teacher says two short sentences. Student repeats.
   The coffee is hot. The coffee is strong.

2. Teacher gestures to combine them.
   Teacher: *The coffee is hot and strong.*
   Student: *The coffee is hot and strong.*

3. Once this routine is comfortable for the student, the teacher gestures to combine them and says
   Teacher: *The coffee is hot. The coffee is strong.*
   Student: *The coffee is hot and strong.*

Restatement

As students become more proficient at speaking English, you can have them restate specific sentences, putting the information in the first person singular.

Teacher: *Tell me that you are going to the library.*
Student: *I'm going to the library.*

Substitute various phrases to reinforce the concept.

Teacher: *Tell me that you are looking for a book.*
Student: *I'm looking for a book.*

Teacher: *Tell me that you are reading stories to your children in English.*
Student: *I'm reading stories to my children in English.*

This is an effective way of encouraging your students to talk without simply repeating what you say.

Another way to encourage restatement is to suggest that the students ask the teacher questions.

Teacher: *Ask me where I went on my vacation.*
Student: *Where did you go on your vacation?*
Teacher: *I went to Arizona on my vacation.*

You can ask advanced students to restate longer and more complicated sentences. They must remember the original sentence, creating new words and ideas on their own.

Teacher: *Last week I saw an accident, and I got a call today to be a witness.*
Student: *You saw an accident last week, and today you got a call to be a witness.*

Again, for advanced students, more difficult structures can be used. You can teach the tenses without using the terms *present, past, future* by modeling and then restating them with the appropriate adverbs (e.g., *today, yesterday, tomorrow*).

Teacher: *Today I am (I'm) having lunch with a friend.*
Student: *Today I am (I'm) having lunch with a friend.*

Teacher: *Yesterday I had lunch with a friend.*
Student: *Yesterday I had lunch with a friend.*

Teacher: *Tomorrow I will (I'll) have lunch with a friend.*
Student: *Tomorrow I will (I'll) have lunch with a friend.*

When the students have practiced and understood how the cue words *today, yesterday, tomorrow* indicate a change in tense, first give a sentence and then only the cue word.

Teacher: *Today I'm playing tennis.*

Teacher: *Yesterday. . .*
Student: *Yesterday I played tennis.*

Teacher: *Tomorrow. . .*
Student: *Tomorrow I will play tennis.*

RESTATEMENT

Ask the students to restate a sentence, putting it in different words.

> Teacher: *Tell me that you are enjoying your vacation.*
> Student: *I'm enjoying my vacation.*

After you teach past and future tenses, give cue words (*today, yesterday, tomorrow*) and have your students restate a sentence using the appropriate verb tense.

> Teacher: *Today I'm riding the bus to work.*

> Teacher: *Yesterday...*
> Student: *Yesterday I rode the bus to work.*

> Teacher: *Tomorrow...*
> Student: *Tomorrow I'll ride the bus to work.*

Sentence Completion

Your students can get additional practice forming correct sentences as well as an opportunity to be creative by completing sentences that you start. You can use pictures to suggest the new vocabulary, or you can leave it to your students' imagination.

> Teacher: *I went shopping and bought. . .*
> Student: *I went shopping and bought six oranges.*

If you have several students in your group, you could have each add one item (a chain drill) and repeat the items suggested before.

> Student: *I went shopping and bought six oranges and two apples.*

If you are working with advanced students, they may want to make more complicated additions.

> Teacher: *On the way to class. . .*
> Student: *On the way to class, I met two men from my country, and we had a nice talk.*

COMPLETION DRILL

The teacher begins a sentence and asks the student to complete it appropriately.

> Teacher: *I have...*
> Student: *I have a new car.*

Continuing Story

To encourage advanced students to speak spontaneously, use the continuing story exercise. The teacher starts the story, setting the stage and giving the students an idea of what is expected. To help the person continue the story, allow for a range of options by leaving the final sentence unfinished. The student can add one or as many appropriate sentences as he or she wishes. The teacher can continue the story, or in a small group or in a class, a second student can add to the story.

Teacher: *I know an old man. He lives. . .*

First Student: *He lives across the street from us and is known to everyone. He enjoys watching the children. He is. . .*

Second Student: *He is very poor, but he brings cookies every day to share with the children. One day. . .*

Third Student: *One day the old man wasn't in his usual place on the park bench. The children missed him and wondered what happened.*

This story could go on and on, with the teacher and students continuing to add their own ideas, creating a mystery, a charming short story, a love story—whatever they want.

What follows is an example of a more advanced continuing story in which both the teacher and students are expected to give longer responses:

Teacher: *The bus came up the street. It was the #20 bus, just the one I was looking for. We had formed a line, and I was in the middle. The man in front of me reached into his pocket and pulled out. . .*

This gives the next person an opportunity to say whatever comes to mind, not taking too much time to think. The students can take more time thinking as the story develops, but encourage each student to stop in midsentence. Each student must speak, trying to be creative in using the English he or she knows. At the end of the lesson, suggest that the students write the story in their own words; then read the story to the group.

The suggested exercises can be used with beginning as well as advanced students. Introduce them simply, and repeat them often until the students understand the concept and see the patterns. Repetition may seem boring to you, but it builds confidence and gives needed practice to the students. It is a long road between saying something once and having it come naturally in a conversation.

CONTINUING STORY

1. The teacher starts the conversation.

   Teacher: *I bought a used car. The color is...*

2. Each student adds as many appropriate sentences as he or she wishes.

   Student 1: *The color is blue. It's a 2004 Ford, four door. I got an excellent deal, and it's in good...*

   Student 2: *It's in good shape. Yesterday, as I stopped for a red light, the car behind me...*

3. Continue as long as the students maintain interest.

4. Each student writes his or her own version of the story.

5. Each student reads his or her story to the group.

Dialogue

A dialogue is a conversational exchange between two or more people in a given situation. An effective way to present and practice the patterns and structures of English is through dialogue rather than in isolation. Try to tie the dialogue to the topic of the lesson if possible. You can incorporate all the techniques presented so far: substitution drill, response drill, transformation drill, chain drill, and backward buildup.

Memorized dialogues are especially useful with beginning students. Free dialogues spring from a topic the students are familiar with and are built with vocabulary and structures the students know.

Memorized Dialogue

A dialogue to be memorized can be taken from an ESOL text, or you can prepare it yourself. You can help your students memorize the dialogue through repetition and response drills. Even at a basic level, dialogues can and should resemble brief real-life conversations. Together, decide on the topic to be used in the dialogue. Be sure to use pictures or props if your students need them to understand. Keep the sentences simple and limited to four lines at first. A sample for a beginning student might be:

Teacher: *Would you like a cup of coffee?*
Student: *Yes, thank you.*
Teacher: *Sugar and cream?*
Student: *No, I take mine black.*

An advanced student could memorize a more complex dialogue.

Gesture for your student to listen, or say, *Listen*. First, say the entire dialogue, performing any activities or using any objects or pictures to aid understanding. By sitting in opposite chairs or by turning your head a different way for each person, you can indicate that you are one person for lines one and three and another person for lines two and four. You can also use cards with names indicating speaker A or B. Or you can use pictures of two people from a magazine as the imaginary dialogue partners.

When modeling the dialogue, be sure to speak as you would speak normally. Talk with normal speed and rhythm. Speak clearly but not too loudly.

- Present the entire dialogue at least twice before you ask the students to repeat it.

- Break it down by sentences. Say the first sentence. Ask your students to repeat it several times until you feel they can say it with fairly good pronunciation. Then do the same for the second sentence, sitting in the opposing seat or showing appropriate actions. Repeat this process for each line. You may have to repeat the lines several times before your students are comfortable with them.

- Repeat the entire dialogue. This time, act it out, and have your students listen.

- Say each line together. Go through the dialogue, and have your students say each line with you. Repeat several times until your students have the dialogue memorized. Be sure your students understand the meaning of the dialogue. Next is the performance.

- You say the first line, your students responding with the second line. Continue this pattern line by line until the students can say their lines readily.

- Reverse the roles. The students say the odd-numbered lines, and you say the even-numbered lines. If you have a small group or a class, you might divide the students into pairs and ask them to practice the dialogue.

- When the pattern is learned, you can substitute words such as *tea* for *coffee* or adapt the dialogue in some other way, keeping the same general pattern.

> **Teacher:** *Will you have a sandwich?*
> **Student:** *Yes, thank you.*
> **Teacher:** *Tuna salad or ham and cheese?*
> **Student:** *I'd like ham and cheese.*

Use pictures to cue the students to give more than one likely response, using substitution drills.

Recording dialogues for review at home is helpful. As students repeat sentences with the audio, they can practice pronunciation as well as the normal rhythm of the language.

For advanced students, use more complex dialogues. Dialogues provide a safe setting for students to practice talking about a subject without having to rely on spontaneity. For the following dialogue, bring pictures of a refrigerator, cheese, meat, and bread to the teaching session. Point to the appropriate pictures and gesture for the students to listen and then repeat the dialogue.

First Speaker: *What's in the refrigerator? I'm hungry.*

Second Speaker: *There's cheese, meat, and bread. Why don't you make a sandwich?*

First Speaker: *Yes, that sounds good.*

Second Speaker: *Why don't you make one for me, too? Or Would you make one for me, too?*

First Speaker: *All right, I will. Or OK, I will. Or Sure.*

With every dialogue, go through all the steps as suggested. In the following dialogue, perhaps the students couldn't repeat the second line. This is a perfect time for backward buildup.

Teacher: *A sandwich.*
Student: *A sandwich.*

Teacher: *Why don't you make a sandwich?*
Student: *Why don't you make a sandwich?*

Teacher: *Meat and bread. Why don't you make a sandwich?*
Student: *Meat and bread. Why don't you make a sandwich?*

Teacher: *There's cheese, meat, and bread. Why don't you make a sandwich?*
Student: *There's cheese, meat, and bread. Why don't you make a sandwich?*

Using pictures, you can change the situation. Instead of a refrigerator, a picture of a cooler or picnic basket could be used. Other food can be substituted in the dialogue. Eventually the students will feel confident enough to adapt the language learned in dialogues to other situations.

After you and your students have gone through a dialogue, suggest that they copy the dialogue onto a piece of paper for home study; if they have difficulty with writing, give them a copy to read at home. You might suggest that they try recording the memorized dialogue at home. They can refer to the printed dialogue if they wish.

One of the most difficult things for teachers to realize is that language must be overlearned. Language learning requires constant review and repetition. "Once over lightly" simply will not suffice. Remember, everything is new, and much repetition is needed to build confidence as well as new vocabulary.

Dialogues are worth all the effort of practice. The rewards come when they lead to real conversation.

DIALOGUE

Dialogue is a conversational exchange between two people. Keep dialogues simple at first, no more than four lines. Incorporate techniques as needed.

> Teacher: What's this?
> Student: It's an orange.
> Teacher: Do you like oranges?
> Student: Yes, oranges are good.

Steps for learning dialogues:

1. Teacher says entire dialogue, making sure student understands meaning.

2. Teacher says first sentence; student repeats first sentence.

3. Teacher says each sentence; student repeats each sentence.

4. Teacher says entire dialogue while student listens.

5. Teacher and student say the entire dialogue together.

6. Reverse the roles if appropriate.

Variations for further practice:

- Substitute words or lines, especially on the teacher's part.

- Add new lines for a longer dialogue.

- Combine two short but related dialogues.

Free Dialogue

Conversing spontaneously in real-life situations is the primary goal of most ESOL students. Prepared or cued dialogues can provide an entrance into free dialogue or discussion. It is desirable to stimulate free dialogue as soon as possible, but recognize that the amount of discussion will be minimal with beginning-level English speakers compared to what you might expect from more advanced students.

Action pictures as well as student-suggested situations can be starting points for free dialogue. For an entertaining alternative, take a sequence of cartoons and cut out the words. Using the situation in the cartoon as the basis for a dialogue, you and your students decide what words you would like the characters in the cartoon to say.

Role playing is an important tool for introducing and practicing free dialogue. As a group, pick a situation for a role play, and then act out a dialogue. Perhaps your students will be visiting a school soon. You could pretend to be the office receptionist. In character, ask your visitors questions. Your students should respond. You might want to record the entire dialogue, playing it back so that the students can hear themselves.

Ask your students to suggest situations where they need help: in stores, in pharmacies, in banks, at doctor's appointments, on the bus, or at work. Act out as many dialogues as seem useful based on these and other relevant situations. Have the students break up into pairs when feasible. Possible scenarios for them to enact could be cashier and customer, pharmacist and customer, bank teller and customer, nurse or doctor and patient, bus driver and passenger, or supervisor and employee.

Dialogues give students a way to practice using English in real-life situations. Write lots of dialogues for them. Write simple dialogues of your own, and suggest that they write dialogues for the situations listed below or others they identify.

- Use the phone to make an appointment.
- Use the phone in an emergency or to tell the teacher that there has been an unexpected event and they won't be at the lesson.
- Talk to a doctor, nurse, or pharmacist.
- Order food in a restaurant.
- Ask directions.
- Return an item to a store.
- Ask the landlord to repair something in the apartment.
- Seek information about work.
- Enroll a child in school.
- Make change.

In such dialogues, your students will be discussing real-life experiences and practicing English that they can use in their daily lives. You will find many ideas for dialogues that focus on immigrants' and newcomers' interests and concerns in Appendix C, page 202: talking with family, filling out forms, doing housework and caring for children, buying and driving a car, communicating in work and social settings, going to restaurants, renting/buying a house, doing house repairs, dealing with health and finance issues.

Idioms

An idiom is a succession of words whose meaning is not obvious through knowledge of the individual words but must be learned as a whole (e.g., *give way, in order to, be hard put to, run up the bill*).

In his book *Doctor to the Barrios* (1970), Dr. Juan Flavier said that when he was trying to get to know the people of the Philippines better so that he could teach them English, he found that it was just as important to know their idioms as to know their more formal language. He gave this example:

One day a farmer asked him if he wanted "kisses honey." He declined because he wasn't sure what was meant. His colleague accepted and the farmer opened an old biscuit tin. It contained shredded tobacco and cigarette paper. Then the meaning became clear. The farmer put some tobacco on the rectangular paper, rolled it expertly, and licked the edge to keep it in place.

Hence, *kisses honey* was a hand-rolled cigarette.

American idioms are just as difficult and just as confusing for the person trying to learn American English. Yet idioms are accepted as part of everyday speech. They cannot be translated directly, and their meanings are not always easy to explain.

He's broke.
Give me a ring.
My new car was a real steal.
I'll drop you a line.

Idioms should be taught, giving explanations of their meanings as they are repeated.

He's broke. He has no money. He's broke.

Rosa, a reliable hotel housekeeper, had improved her English and was promoted to a supervisory position responsible not only for several other workers but also for the appropriate paperwork. One day she received a note from her manager, "You make this job look like a piece of cake."

Upset, Rosa checked back on the rooms she was responsible for and on all her work. Finally, she came to her boss saying, "I'm so sorry about the cake, but where was it?" She didn't know that "piece of cake" was an American idiom, and her boss meant "You make it look easy."

Provide several explanatory sentences so that your students can understand the meaning of each idiomatic expression and become comfortable with it. Even though English speakers understand the meanings of many idioms, it is often not easy to explain them to someone else. There are many books on idioms that could help you. Also, ask students to bring to class idioms that they would like to discuss.

Sentence Structure/Grammar

When we think of the structure of the English language, most of us do not analyze why we say something a certain way. We say it the way we do because it sounds right. For example, we wouldn't say, *I to work go,* but rather, *I go to work.* We wouldn't say, *This pencil not is sharp* or *This pencil not sharp is.* We'd say, *This pencil is not sharp.*

Even those of us who have studied formal English grammar do not always know which rules we follow when we speak, but we generally know implicitly what is right. Your aim as a teacher is not primarily to teach grammatical rules but instead to teach standard usage so your students will get a feel for the accepted form of spoken English.

After a while, grammatically correct sentences will begin to sound right to your students, and you can avoid teaching many confusing rules about language and grammar. Often a student will want to know why something is said in a certain way, but avoid talking about grammatical rules unless you are specifically asked to do so. Instead, teach correct usage by demonstrating properly structured phrases and sentences throughout the lessons. If students do ask, avoid lengthy technical explanations.

In teaching sentence structure, you should be aware that proper word order is essential for accurate communication in the English language and that the same words can convey a totally different meaning when their order in a sentence is changed. For example, every native English speaker knows that although identical vocabulary is used in these two sentences, they describe two totally different experiences:

The dog bit the man.
The man bit the dog.

With beginning students, use sentences that can be illustrated during your tutoring session. Of course, use vocabulary relevant to your students' lives whenever possible.

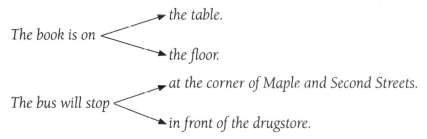

The book is on — *the table.*
the floor.

The bus will stop — *at the corner of Maple and Second Streets.*
in front of the drugstore.

At times you may want to prepare simple grammar checks for the students by having them decide which of two sentences is correct according to the picture.

For simple grammar contrasts (singular vs. plural, male vs. female, now vs. every day), prepare several sentences. Say them and have the students indicate which category each fits into.

Teacher: *He's swimming.*
Student: *Now.*

Teacher: *He eats at Big Burger.*
Student: *Every day.*

Teacher: *They work at the factory.*
Student: *Every day.*

Teacher: *They're riding the bus.*
Student: *Now.*

If your students want detailed help with English grammar, you could point them toward one of the many books available or suggest that they explore relevant information on the Internet (see Appendix M, page 236, for suggestions). Be selective with textbook activities so as not to overdo isolated drill work. It is important for students to have sufficient practice with correct grammar, especially if they ask for it, but the goal of language learning is effective usage rather than memorization of rules. You and your students need to work out the proper balance between structured grammatical exercises and free conversation. That balance will differ depending on students' educational backgrounds, learning styles, and purposes for learning English.

Expanding Vocabulary

Words are heard, spoken, read, and written. For real competence in English, your students will need an ever-expanding vocabulary. Instead of asking students to memorize vocabulary lists, introduce new words within known structures or within similar word group meanings. Substitute new words into sentences and patterns you are already working on. Use actions, objects, pictures, questions, or a bilingual dictionary to ensure that your students understand meanings. When you introduce new vocabulary words, talk about their stress patterns as well as their meanings.

New Vocabulary Within Known Structures

We all remember new vocabulary better if we learn the words not in isolation but in sentences and preferably with images. For example, if the words to be learned are *coat, hat,* and *tie,* you could use a simple substitution drill, putting the new words in sentences:

> *He's wearing a coat.*
> *He's wearing a hat.*
> *He's wearing a tie.*

If the words are more difficult to understand, such as *beautiful* or *kind,* you could use pictures or a bilingual dictionary to convey the meaning. Presenting new words in sentences helps with comprehension.

Writing down new words is helpful. You or your students might want to write labels that they can post on objects around their homes or at their workplaces. Encourage your students to bring in pictures or descriptions of objects for which they want the English words. This is a good way to start developing personal word lists.

New Vocabulary Within Word Groupings

It is helpful to teach new vocabulary words in groups and in context:

- Words associated with particular situations, such as *doctor, clinic,* and *medicine* or *act, acting,* and *actor*
- Words illustrated by pictures or objects at hand, such as *table, chair, purse,* or *door*

- Words related to everyday needs, such as days of the week, months, numbers, colors, parts of the body, or shopping list items

Vocabulary that relates to student needs and interests is always more easily learned than abstract vocabulary. Illustrate the new word in a sentence to teach the meaning rather than simply giving a definition. Students will usually learn the meaning by associating the new word with other English words they already know—*divide, dividend, division.*

> *A person who works for a company is an employee.*
> *The person who hires him is his employer.*
> *A person who has a job is employed.*

Placement of a single word sometimes makes a big difference:

> *She has a few friends* is so different from *She has few friends.*

When your students know some basic words, *understand, possible, regular,* you might want to show how adding different prefixes changes the meaning of these same words: *misunderstand, impossible, irregular.*

After your students have heard these new words, understood their meaning, and repeated them, they should read them and finally write them down.

Word Cards and Vocabulary Notebooks

All learners want to see progress. One concrete measure of progress for ESOL students is the number of vocabulary words they know. To help them keep track of their increased vocabularies, have your students put each vocabulary word on a 3 × 5 index card or a quartered card or in their own vocabulary notebooks. If a student can say the word, recall its meaning, and use it correctly in a sentence on three separate occasions, then that word can be considered "known."

Put one check mark by a word if a student says it correctly without having heard it modeled (from picture, action, and so on).

> *refrigerator* ✓
> *stove* ✓

Put another check mark if a student uses the word correctly at a second lesson.

> *dishwasher* ✓✓
> *silverware* ✓✓

Put a third check mark if a student uses the word correctly at a third lesson. By then one can assume that the student knows the word.

> *toaster* ✓✓✓

Your students might want to add their own notes on the backs of the cards or in their notebooks, perhaps noting how the word is pronounced, writing in their own language, putting the word in a sentence, or drawing a picture to illustrate its meaning. Students often feel they are not learning new English words fast enough, and a pile of these cards is concrete evidence of the number of new words they are learning. These cards or notebooks can be reviewed for home study.

Encourage students to jot down new words they've learned or want to know more about in a notebook, perhaps organizing them by categories—foods, colors, clothing, animals, etc. This might be a good time to show students how to look up new words in a dictionary.

When your students can use the new vocabulary words to create original sentences, you can be assured that they are growing toward independent speech.

Free Conversation

Free and easy conversation that is interesting and informative is what you should strive for in your lessons. Keep the students talking. The key often is to find a topic of interest to start the conversation. Often a question or a request for the students to tell you about something can lead the way. A list of suggested conversation starters is in Appendix G, page 212.

If you will stop, look, and listen to your own small social groups, you will note that some individuals tend to dominate the group (the talkers) while others sit back quietly (the listeners). This is natural in most groups and probably will happen even when you are tutoring only one student—that person could be shy and resist trying to talk or might be adventuresome and willing to try new and difficult words. Individuals, whether alone with a tutor or in a small group or classroom setting, can be encouraged to become both talkers and listeners. This is the responsibility of the teacher and can be done through games as well as through free or directed conversation.

IMPORTANCE OF PRACTICING LISTENING AND SPEAKING SKILLS

Even native English speakers do not always understand what is said to them. Perhaps the listener wasn't paying attention, or there was background noise; maybe the speaker didn't speak clearly or with proper stress and intonation. Establish with your students some appropriate ways to communicate lack of understanding.

> *Could you repeat that, please?*
> *Excuse me?*
> *Pardon? I didn't understand what you said.*

Practice these and other similar expressions with your students. They will find these expressions very useful as they develop their listening and speaking skills.

Students might want to structure their learning more by setting aside some time each day, or even a whole day each week, when only English is spoken in their family.

> *While working with a young English teacher in China, I found that her dream was to have her two-year-old son speak English. In China all adults work, so the grandparents, if they are retired, are often responsible*

for raising young children. This woman's parents only spoke Chinese, so she wondered how she could help her son get practice in English. She admitted that at the end of a busy day, neither she nor her husband (who also spoke English) felt like communicating in English. I suggested that perhaps they'd want to set aside just one hour a day—perhaps an hour in the morning or an hour right after dinner—when only English was spoken. Since her son's primary caregivers spoke no English, the only way her son was going to get enough exposure to English to eventually pick it up was if she and her husband spoke English around him regularly.

SUMMARY

Be aware of your students' interests and needs. You can use any and all the suggestions given—mix and match. Find your students' strengths and weaknesses by checking the Learner Profile Sheet in Chapter 4 (page 69), adapting the targeted instructions to your students' English levels, and focusing on their interests, needs, and goals. The Quick Reference Guide—Techniques, Strategies, and Activities in Appendix O, page 245, will refer you to specific pages for particular techniques or strategies.

One teacher saw that a student had an ad for a refrigerator on her desk. She found that the student needed a new refrigerator and wanted help finding a good one at a fair price. The other students in her small group agreed that this would be a good project. Their home assignment was to find out all they could about refrigerators.

Wonderful, lively conversation brought out much needed information. By examining different ads, they were doing comparison shopping. Some students wanted to know whether they could bargain as they had done in their home countries. How much more would it cost if they didn't have all the money right then and needed credit? They debated whether it was worthwhile to wait and save the money rather than make interest payments.

Ask your students what *they* want to discuss. You can choose lesson topics according to their interests. Once they decide on a topic, you and they can bring in props. Gardening, buying a car, sports, travels, family activities—the list of possible topics is endless.

Don't forget that *National Geographic* magazines contain colorful pictures of scenes from nearly every country. They also have many images on their website, http://www.nationalgeographic.com. Upon seeing a picture of her country, one student actually cried. She was just bursting to tell the group more about her country. Before this, the teacher hadn't had much success with getting her to speak in English—she was too embarrassed. Seeing a familiar scene gave her the incentive to talk.

TECHNIQUES, STRATEGIES, AND ACTIVITIES FOR TEACHING READING AND WRITING

All the techniques and activities that have been discussed in this book up to now stress listening and speaking in English, reinforced immediately by reading and writing. You will also need to know specific techniques and strategies for teaching reading and writing in English to students who may be either literate or illiterate in their first language.

READING ENGLISH (RECEPTION)

For students who know little or no English, reading will probably be limited to the lesson material, but be aware that there are signs or labels that your students must read daily. Include them in your lessons. Thus, survival skills such as reading street signs (e.g., *STOP, EXIT, EMERGENCY*), labels on medicine bottles (e.g., *take one tablet twice a day*), and ladies' and men's room signs should be taught early. To keep instruction centered on learners, you'll want to focus reading and writing lessons on your students' interests and goals, adapting the drills and exercises to those interests.

Determine Your Students' Current Reading Levels

Chapter 6 included an extended discussion of ESOL student profiles:

Group A • Students cannot understand, speak, read, or write any English and are illiterate in their native languages.

Group B • Students cannot understand, speak, read, or write any English but can read and write in their native languages. There are two subgroups:

1. Native language—Roman alphabet
2. Native language—non-Roman alphabet

Group C • Students can read and write English but have limited speaking and understanding skills.

Group D • Students are Generation 1.5 and have attended school in the United States for some time. They are fluent speakers of English but may have problems with reading and especially with writing.

Group E • Students can read, write, speak, and understand English, but with limited proficiency.

After a few sessions with your students, you should be able to identify the profile that describes each student. (Check their skills by referring to the language functioning levels in Appendix B, page 197.) Knowing the backgrounds, abilities, and goals of your students will help you determine how much to stress independent reading and writing.

For students who write with Roman letters, writing in English will come more easily. But for students whose native language uses non-Roman letters, reading and writing English may be more difficult. For students who cannot write in their own language, you may have to start at the most basic levels—even holding a pen may be new to them.

If such facilities are available, you may want to consider having students in Group A learn to read and write in their first language as a first step to English. Because of the tremendous growth of Hispanic and Latino populations in America, there are often opportunities for native Spanish speakers to learn to read and write Spanish. You'll find more on this later in this chapter and in Chapter 12.

Diagnostic Tests

Informal assessments can identify and measure students' progress with specific reading and/or writing strategies and skills. *READ: Reading Evaluation—Adult Diagnosis* (Colvin & Root, 1999) was designed especially to assess adult reading levels and suggests gaps in learning and how they can be addressed. The *READ* assessment covers the following skills:

1. Basic sight word recognition
2. Specific word analysis skills in relation to:
   - Names and sounds of letters (consonants)
   - Blends (*bl, br*)
   - Word patterns (*mat, sat, fat*) (vowels)
   - Reversals (*was* for *saw*)
   - Variant vowels
3. Level of reading ability
4. Level of reading and listening comprehension

The information you get from *READ* will help you decide which skills need reinforcement and what portion of your lessons should be devoted to each skill.

Ongoing Assessment

As described in Chapter 6, ongoing assessment is most important. Portfolios— folders where records for individual students are kept—are described in that chapter. As lessons include more reading and writing, you'll want to add records of articles and books read as well as student writing to portfolios. When your students read aloud, note their weaknesses as well as their strengths. Do they read word by word? Do they need help with intonation and rhythm? Do they miscall specific words? Keep those notes in the portfolios, too.

Techniques for Teaching Reading

Your students want to learn to read and write English independently, and you can help them acquire these skills. Word recognition occurs when readers can easily identify and say a word. You'll learn different techniques for identifying words such as sounding them out (phonics), seeing and identifying words by sight (sight words), and seeing known word patterns or families and connecting them with new consonants (patterned words).

Drills and exercises are important, but comprehension is the heart of language learning. Little is accomplished if students can read and say words and sentences correctly but have no idea of their meanings. Without knowing certain background information, without having actual real-life experiences, without understanding the cultural context in which language is used, students often do not completely comprehend what is said. No lesson should be considered complete until the teacher is satisfied that the words, phrases, and sentences are completely clear to the students. Comprehension is an integral part of language learning; in fact, it is the true foundation of language acquisition.

> The story is often told of the boy who was asked to read aloud a passage in French. When he finished, the teacher asked him to summarize what he'd read. "I can't, sir. I wasn't listening," he commented.

When reading aloud, language students often concentrate so hard on pronouncing the words correctly that they have no idea what they have just read. Do not ask your students about their understanding of material they have read aloud for the first time. It is very difficult for anyone to grasp meaning while focused on decoding and pronouncing. Although reading aloud gives you important opportunities to check on reading levels, on pronunciation, and on fluency, you can be sensitive to your students' needs by providing silent reading preparation time before asking them to read aloud.

Because people learn in different ways that are not always predictable or even completely understood by experts on cognition, it's important for you to know and be able to use different teaching approaches. Condensed descriptions of several techniques will be included here, but you may want to read *TUTOR 8* (Colvin, 2009) for additional information on how to use these techniques as well as more information on learning styles, learning disabilities, and learning differences:

- Language Experience
- Sight words
- Phonics
- Word patterns
- Comprehension
- Process writing

Language Experience

In Language Experience activities, a student recounts in his or her own words a personal experience, a news item, a description, a public happening, or anything else of interest. In this technique, you write down the student's exact words, demonstrating the connections between thought and writing and between oral language and written language. Even if your students can't yet read the words, they can see how spoken language looks when it becomes written language. The teacher also receives insights into the students' worlds that can guide selection of teaching materials.

If you are tutoring one student, begin a Language Experience activity by inviting him to tell you something of interest: why he came to America, something about his country's history, his dreams for the future, his hobbies, or issues or problems he is facing (such as looking for a job). Ask questions and pick up ideas from your conversations together. If your student still hesitates to talk, use pictures or articles from magazines or newspapers as a focus for discussion.

If you are teaching in a small group or in a classroom setting, let the group decide on a topic for their Language Experience project. Take the first three subjects they suggest, and let them choose one by voting. You can do Language Experience stories on the remaining subjects later. Your students might want to talk about becoming U.S. citizens or about a story heard recently on TV, or they might want to share something that happened in their daily lives—an accident on the way to class, the birth of a new baby, a son's high school graduation. You might want to write down key words they use as they discuss the project to help them remember their ideas.

After having a discussion and using the key words as a guide, have the students dictate the story. This can be done individually or as a group project.

Print the students' words on the board, or if you think they're ready, suggest that your students write the words. Even if beginning-level speakers dictate something incorrectly, write down what they say. Using their exact words shows respect for their thoughts and gives them the confidence to speak out. You might suggest that you read the story together. Ask if they want anything changed—often students self-correct. Later, you can edit the story and explain the corrections. Students eventually want their work to be in proper English.

For advanced students, record the exact words, but offer an opportunity to self-correct. They often know grammatical rules but have not incorporated them into their own spoken language. They sense that something isn't quite right, and when they see their errors in writing, they may be more apt to correct themselves. Follow your students' lead. Suggest that you'll work on more detailed grammar later as the need arises.

Whether you capture the students' words on the board, on paper, or on a computer, do make a copy of the story for each student, and always keep a copy in your students' portfolios.

As you read the entire story aloud, let your hand follow the words. Remind the students that these are their own words. Then reread the first sentence, again following the printed words with your hand. Ask the students to read that sentence. Continue with the same procedure until they can read the story fairly well. If you are working with more than one student, you might then have individual students read the story aloud.

Ask the students to pick out five to ten words from the story that they would like to learn first. Write each word on a small card (3 × 5 cards for group teaching, cut into smaller units for one-to-one). Have the students look at each card carefully, reading the word and putting it under its duplicate in the story. Mix the cards up. Then ask the students to read them, referring to the story when necessary.

Have the students reread the story, first as a group, then individually. Be sure to give them copies for home practice. If you have one student, give the student the original and keep one copy for the student's portfolio. With a small group or a class, you might suggest that they copy each story from the board. Recording students as they read their own stories gives helpful evidence for later evaluation. Self-correction takes longer in a new language. When you find that your students are able to hear "what sounds right," you will see them begin to work more independently.

Often this is just the beginning of a story—the students may have more to say on the subject and may want to continue the story at the next lesson. Your students can now claim to be authors. They might want to add illustrations and even make their stories into little booklets.

You can reinforce sentences from a story by cutting them in strips and mixing them up. Ask the students to arrange the sentences in the right order. This is "sentence unscrambling," described later.

All students like stories about themselves and their experiences or interests. Use these stories as the basis for teaching word recognition, phonics, and word families or patterns, as well as for vocabulary development.

Examples of ESOL Language Experience Stories

One student, Maria, said:

> *America my new country. Portugal my home country. I make new friends. Miss old friends.*

Maria was pleased to see the words she said in writing. She had spoken in English, and she knew the teacher understood her, and she now saw her own words in print. It was only later, when Maria had more lessons, that she decided she wanted to edit and rewrite her story. Her edited story said:

> *America is my new country. Portugal is my home country. I am making new friends. I miss my old friends.*

A small group of students from three different countries dictated this story:

> *We come America from Vietnam, Poland, China. We want learn English, become good citizens. America like small United Nations.*

Much discussion followed, and they asked the teacher if that was "good English." They wanted it right even from the beginning. Because *they* asked for corrections, the teacher repeated the story with correct grammar. They insisted their story be in proper English, and they changed it to say:

> *We came to America from Vietnam, Poland, and China. We want to learn English and become good citizens. America is like a small United Nations.*

The words the students elected to learn first were these: *America, English, citizens, United Nations.*

Margarita, a Spanish-speaking social worker from Bolivia, wanted her teacher to help her write a report to be read to the case conference group she belonged to. She could speak and read English, but her writing was limited. Here is what she dictated:

> *I have big problem in community. Is about one mother. She have six children. She not well of the mind. She no feeling well in mind and she go to hospital to get especial attention medicine. We have problem of children now. What do with children?*

Margarita knew that her English was inadequate and was embarrassed to present a report in poor English. She asked if the teacher would please help her put it into "good English." The rewritten story came out like this:

> *I have a big problem in my community. It is about a mother. She has six children. She is not well mentally. She must go to the hospital to get special medical attention. We have the problem of the children. What shall we do with them?*

Margarita read the rewritten story. She was delighted, knowing that she wouldn't be embarrassed at the meeting. While she wasn't able to put her thoughts into standard English yet, learning to do so became a priority for future lessons.

Many literacy programs and schools are collecting their student stories and publishing them for other adult learners to read. What better reading material for new readers than stories written by other learners!

Using Language Experience as a class project can be fun and helps unite the class. I used it in a difficult situation when I was working in Africa.

> *While working in Zambia, Africa, I was invited to visit a rural prison to talk to a class of prisoners. Seldom is one invited to a prison in Africa because of the very bad conditions, and this was no exception—dirt floors, barbed wire, inadequate food. The 20 men were barefoot and wore mealie-meal sacks as shirts. They leaned on a tall table, eyes down, no interest, resigned to their fate. The instructor stood in front of a broken blackboard, writing and saying words in Bembe, the local language. The students reluctantly repeated the words—all learning is by rote here.*

> *I was introduced. They looked up but showed no interest. What does one say to a group of unmotivated prisoners in a language you don't know? Through a translator, I asked the teacher to ask the students what they liked to do. He gave me a quizzical look indicating "You're supposed to teach." The teacher asked, but the students gave no response. I pointed to one student and repeated the question in Bembe. He gave me a look of surprise suggesting "You're asking me? I've never been asked, only told what to do." He finally said the word in his language for "farming."*

I pointed to a second student. He said, "Woodworking." By this time, all were clamoring to talk. I pointed to a third, who said, "Dance." I had them vote, and they chose "farming."

After much animated discussion, they came up with this sentence: Farming is important to give us food.

How I wished I could have stayed longer both to train the teacher and to work more with these prisoners who had responded so enthusiastically to just one short Language Experience story activity.

LANGUAGE EXPERIENCE

1. Invite your students to talk about something of interest to them. Identify key words.

2. After discussion, have the students tell their story, using the key words as a guide.

3. Write the story the students dictate, using their exact words. With advanced students, suggest that they write the words themselves. Some students will self-correct; others will ask the teacher for corrections. Let the students decide.

4. Read the entire story aloud as the students silently follow the words.

5. Read each sentence and ask the students to repeat it after you.

6. Ask the students to select five to ten words that they would like to learn. Write the words separately on word cards. Teach students to read them as sight words.

7. Have the students reread the story aloud, and give them opportunities to revise or edit.

Sight Words and Context Clues

Sight words are words that students recognize and understand immediately. They are learned as whole words. In addition to words gathered from Language Experience stories, there are four specific types of words that can be taught as sight words:

1. Survival words: *danger, exit, emergency*
2. Service or utility words: *the, of, why*
3. Irregularly spelled words: *have, of, laugh*
4. Introductory words in word patterns: *run, sun, fun, bun*

The teacher and the students together select from the context of the lessons, from the list of commonly used words, or from a list of survival words which words are to be learned as sight words. Usually five to ten words per session are all that should be attempted. Print the words on the board—or have your students write them on index cards, one per card. Quartered index cards are also convenient for individual students. Use larger cards for a group. Teach one word at a time.

Say the word as you point to the word or show the word card. Have the students repeat the word. Ask your students to use the word in a sentence. Have the students look again at the word and repeat the word. Go on to the second word, repeating the process. When you have taught five to eight words, shuffle the word cards and ask the students to read each card.

Generally, if students can read a word out of context on three separate sessions, they know the word, and it can be put in a known words file. These can be reviewed periodically to emphasize the many new words the students have learned. The word cards give them something tangible to take home and study.

After or sometimes during a conversation, you and your students can select important new words to write on word cards. Thus, natural conversation can also be a stimulus for building personal word lists that can be taught as sight words.

As you read, you may come across a word you don't know. Sometimes you stop and look it up in the dictionary. Other times, you just read on, guessing at the meaning. And most times you're right—you get the meaning from the context of the article or story you're reading. As their vocabularies increase, your students will be able to do this, too. Let them know that it's another way of learning the meaning of words.

SIGHT WORDS

1. Students and teacher select words to be taught as sight words.

2. Ask students each to pick five to ten words to be learned one at a time.

3. Write a word (in manuscript)—or have students write it—on a word card.

4. Read the word aloud while showing the card; ask students to repeat.

5. Ask students to use the word in a sentence.

6. Go to the next sight word. Repeat the process.

7. Shuffle the word cards, and have students practice rereading them.

Sentence and Story Unscrambling

You can give students who read some English, even those at a lower level, a chance to think about language by having them unscramble sentences. On individual cards, write words that the students know. (Make sure that the words together would make a meaningful sentence.) Ask your students to put them in order. They may or may not be in the order you had in mind, but they must make sense. For example, with these words

coffee   sandwich   a   I   ordered   and

The sentence could be
   I ordered coffee and a sandwich.
or
   I ordered a sandwich and coffee.

The sentence can be as simple or as complex as the students can handle.

the   vegetables   bought   store   father   at   The

The father bought vegetables at the store.

You can scramble lines of dialogue rather than individual words. Ask your students to put the lines of dialogue into a meaningful order. Or you can jumble the sentences of a paragraph and suggest that the students put the sentences together so that they make sense. You can also cut apart a comic strip and have the students put the frames in the proper order. These are sometimes called strip stories.

Phonics and Letter-Sound Relationships

Effective reading necessitates that students make accurate connections between sounds and letters or groups of letters. Many languages are phonetically regular (i.e., letters or groups of letters always represent the same sounds). While English is not phonetically regular, especially the vowel sounds, most consonants represent a constant sound. Students who can read and write in a language with Roman letters will probably know that the sounds the same consonants represent in their language are similar to the English sounds. For students who cannot read or write in their own languages or for those whose written languages do not use Roman letters, understanding phonics will probably be more difficult.

Teaching consonants

/m/   /s/   /f/   /p/   /b/   /t/

The sounds of the consonants in English are more constant than the sounds of the vowels. To help your students with their consonants, work with them to create a letter-sound dictionary. Use one sheet of paper, an index card, or one page of an address book for each letter. You might start with *m, f,* and *s.* Because the sounds of these letters are sustained, they're usually easier to learn, while the sounds of letters like *b* and *d* are more difficult to isolate. Indicate the sounds of letters by writing them with slash marks on either side: */m/, /f/, /s/.* Consonant digraphs, in which two letters together represent one sound (*ch, sh, th, wh,* or *qu*), are taught the same way consonants are taught.

You may want to start with a consonant in your student's name or in his or her country—for example, the *m* in *Marta* or *Manuel*, the *s* in *Sam* or *Sergio*, or the *f* in *Fanny* or *France*. Start with letters that might be most useful to the students. It is not necessary to learn the sounds in alphabetical order; you can put them in alphabetical order later. Detailed discussion and instructions, including suggested key words for every consonant, are included in *TUTOR 8* and should be reviewed, but here is the abbreviated version.

1. Identify the letter by saying its name and writing it in manuscript.

   This is the letter m. *What is the name of this letter?* (m)

2. Ask the students to listen to the beginning sound.

   Listen for the sound of m *at the beginning of these words, and repeat the words:* motor *(motor),* mother *(mother),* milk *(milk).*

3. Ask the students to pick a key word and write the key word under the letter.

   Which of these words—motor, mother, milk—do you want to use to help you remember the sound of m? (motor). (If you are teaching more than one student, you might have the students vote on the key word they want.)

   m
   motor

4. Ask the students to produce the beginning sound.

   Think of the beginning sound in motor, *and say the first sound.* (/m/) /m/ *is the sound of the letter* m.

5. See if the students recognize the sound in other words.

   Here are other words. Listen. Do they start with the /m/ sound? Country. (No) *Miles.* (Yes) *Telephone.* (No) *Moon.* (Yes) *Family.* (No)

6. Put the sound at the end of words.

   I'll move the /m/ sound to the end of some words. Listen to the last sound, and repeat the words—rim (rim), *them* (them), *thumb* (thumb). (Note to the teacher: It doesn't matter whether the spelling is regular as long as the last sound is /m/.)

7. Have the students produce the ending sound.

   What is the last sound in these words—room, limb, stem? (/m/)

8. Review the name of each letter, its key word, and its sound.

   What is the name of this letter? (m) *What is your key word?* (motor) *What is the sound at the beginning of the word?* (/m/)

9. Have the student write the letter.

   Please write an m. (The student writes an *m*.)

10. Explain and write the capital letter.

    This is a capital M, *the same name, the same sound. Write a capital* M. (The student writes a capital M.)

    m   M
    motor

PHONICS—TEACHING CONSONANTS

1. Identify by name the letter to be taught.

2. Students listen for beginning sound of words starting with that letter.

3. Students pick key word.

4. Students produce beginning sound.

5. Ascertain that students recognize sound in other words.

6. Put letter and sound at end of words.

7. Students produce ending sound.

8. Review name of letter, key word, and letter sound.

9. Students write letter.

10. Explain and write capital letter.

Word Patterns (Teaching Vowels in Pattern)

fat	mark	sight
cat	park	might
sat	lark	light
mat	dark	right
brat	stark	bright

Vowels in English have many sounds. Note the different sounds of the letter *a* in the following words:

can   *came*   *call*   *car*

English may not always be phonetically regular, but it is generally a patterned language: *-an, -ame, -all,* and *-ar* are constant patterns. You can teach vowels through their various patterns.

can	*came*	*call*	*car*
pan	*game*	*fall*	*tar*
ran	*same*	*ball*	*bar*

Learning words by seeing word patterns helps students notice the relationships between clusters of letters and the sounds they represent. Parts of words that sound alike are often spelled alike.

Choose a patterned word from the words your students already know. Use a simple consonant-vowel-consonant (C-V-C) word first, such as *can*. This word will provide a clue that will help them figure out the other words in that pattern. Be sure the students understand the meanings of the words you use, know about rhyming, and are familiar with some of the consonant sounds. This will help them to master the word pattern technique. Teaching words in pattern may seem simple, but it is well worth practicing because of its value.

Be sure you have taught the sounds of the initial consonants you will be using in the pattern. It is helpful to write the words as they are spoken, listing them in a column so that similar letters in the pattern can be seen as well as heard. Here are the basic steps for teaching words in pattern:

1. Write the first word in the pattern: *man*
followed by the second patterned word: *pan*

2. Explain as follows:
If m-a-n is man, what is p-a-n?

3. If the student responds correctly, *pan*   *ran*
add more words in pattern.   *can*

   Ask the student to read them.

   If the student gives no response or responds incorrectly, think about possible learning blocks.

   • He or she may not remember the sound of the consonants (*p, r, c*).

   • He or she may not remember the sound of the vowel cluster (*an*).

   • Ask the student to identify the letters that are the same in all the words.

4. Make word cards for the words in pattern.

English has many unusual spellings, but once a pattern is learned, your students will find they can read many more words. All the word patterns in English are listed in Appendix K, page 222.

high	*oil*	*ought*
sigh	*soil*	*bought*
nigh	*toil*	*fought*
thigh	*boil*	*sought*
	broil	*brought*
	spoil	*thought*

When you're using patterned, rhyming words, be aware that some words in English rhyme but are not patterned—*kite, right,* and *height,* for instance, or *shoe, blue,* and *do.* When teaching "families" or patterns, be sure that the words have the same ending spellings.

TEACHING VOWELS IN WORD PATTERNS

1. Write the first word and a second word in pattern. *map*
   sap

2. Say: *If m-a-p is map, what is s-a-p?*

3. Add more words in pattern; ask student to read them. *tap*
   cap

   If answers are incorrect, check
   - Does the student know the sounds of the consonants?
   - Does the student know the final letter cluster?
   - Ask the student to identify duplicate letters.

4. Write word cards with patterned words.

Reading to Expand Vocabulary

Your students' spoken vocabulary has greatly enlarged. Now you want to concentrate on enlarging their reading and writing vocabularies. Most literate Americans who have expanded their vocabularies have done so by reading, reading, and reading some more. Encourage your students to read everything around them. You can use print materials—labels, TV ads, billboards—as the basis for further discussion to help stimulate vocabulary development and fluency of expression. The more one reads, the bigger one's vocabulary, and the bigger one's vocabulary, the more one can read.

While we encourage our students to listen and speak before reading new material, there comes a time when they should begin independent reading. The timing varies from student to student, but when students can read fairly well, you might encourage them to read material that is slightly above their level. Suggest that they read fast, skimming each page. When they ask for help with unknown words, have them guess the meanings, using context clues. All proficient readers do this—they learn new words just by reading; they don't look up the meaning of each word they read. ESOL students can be taught to figure out the meanings of new vocabulary words in their reading as well, but do also encourage them to use a dictionary.

Graded Reading Material, Grade Equivalents, Readability Formulas

You can find material that is graded at your students' reading levels, giving them the confidence that they *can* read at a fairly consistent speed with comprehension. If they are parents, you might suggest that they read children's books to their children. These probably will be below their reading levels, but they can read them easily and will get practice reading aloud to their children.

You'll find that students generally are motivated to read beyond their reading levels if the subject matter is of special interest to them. So finding their interests (sports, cooking, etc.) and their needs (ads for things they're shopping for, bills that must be paid, job applications, etc.) will open doors to suggested reading materials for their lessons.

As you assess your students' strengths and weaknesses in reading through the *READ* assessment, you will learn not only the levels of their reading and comprehension but also the grade equivalencies. While we don't want to put adult students in school grade levels, it's helpful to know approximate grade equivalents as you look for appropriate material for students.

Most materials written for adults are not graded, but you can easily find the approximate grade level of any reading material by using one of the many available readability formulas. Most such formulas suggest that you take several random 100-word samples and then count the number of sentences and the number of words. Some formulas consider word length or count "hard" or "unfamiliar" words; others look at the number of syllables in individual words. When you have the required numbers, you enter those figures into the specific readability formula. Read Burke and Greenberg's paper (2010) to learn more about the formulas and their use in the adult literacy field. For details about specific formulas, you can look them up on the Internet:

- Fry Readability Graph
- Gunning FOG Readability Formula
- Dale-Chall Readability Formula
- Flesch-Kinkaid Grade Level Formula
- Spache Readability Formula
- SMOG Readability Formula

Check the material you're examining with two different formulas, and average the result to get a fairly accurate level.

You can also get "graded readers" written at different English proficiency levels from most publishers. These often present classic novels in much simpler and shorter forms.

Reading Aloud—Fluency

Reading poetry or excerpts from plays aloud can provide excellent pronunciation practice. Students can learn real-life stress, rhythm, and intonation patterns without specific drills. You can have the students read with you or "shadow" your reading, following your natural speech patterns. You could also read aloud articles or stories of interest to the students as they follow your speech rhythms and intonation. If possible, set up a recording device, so students can read aloud and then listen to their own pronunciation, rhythm, and intonation.

While discussing helps for spoken English in Chapter 7 (page 80), we talked about "pausing" and suggested that you put slash marks (/.../) between connecting words for pausing or taking a breath. This is perfect for helping your students read fluently. For beginning students, use shorter segments.

I'm going / to school / to pick up / my children.

Use longer slashed segments for more advanced readers.

He's going to the mall / to meet two friends / to see an exciting movie.

Adults are called upon to read aloud more often than you think—reading from the Bible at church, reading to their children, reading aloud an advertisement to a peer group, reading aloud a letter from a loved one.

Comprehension in Reading

As important as phonics, spelling, and grammar are, understanding the intent of any message (comprehension) is the key to communication. Even those with limited reading skills can get information when stories and books are read to them.

We've discussed checking comprehension throughout the students' lessons—Total Physical Response, questions, paraphrasing. Continue to check comprehension as your students read, for reading just words and sentences without understanding is not truly reading. Suggest that they read a story silently first and then ask you questions about things they didn't quite understand. Scanning reading material is a skill more advanced students will need—they can quickly scan each page looking for specific pieces of information.

Ask the students questions—both factual and inferential. *When, where, what, who, why,* and *how* questions can yield needed information as well as check how well your students understand.

When did the action in the story happen?

Where was the boy when his mother left him?

What was the man thinking when he committed the crime?

Who are the most important characters in the book?

Why do you think the story ended the way it did? Could there have been another ending?

How did the detective find the clue that led to the robber's arrest?

Have your students retell a story they've read. To retell the story in just a few sentences, they will need to identify the main idea and a few important details. They can add further details and descriptions later. Identifying the main idea and outlining a story can be a first step toward helping students write their own stories.

Beginning students might be more comfortable retelling stories paragraph by paragraph, but more advanced students can be asked to paraphrase an entire story. Some may be more comfortable jotting down key words to help them remember the action sequence.

Bring a cake mix box or the directions for fixing a flat tire. Show the pictures on the carton, and have your students read the directions. Their job is to tell you or the class, in sequence, what to do to bake a cake or fix a flat tire.

The Cloze Procedure

Cloze is one procedure used to check comprehension. Words are deleted from a passage, and as they read the passage, students insert the appropriate words. The technique also gives opportunities to use context clues (guessing) for appropriate words as well as to add new vocabulary words, encouraging students to think critically.

While there are adaptations of the cloze procedure, these are the well-accepted steps:

1. Select a passage of appropriate grade level and length that can be easily read by your students, and ask them to read it silently.

2. Using the same passage, leave the first and last sentences and all punctuation as they originally were.

3. Select words for omission. One way to do this is to insert a blank line in place of every xth word. Don't eliminate more than every fifth word, or there will not be enough context left to identify the missing words.

4. Make all blanks of equal length to avoid giving visual clues as to length of words.

5. Have the students read the entire passage silently before they fill in the blanks. Encourage the students to fill in all the blanks if possible.

6. While there is no time limit, jot down the time it took each student to complete the task for your own records.

7. Ask the students to reread the completed passage with their own inserted words.

Cloze exercises can be adapted for beginning, intermediate, or more advanced students. For beginning students, read the story aloud and give them a choice of words for each blank. For intermediate-level students, you can give the first letter(s) of the appropriate word for each blank space. For more advanced students, give no clues. For example, in a story about Monica's garden, you could use any of the following cloze variations:

> Monica was growing a small garden. Her most popular vegetable was tomatoes, but she found that growing broccoli plants gave her bigger profits.

> Monica was growing a small _____ (garden, plant). Her most popular vegetable was _____ (tomatoes, lettuce), but she found that growing _____ (tomatoes, broccoli) plants gave her bigger profits.

> *Monica was growing a small g_____. Her most popular vegetable was t_____, but she found that growing b_____ plants gave her bigger profits.*

> *Monica was growing a small _____. Her most popular vegetable was _____, but she found that growing _____ plants gave her bigger profits.*

Using the cloze procedure for your students' Language Experience stories can give them an opportunity to change one or a few of their own words, substituting words they later think better express their feelings. For instance, here's what one student originally wrote:

> *José was in the dark basement when he heard a loud noise.*

The teacher chose to delete every sixth word.

> *José was in the dark _____ when he heard a loud _____.*

The student knew the words he had first written but asked if he could change the words. He had learned new vocabulary and wanted to include new words.

> *José was in the dark cellar when he heard a loud explosion.*

WRITING ENGLISH (PRODUCTION)

While only a limited percent of an average person's personal communication is given to writing, that skill becomes ever more important as one goes on to more education, as one advances in one's job, as one wants to record personal and professional information, and as one uses the computer more.

Writing is one of the four skills—listening, speaking, reading, writing—involved in learning a new language. Writing is one form of giving information, and writing in English is a highly useful communication skill in today's world. While help may be available, a student's independence is enhanced if he can fill out his own job applications or take notes during a lecture, if she can write her own letters, write her own reports, or write her own checks and financial reports—the list is endless. Writing will also help students see what they have learned and help them remember it.

Most of the drills suggested in the speaking segment of this book can be used for teaching writing. Students can *write* Language Experience stories instead of dictating them. The same life experiences, stories, and interests can be expressed in writing just as they were expressed orally. Students can write stories they learned as children to read to their own children, thus keeping their traditional stories alive. If your students can write Roman letters, they can start writing just as soon as they have heard and understood, spoken, and read even a few words.

Manuscript and Cursive Writing

Even the lowest-level ESOL students must be able to read and write their names and addresses as well as say them. Teach your students to write in manuscript (print) first because it most closely resembles the print they will read. Books, magazines, or anything typed will be in print. Signs, labels, and job applications are other examples of printed texts. Cursive writing (script) should probably be taught after your students are fairly comfortable with printing. However, some adults will want to write their names in cursive early, for that's the signature they need for job applications, credit cards, wills, and many official documents. You'll find that many students aren't interested in learning cursive, for with the rise of computers, they really don't need it in their daily lives anymore.

When you teach basic writing of Roman letters in manuscript, you will note that only two letters, *a* and *g*, are slightly different in manuscript and print. In manuscript you write ɑ and ɡ, while in print they look like this—**a** and **g.** You might want to practice your own manuscript and cursive writing to make sure your students can read your writing. Models for the manuscript and cursive alphabets are in Appendix E, page 208. Even if your students cannot write in their own languages, they don't necessarily need to begin by writing the alphabet. They can learn letters by copying the letters in their names or in words they need to know.

Process Writing

How and when should you begin teaching writing, and what skills do you start with? After your students have learned to read and write their names, addresses, and phone numbers, they've probably learned to write some of the words and sentences they've learned as they developed their listening, speaking, and reading skills. A good beginning is to have them write lists of things they want to remember—shopping lists, chores they want their children to do or that they want to remember to do themselves, or birthdays and anniversaries of family and friends, for instance. Remember, writing is another form of communication, so getting thoughts and ideas across in writing is more important at the beginning than correct grammar.

You can support even beginning writers by helping them plan and showing them a process through which they can write. We'll focus on both a simple story for a beginning writer and a more complex report with which an advanced student might need assistance.

1. A **trigger event** starts a discussion. This could be a picture, a special interest in a student's homeland, or a discussion of a hobby or of family. Time spent in discussion of trigger events will stimulate good ideas for writing.

   One tutor found her student wanted to tell of her latest knitting project.

   A beginning class decided they wanted to write a story that they could later read to their children. They were all from China, and they wanted to tell their children a story of past events in their lives.

   A small group of advanced students wanted to write a report to their individual bosses telling of their English classes and asking for opportunities to advance themselves.

2. **Prewriting** activities include discussion of the selected topic. The writing activity could be a simple description of a picture or the retelling of a news event, or it could respond to a real need. The teacher can lead the discussion, asking questions and encouraging students to participate. The students must then decide which type of writing task they want to do. They may want to write a letter, a report, or a story.

> *The one-to-one student became excited as she explained how the knit blanket would be used for a new baby.*

> *The beginning class talked of their experiences working on communes in China, while the more advanced group talked about what they had already learned and how they felt it was preparing them for more responsibilities in their jobs.*

As you brainstorm together, write key words that seem to pop out during your discussions. These key words become a simple outline of what the students want to write.

3. Using the key words as a base, the students can begin to **write**. This can be an individual project or a group project. If students write individually, assure them that you are not looking for correct spelling, proper grammar, or correct punctuation. At this time, you want them to get their ideas down on paper. If the students write in groups, have them select one person to write on the board or flip chart what the others dictate. Again, spelling, grammar, and punctuation are not a concern at this time.

The individual student chose these key words: *knit, blanket, fanci, paturn, #5 needles.*

> *My knit blanket has a fanci paturn, and I use #5 needles.*

The beginner class came up with these key words and story, forgetting about spelling and grammar.

> *hard work   comyune   shar*

> *Work is hard on comyune. Comyune is vary big farm where we all share. Even children work.*

The more advanced group decided to write their story as individuals because each wanted to take it to his or her boss.

> *Proud   read/write English   help children   better life   better job*

> *I am proud that I have studied hard and that I can now understand, speak, read, and write English. This means I can help my children with school work. I can shop better. I can do better job.*

4. Next, have the students **read aloud** what they have written. Accept their words and their pronunciations. Comment on grammar or pronunciation only if they ask for help; you can work on that together later. Let them know that you understand what they have written. Then **discuss** the

content of what they have written, asking for clarification of ideas where necessary.

5. Based on this discussion, the students will often suggest changes to their writing. They are **revising** and **rewriting** their own work—a most important step. They can continue to revise and rewrite until their work is the way they want it. As a final step, encourage your students to type their work on a computer, or suggest that you will type it for them. Give copies to the students.

In our examples, each group of students asked the teacher to correct any misspelled words. As they talked, they realized that some of the sentences just didn't "sound right." With the teacher's help, they made corrections.

My knit blanket has a fancy pattern, and I use #5 needles.

Work is hard on the commune. A commune is a very big farm in China where we all share, and even the children work.

The more advanced group decided to write their stories individually. Here is one example:

I am proud that I have studied hard and that I can now understand, speak, read, and write English. This means I can help my children with their schoolwork. I can shop better and can understand discounts, bargains, and how to get credit if I need it. I feel more confident and I hope more doors will be opened at work so that I can do an even better job.

Several lessons later, the one-to-one student brought her knit blanket to show her tutor. The beginner class was ready to print their story, for which one member of the class had made simple illustrations. The advanced group continued to edit and change wording, each making a personalized report to give to his or her supervisor.

PROCESS WRITING

1. Select trigger event

2. Prewrite

    a. Discuss

    b. Decide on the writing task

    c. Brainstorm and write key words

3. Write

4. Read, respond, and discuss

5. Revise and rewrite

Journals and Letter Writing

Many ESOL students are interested in and willing to try writing their own experiences and thoughts if they are assured that their work will be kept confidential. Encourage them to write even a sentence or two each day in a journal. They can review their writing later if they want to or use it as a nonthreatening way to practice putting their thoughts down on paper. This daily activity will not only give practice in writing skills, but it can be used as a reference for areas where students want help. When trying to think of a real-life dialogue that they'd like to practice, students can refer to their journals, reminding themselves of times when they were at a loss for effective words.

Letters to and from people who are important to the students can be meaningful. Students may want to write letters to their families and friends in their native languages, or they may want to try writing in English—letters to their children's teachers, letters of complaint for defective merchandise, letters to accompany job applications, or letters to you. They may or may not want to share their journals, but often they'll ask you to look over a letter they've composed, especially if it is a business letter.

Dialogue Journals

Some students may want you to read their journals and respond to what they have written. Dialogue journals are just that—writings back and forth between individual students and their teachers. They are similar to spoken dialogues, but this time they are written, and they contain thoughts that individual students want to share with their teachers.

These interactive journals will give you insight into your students' lives as well as an opportunity to see where they need help. You can use dialogue journals as a part of home assignments, or you can set aside perhaps 10 minutes during the lesson for students to write in their journals. Students with limited writing skills can draw pictures or answer *yes* or *no* to your simple questions.

Each student writes whatever he or she wants—a happy or sad thought, an incident that just happened, a news event—and gives the dialogue journal booklet to you, the teacher. Never correct journal entries. If something is incomprehensible, just ask for clarification when you write back. Write at a level similar to the student's and in careful manuscript. Respond with your reaction to the student's words, perhaps sharing new thoughts. If a student has asked you to correct her English, don't use a red pen. Instead of crossing out an incorrect structure, model the correct one. This gives each student more reading material as well as the courage to write with confidence, knowing that there will be no corrections or criticisms unless they are requested.

Grammar and Sentence Structure

Some ESOL students feel that grammar and sentence structure are basic to learning English. It is often difficult to assure them that they will learn correct

English grammar and sentence structure not by following rules but by listening to fluent speakers like you and by reading. Most of us do not stop and think about the correct way to say or write something—whether the noun comes first, or whether we are talking in the present, present progressive, past, or future tense. We just know when it sounds right. We want to help our students get a feel for the language, too. And grammar rules can come later.

Language is best learned in real-life contexts, whether in general conversation, reading, or writing. Rules of grammar should probably be delayed until after students have used English in specific real-life situations. After students can understand, speak, and have general conversations, you can explain pertinent grammar rules. This can happen even after students understand and can only say simple sentences like *I go to the supermarket*. If they want rules, you can explain, for example, that in English the subject goes before the verb. We never say:

To the supermarket go I.   or   *I to the supermarket go.*

The correct way is *I go to the supermarket*.

The many excellent grammar textbooks currently available have multiple suggestions and drills for practicing correct sentence structure and giving rules. Use them creatively to supplement your lessons.

Some students want help in more advanced grammar usage. For example, you might want to teach the present progressive tense. You could do this by bringing objects to help your students understand (pennies to count, cookies to eat, paper clips to put in a box). Tell the students to count the pennies, eat the cookies, or put the paper clips in the box. Then ask the students what they are doing. As they are counting the pennies, they may say, *I count pennies*. You may want to model the correct answer first, or you may want to let them try for themselves. They may get the correct answers because they have heard similar English sentences. You might get these answers:

I count pennies.
I eat cookies.
I put paper clips in the box.

You can model the correct replies and ask them to repeat:

I am (or *I'm*) *counting pennies.*
> (*you are/you're - we are/we're – they are/they're*)

I am (or *I'm*) *eating cookies.*
> (*you are/you're – we are/we're – they are/they're*)

I am (or *I'm*) *putting paper clips in the box.*
> (*you are/you're – we are/we're – they are/they're*)

If you are working on the past progressive verb tense, have the students do the same activities (count pennies, eat cookies, put paper clips in a box). Ring a bell, clap your hands, or knock on the table to stop the activity. Ask your students what they were doing when you gave the signal to stop. The correct responses would be:

I was (We were) counting pennies.
I was (We were) eating cookies.
I was (We were) putting paper clips in the box.

It is not important whether they, or you, can name the verb tense. It is important that they know what tense to use when talking about an action that they are or were doing.

For present, past, and future tenses, you could use a newspaper ad showing groceries and their prices. Say that you are going to plan a shopping list. Ask your students to indicate what to buy by stating it in a sentence:

Today we are buying (or we're buying) tomatoes. The price is $. . . .
Yesterday we bought bread. The price was $. . . .
Tomorrow we will buy (or we'll buy or we're going to buy) lettuce. The price will be $. . . .

You can vary the items by using different ads—such as those for clothing, hardware, or household items—depending on students' interests.

Teacher-made exercises can be used for practicing various parts of speech or grammar. Use any material of interest to your students. Copy an interesting article (a newspaper article about sports, a travel story of a faraway place, a descriptive article on food, etc.). White out whatever part of speech you're working on (e.g., all prepositions). Read aloud the entire article to your students. Then read the article again, but omit the prepositions, and ask the students to supply them. If it's a beginning group, make a list of the prepositions available. If it's an advanced group, let them supply the missing words. Finally, give the students copies of the article with blanks where the words are missing. Ask each of them to fill in the correct words. You can create this exercise with missing nouns, verbs, adjectives, or other grammatical forms.

Spelling and Punctuation

Spelling in English is difficult because it is not phonetically regular. While correct spelling isn't essential for general communication, it is important when writing reports or important letters, filling in business documents, etc. When we write on a computer, we have the luxury of a spell checker, so students may not have learned correct spelling of many words. Those who send text messages on their cell phones may also have developed a habit of using contractions and abbreviated ways of saying things. Go back to the word pattern exercise in this chapter (page 127). This can be most helpful to students—once they have learned a pattern's spelling (*l-i-g-h-t*), they know how to spell other words in the same family (*might, fight, blight*).

Encourage your students to look up words in the dictionary when they're not sure of the spelling. But there are some helpful rules, too. Just ensure that any rule you suggest is correct at least 50 percent of the time. There are simple rules like these:

> *i* before *e* except after *c*

> Adding an *e* at the end of a C-V-C word usually makes the vowel long:
>
> | | | |
> |---|---|---|
> | hat | cap | hid |
> | hate | cape | hide |

But know that there are exceptions: *give, have.*

Continuing Stories

We discussed continuing stories in Chapter 7 (page 104). Students often hesitate to begin a story. Suggesting a theme by saying or writing a first sentence can open the door for them and get them started. Give one or two sentences to set the scene, but stop in mid-thought. Students are usually willing to quickly add their own words and create their own stories.

> *Jose and Maria were holding hands as they walked quietly along the seashore. Suddenly they heard a scream. . .*

What fun when the students read aloud the stories they wrote after such a prompt, for each one will be different. Some students may want to work as suggested in the Process Writing section (page 134): thinking about the topic, writing key words as a simple outline, then writing the story. But most will just write whatever comes to mind, knowing they can edit and correct it later.

Note Taking in Lectures

Many scholars come to the United States for advanced studies, but they may have problems understanding the lectures. In the listening section, Chapter 7, I suggested ways to help them. When they can understand our quickly spoken English more easily, they want to take notes. Some may want to type notes directly into their computers, but many want to jot down key words and new ideas as they are listening. If they record the lectures, they won't feel the pressure of losing any part of them. Then they can practice taking notes to jog their memories.

A BALANCED SEQUENCE IN TEACHING ESOL

Throughout this book, we have suggested a balanced teaching sequence: listening followed by speaking, reinforced by reading and writing, and ensuring comprehension in each area. We suggest the following sequence when you present new material to students who particularly want help with listening and speaking skills balanced with reading and writing. It is especially helpful to intermediate and advanced students who can read and write English fairly well but have difficulty understanding and speaking English at the same level.

LISTEN

1. Tell or read aloud any story or other new material of interest to the students at their comprehension level, motioning for or asking the students to *listen*. Don't give them a copy of the text. Use pictures, props, and gestures to aid comprehension. Read one sentence, one paragraph, or one segment at a time depending on the level of listening skill. After each sentence, paragraph, or segment, review any new vocabulary and explain the meanings of unknown words to the students if they cannot guess them from the contextual clues. You might want to make slash marks in the text, ensuring that you read fluently and in small enough chunks for them to understand and remember.

SPEAK

2. Read the same paragraph aloud again, this time phrase by phrase or sentence by sentence, as a model for pronunciation. Have the students repeat each phrase or sentence aloud.

3. Ask individual students to tell in their own words what they heard you read aloud, paraphrasing

4. Continue the above procedure, paragraph by paragraph or segment by segment to the end of the text.

READ

5. Give the students a copy of the material you read aloud. Ask them to read it silently to themselves.

6. Ask one student at a time to read aloud. Adults are often asked to read aloud to a group—instructions from a manual, stories to children, or passages during a religious meeting. Reading aloud during the lesson helps build confidence and is a good way to check pronunciation.

SPEAK

7. Discussion: For intermediate or advanced students, ask questions and ask for opinions. Examples of critical-thinking questions are *Why do you think the author said. . . ?* or *What do you think would have happened if* (change the story). . . ?

WRITE

8. Homework: Have the students paraphrase the story in writing, using their own words. This will give you the opportunity to check comprehension as well as grammar, spelling, and punctuation for future lessons focused on writing issues. It will also give you a sense of your students' writing fluency and style.

9. Respond positively to written homework. All English lessons should include all four language skills for new material: listening, speaking, reading, writing. If you don't have enough time in one session to cover all four skills, you should review what was done in the previous session and move on to the skills you omitted last time.

*Nyeng, a **beginning-level** ESOL student from Vietnam, was hesitant to shop at the huge supermarket. She wanted to know how to ask where items were and how much they cost. Her teacher prepared a dialogue asking the appropriate questions and giving answers. Nyeng listened, repeated, and then paraphrased the dialogue* (**Listen, Speak**). *She couldn't read, so that skill had to be skipped for the moment, but the written dialogue became the text for her beginning reading and writing lessons* (**Read, Write**).

*Two young men at the **intermediate level**, Mikael from Latvia and Bong from Vietnam, were craftsmen at a local furniture factory. They had been given a manual to read on the care of expensive tools. Their supervisor was going to question them on its contents. They asked their teacher to help them understand the material. When their teacher suggested they might want to write a summary of the manual, they were excited but overwhelmed. They thought they could never do it.*

Their teacher read aloud paragraph by paragraph from the manual, asking questions and having them paraphrase what she had read (**Listen, Speak**). *After all, they knew more about these expensive tools than the teacher did. Silently they read the manual, even though it was much higher than their general reading level* (**Read**). *Together, they wrote key words on the board. From the key words, they had a good discussion on the contents of each chapter. Then she asked each to write a short summary of the manual using the key words as an outline* (**Write**). *They were hesitant, but they tried. Their ability to understand and talk about the material surpassed their reading and writing skills. But they did get their thoughts on paper—and after a bit of editing, they were delighted to share their knowledge with their supervisor.*

*Four young mothers, **advanced-level students** Ruo from China, Tatiana from Russia, SunHwa from Korea, and Christine from Brazil, wanted to be able to go to PTO meetings and neighborhood group meetings and be able to understand what was being said. Often several people spoke at the same time, and they spoke rapidly. The women could understand written material but had problems understanding spoken English, especially if it was in the form of a lecture or speech. They found their common interest was family life and values in the United States.*

Focusing on their common interest, the teacher read a short article about family life in the United States in the early 2000s (**Listen**). *She brought in information on family life in the early 1900s, and they had a discussion comparing the two eras* (**Speak**). *She gave the students a copy of the article she had read to them* (**Read**) *and suggested they jot down key words or phrases, highlighting the material* (**Write**).

They worked on new vocabulary words, questioning and paraphrasing, and had a lively discussion interspersed with information on family life in each woman's native country. The teacher suggested that each one write a short report on family life and values in the United States, using their key words as a guide (**Write**). *Their initial objective was to get their ideas on paper, not to focus on grammar, structure, or spelling.*

At the next session, each student read her paper aloud to the group (**Read**). *The others listened* (**Listen**) *and then added their own ideas or asked clarifying questions* (**Speak**). *It gave the teacher an opportunity to check pronunciation, grammar, etc. Each student edited her own paper, and they took great pride in the project, knowing they had listened with comprehension; discussed, questioned, and paraphrased; taken individual notes; and written reports.*

*After the opening of China in the early 1980s, many Chinese students came to America to continue their studies. They had passed **written English language examinations at high levels** and felt confident of their ability to live and learn in the United States.*

They were shocked to find that they struggled to understand their classmates and to understand English spoken in restaurants and shops. The lectures were beyond their listening comprehension. In addition, their American colleagues had difficulty understanding them.

Their English lessons in China had focused on reading and writing. Their listening/understanding and speaking skills were hardly adequate for university work. While they were scholars in their subject matter and they could read and write English very well, they desperately needed the survival skills of listening/understanding and speaking English.

When I suggested that they close their books and put their pens down, they were amazed, insisting they must have the printed material in front of them if they were to understand it.

Going through the sequence of getting new material first through their ears was new to them, but as they realized the importance of understanding what was said in English, they were able to eventually live and learn well in America.

Adjust the order of the various communication skills to the needs and learning styles of individual students. Be sure to include all the skills—if not in a single lesson, then in your general working plan for your students.

> **A BALANCED SEQUENCE IN TEACHING ESOL**
>
> 1. Learners hear and understand English spoken, read, or recorded.
>
> 2. Learners repeat the same English sentences or story.
>
> 3. Learners paraphrase aloud what they heard.
>
> 4. Learners read the same material.
>
> 5. Learners write in their own words what they heard, said, and read.

SUMMARY

Use and adapt the techniques and exercises described in this chapter to help your students pursue their needs and interests and attain their goals. Include all four skills—listening/understanding, speaking, reading, writing—but adapt to each student's needs and learning style. No techniques or strategies should be used in isolation. Once learned, they can be adapted to the interests and concerns of individual students. Remember—the goal is communication.

After your students can understand and speak English competently, encourage them to read new material for pleasure or for knowledge, and encourage them to write, to put their ideas and concerns on paper. As a general rule, all of the language communication skills should be integrated into your work, regardless of the levels of your students, even if you are only stressing one or two of the skills in a particular lesson.

A communicative approach, as suggested in this book:

- stresses comprehension
- uses all four language skills—listening, speaking, reading, and writing
- encourages the use of authentic real-life material and vocabulary
- is learner-centered and learner-directed
- is collaborative, in that the students and teachers work together and are involved in all parts of the lessons

Mix and match the suggested techniques, exercises, and activities, and adapt them to the materials and vocabulary your students need.

RESOURCES AND MORE ACTIVITIES

9

Survival Kit
Students' Names, Addresses, and Telephone Numbers
Letter Names

Visual Aids
Real Objects
Pictures, Picture Files, Picture Dictionaries
Progressive Picture Stories
Clocks and Time
Calendars
Telephones and Cell Phones
Numbers and Money
Maps and Directions
Family Trees
Simple Drawings

Bilingual Dictionaries

Textbooks And Workbooks

More Activities
Role Playing/Skits
Field Trips
Music
Holidays and Parties
Games
Listening Games
Vocabulary Games
Conversation Games
Communication Games

Summary

There are many resources and activities to help your students become proficient in English—some with lessons on specific topics such as shopping or health issues, and others that focus on specific skills such as grammar, pronunciation, or idioms. Your library and program resource files will have suggestions, but you need to be creative and to work closely with your students to identify which specific skills and topics of interest to focus on. Many teachers create their own materials, adapting to their students' needs and interests.

SURVIVAL KIT

In order to meet many basic needs in a society whose dominant language is different from one's own, learning to understand and speak, read, and write specific words and phrases in that language is very important. Such mastery is what we refer to as "survival skills." Teaching these survival skills should be a part of early lessons with any students who haven't yet developed them. We recommend that early in your teaching you check out individual students' abilities to handle these skills so that you know which need further development and practice. Many examples of survival skill activities can be found in the Performance-Based Curricula and Outcomes guide to the MELT Project in Appendix C, page 202.

As you prepare for your first lesson, get the necessary items for a survival kit to keep in a folder or bag for easy reference. It will not only help you in your first lesson but will also provide lesson topics relevant to your students' needs for portions of future lessons. Keep *I Speak English* close by. Use the index to find specific helps or suggestions. Here are some suggested items. Add others as you see the need.

- Students' names, addresses, and telephone numbers
- Letter names
- Neighborhood, United States, and world maps
- Picture dictionary or your own collection of pictures
- Number cards
- Price tags
- Money—coins and "play" bills
- Students' clothing sizes
- Cardboard clock
- Calendar
- Colored paper strips
- Sample restaurant menu
- Bus/train/plane schedules
- Bilingual dictionary
- Mirror for use in teaching pronunciation

Students' Names, Addresses, and Telephone Numbers

Most ESOL students can repeat their names and addresses in English. Stress the importance of keeping a written copy of this information with them. Often native English speakers cannot understand non-native English speakers because of strong accents and hence cannot give proper directions when asked. By modeling the correct pronunciation of students' addresses and telephone numbers, you help them avoid an embarrassing or frightening experience. Record that information on a tape or digital recorder to give your students opportunities to practice at home.

Letter Names

When someone cannot understand a word as spoken, the listener often asks the speaker to spell it. Whether students' native languages use the Roman alphabet or not, they need to learn the names of the letters in English.

You can use regular or quartered 3" × 5" cards, writing both a lower- and uppercase letter of the alphabet on each card. To teach letter names, pronounce the name of each letter, point to the letter, and have your students repeat it. You might start with the names of the letters in your students' names, writing the letters in manuscript as you repeat the letter names.

> L-u-p-e R-i-v-e-r-a

You may find certain letters are confusing to your students because they sound or look somewhat alike:

> *a* and *e*
> *i* and *y*
> *c, z,* and *s*
> *b, p, v,* and *f*
> *g* and *j*

Have your students repeat the names of letters until they can say the name of each letter as you point at random and point to the correct letter as you say the letter name.

VISUAL AIDS

Tools for teaching conversational English are endless. Using visual materials helps promote understanding and gives your students opportunities to associate words with actual objects or pictures. Picture dictionaries are available, but you may want to create your own library of pictures of objects or activities according to student interest. Although visual aids are particularly important with beginning-level students, they can be used creatively with all students to stimulate vocabulary development, free conversation, and student writing.

Real Objects

The most practical visual aids for building conversation and expanding vocabulary are real objects such as tables, chairs, windows, pencils, books, clothing (yours and your students'), or whatever is available. After the students can say the words and identify the objects when you or other students say them, you might want to label the objects or have your students label them so they can practice reading the labels. Use all the techniques you have learned, including asking questions.

How many windows are there?

What color is my sweater?

Suggest that your students bring in objects or pictures of objects they want to identify in English. Common everyday items can stimulate conversation—a watch, articles of clothing, pots and pans, a cell phone, a picture of an article in an ad.

A handbag suggests words like *handle, leather,* and *mirror.*

A sewing kit suggests *needle, thread,* and *scissors.*

A box of cereal suggests words like *box, cardboard,* and *top.*

A dish suggests *round, glass,* and *bottom.*

There are endless ways to encourage conversation. Gradually encourage the students to ask questions. This not only provides speaking practice but might even satisfy your students' curiosity about why Americans use or do certain things. If you are teaching a lesson on how to open a bank account, bring deposit and withdrawal slips and, if possible, a bank statement adapted to ensure privacy. The more the senses are employed, the more likely the learning will stick. An actual orange has weight, color, and fragrance, and its name will be fixed in the students' minds through their senses of touch, sight, and smell. Use real objects whenever possible; if you can't get real objects, use pictures.

Pictures, Picture Files, Picture Dictionaries

It is sometimes impractical to bring real-life situations into your teaching sessions, but you can always bring in pictures. Encourage your students to bring in pictures they would like to discuss—of their homes, work, or social situations. If students have cell phones that take pictures, suggest that they take pictures of typical meals or unusual situations. For introducing new words, even in a simple substitution drill, pictures can reveal a meaning immediately and help make it memorable.

Pictures from catalogs, magazines, newspapers, calendars, advertisements, maps, photographs, or postcards can be useful for teaching English. It is wise to collect these illustrations before a need arises. A doctor's office, a beauty salon, or a barbershop may be a good place to pick up free issues of magazines with useful pictures. The Internet could be another good source of illustrations.

File your pictures by topic for ready reference. Mounting pictures on heavy paper or cardboard keeps them from getting ruined. Pictures generally fall into two categories:

- Illustrations of a single object or action
- Illustrations depicting an entire situation

As you start to collect pictures, you might find the following suggestions helpful:

- Collect anything you think you might use. It is often difficult to locate pictures you need for a specific lesson when you want them.

- Select pictures that illustrate a specific object, place, individual, scene, or action.

- Select pictures that depict an entire situation that could be used as a topic for conversation (e.g., a family picnic).

- Collect pictures that illustrate contrasts (e.g., big/small, fat/thin, happy/sad, wide/narrow) or that represent concepts that are difficult to describe (e.g., above, under, between, up, down, numbers, colors).

- Look for pictures that depict emotions (e.g., love, hate, jealousy, arrogance, kindness).

- Although many pictures in your file will reflect American culture, include some pictures of other cultures as well. Ask your students to share pictures of their native cultures.

- Avoid using pictures with extraneous printing on them that may be confusing.

- Set up a simple set of categories:
  ° Animals (cats, dogs, other animals)
  ° Body (arm, leg, head, hair)
  ° Clothing (men's, women's, children's)
  ° Colors, shapes, sizes (red/blue, round/square, big/small)
  ° Family (mother, father, children, grandparents)
  ° Food (vegetables, meals)
  ° Household (kitchen appliances, bedroom, bath)
  ° Occupations/jobs (clerk, carpenter, team leader)
  ° Problems (hospital scenes, inadequate housing, etc.)
  ° Recreation/sports (soccer, baseball, swimming)
  ° Seasons (spring, summer, fall/autumn, winter)
  ° Transportation (boat, bus, car, plane, train)

Add any other categories you think might be helpful on the back of the pictures, identify them, and write questions or suggestions for using them.

A picture dictionary with identifying words in two languages is a big help, especially when you're desperate for something new to do. Let the students pick out the picture or pictures they want to discuss. It might be as simple as pretending you're at a supermarket and picking out fruits and vegetables. Or it might be more complex—looking at a picture of an airport, for instance, where students can describe what is taking place and have an opportunity to ask questions.

Progressive Picture Stories

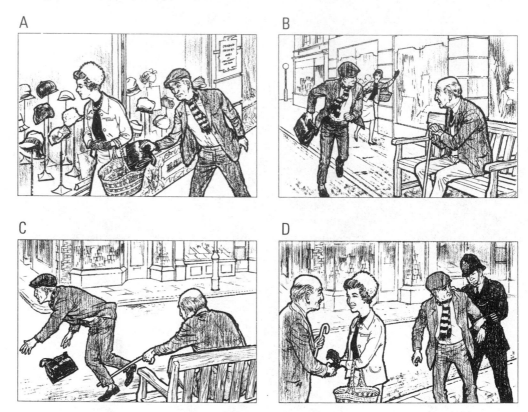

From *Progressive Picture Compositions* by Donn Byrne, page 30. Pearson Education Limited, copyright Donn Byrne 1967. Used by permission.

Words tell stories and so do pictures. You can use pictures in sequence to tell a story and to give your students practice with their listening and speaking skills, ensuring comprehension. There are commercial books with picture series that tell stories. You can use comic strips with the words deleted or even stick figures to make up your own stories. Have the students look at all of the pictures. Ask them to talk about the pictures, telling what they observe—what the characters are doing, where they are, what time of day or night it is, etc. Then have them tell you the story, following the sequence of the pictures. You write the story on the board or on paper—this is another form of Language Experience—and have them copy it. If the students are more advanced, they can write their own stories. It's fun to see how different people interpret the same pictures.

You might want to photocopy a series of pictures or a comic strip, separate and mix up the sections, and give your students an opportunity to put them in the correct sequence. You can ask more advanced students to paraphrase or tell the story in their own words.

Clocks and Time

Americans are usually very time conscious. Many activities in this country are governed by the clock. If you are working with your students on telling time, you may want to use a digital clock, or you may want to use their wristwatches. If you are using a traditional clock, you can bring a clock and adjust the hands, or you can make a clock face out of cardboard or a paper plate.

In America, if a bus is scheduled to leave at 10:42 a.m., it doesn't mean "about" that time. If you have a dental appointment at 9:30 a.m., you had better be there a few minutes early. Because this concept of time and punctuality is not universal, you should discuss the ideas that many Americans have about time. Encourage your students to write their appointments in a date book.

To teach time with either type of clock, start with the hours: 1:00 is *one o'clock,* 2:00 is *two o'clock,* etc. Then 1:30 is *one-thirty,* 2:30 is *two-thirty.* Follow this by 1:15 is *one-fifteen,* or *fifteen after one,* or *quarter past one.* Be consistent; use only one form to begin with, and give alternates later. Take your cue from your students if they speak some English. For example, if they say *quarter to two,* reinforce that before giving alternates.

Realize, too, that as much as Americans tend to go rigidly "by the clock," some situations vary from this rule:

- For an air flight time of 1:30, you should arrive at the airport at least one hour early (two hours or more for international flights) because the plane actually leaves the ground at 1:30 and usually boards 30 minutes before departure time.

- For a clinic appointment at 2:30 p.m., you should arrive a few minutes early.

- A 9-to-5 job means exactly that: arrive before nine to be ready to start at 9:00, and work until 5:00, except for lunch and breaks.

- An invitation to a reception or a party "from 6 to 8" means you arrive sometime after 6:00 and leave at or before 8:00. Guests are not expected to arrive before the stated time.

Calendars

Students should also learn how to use a calendar if they do not already know how. In fact, a calendar is a useful device for teaching and practicing English. You might want to provide your students with calendars, indicating the days of your lessons as well as other important information.

Your students may or may not be able to say the names of the months or the days of the week. Model them and have the students repeat. But also be sure your students hear and understand them. You could say *Tuesday*, and ask the students to point on the calendar to the appropriate column.

One student couldn't understand why his fellow workers laughed when he said he'd be back on *thirsty*. He said, with a question in his eyes, *Sunday, Monday, Tuesday, Wednesday, Thirsty?* Gently the teacher explained the difference between *thirsty* and *Thursday*. Incorrect pronunciation can completely change the meaning of a word.

Telephones and Cell Phones

Most people in America consider the telephone or a cell phone to be a necessity. However, it is much more difficult to converse on a telephone than to talk directly to a person because you cannot see the speaker's face, eyes, or gestures. If you have visited a country where you knew little of the language, you know what a frustrating experience talking on the telephone can be.

Many practical lessons can be planned around the use of a telephone. It provides an excellent introduction to dialogue, because a telephone conversation is just that—a dialogue between two people. You can use a toy telephone, or you may want to draw a set of numbers resembling a touch-tone keypad. Be sure your students understand that the area code must be entered if the call is to a number in a different area. You and your student, or two students back-to-back, can simulate a real telephone conversation. Then, for reinforcement, students can actually call you and each other from their own phones.

Numbers and Money

Numbers should be among the first items taught. They are important in everyday life. Think how often they are needed: telephone numbers, house numbers, prices, weights, and sizes.

Numbers must be exact. Whereas mispronunciation of some words or poor grammar can be tolerated, a mispronounced number cannot. When discussing prices, even knowing where to put the word *dollars* is important. *Two hundred fifty dollars* is very different from *two dollars and fifty cents*.

How would you say these numbers?

1776	You would probably say *seventeen seventy-six* because you assume it's a date. But it could be *one, seven, seven, six* or *seventeen hundred and seventy-six* or *one thousand seven hundred and seventy-six*.
437-8381	*Four, three, seven, eight, three, eight, one* because you assume it's a telephone number. But it could be *four hundred thirty-seven dash eight thousand three hundred eighty-one*.
$3.50	*Three dollars and fifty cents* or *three fifty* or *three and a half dollars*. All mean the same thing to most Americans.
1249	*Twelve forty-nine*, for example, for an address, or *one thousand two hundred forty-nine*.
6.2	*Six point two* or *six and two-tenths*.
1/10	*One-tenth*.

Imagine how confusing it must be to students to learn that we say the same number in many ways. Your students must not only be able to say the numbers, knowing which numbers they mean (*seventy-nine* is 79 and *ninety-seven* is 97), but also to recognize them when they hear them. If *seventeen nine* (179) is heard when you say *seventy-nine* (79), there will probably be many problems. Students may have difficulty distinguishing among *nine, nineteen, ninety,* and *ninth* or *five, fifteen, fifty,* and *fifth*.

To help them, give your students a list of the first 10 numbers. Point to each number as you say it, and ask them to repeat it several times. Review at the end of 10 numbers. When you feel your students know the names of these numbers, point to them at random, asking for the names of the numbers. This is a bit more difficult, and you may find your students counting silently (*one, two, three, four, five, six*) to get to *seven*. Then say a number and have the students point to it. Usually it is more difficult to hear and point to a number than to see the number and say its name.

Reverse the roles. Have a student say a number, and you or another student point to it. Sometimes one number will be spoken when another is intended. Perhaps a student will say *eighteen* (18) and mean *eighty* (80). This will make quite a difference if it refers to a price or an address.

Continue introducing numbers 11 through 19. Then teach 20, 30, 40, 50, etc.

Teach numbers that are said individually (telephone numbers and some addresses) before moving on to numbers said in chunks. Teach the different ways of saying prices: $2.98 is *two dollars and ninety-eight cents,* or *two ninety-eight* for short. Reverse the process and have the students take turns giving the prices. Write down the figures that they dictate. Are they what they intended?

Continue by asking questions or giving directions where the students must think in numerical terms:

> *How many windows are there in the room?*
> *How many days are in a year?*
> *Turn to page 362.*

If the students can add, divide, and multiply in their own languages, provide simple mathematical problems in English. This will help to develop their fluency and build their skills.

Even your more advanced students will need a lot of repetition hearing and saying numbers. Vary the ways you give this practice. You can dictate numbers, using statistics, prices, times, and telephone numbers. Give the students opportunities to hear big and complex numbers as well as simple or more familiar ones. Repeat your dictation at least once, so students can hear the numbers again and check their own papers to be sure they've written what they heard. If you have a small group or a class, ask each student to prepare a list of numbers and then dictate them to another student or to the group. Thus, students must pronounce the numbers so that others can understand them. If you are teaching only one student, record another person's voice for your student to hear. Give the student an opportunity to dictate numbers to you as well.

Most countries use the metric system. Some organizations in the United States are gradually changing over to this system. Until the metric system is universal, your students must know our present system of measurements: an inch, a foot, a yard, clothing sizes. You can help your students with their personal shopping by preparing a written list of each one's sizes after converting them to the American system. For example:

> suit: size 36 regular
> shirt: 15/32
> underwear: 34–36 medium
> socks: size 9–12
> shoes: size 10B
> dress: size 14

It is important for students to know their height in feet and inches and weight in pounds when filling in medical and insurance forms. You could help them take their own measurements and weigh themselves by bringing a tape measure and small scale to a lesson. It might be helpful for them to know that some American women might tell you how tall they are but will seldom divulge their weight or their age because youth and slimness are glamorized in America.

Maps and Directions

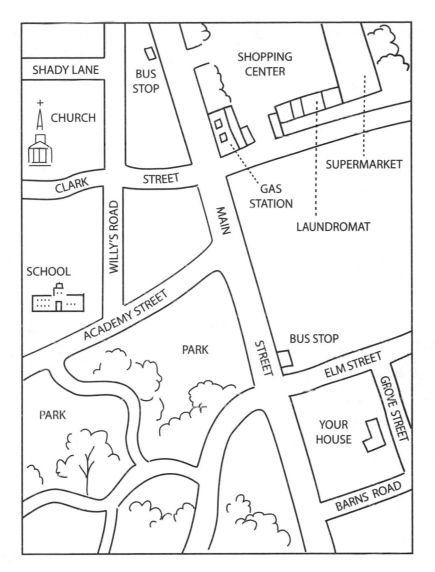

Some non-English speakers are hesitant to venture from their homes. Their fear of getting lost because they cannot communicate is real, so it seems safer to stay indoors or nearby. You can help your students feel more comfortable about venturing out alone by working with them to make a simple neighborhood map.

First, discuss how the students get from their homes to the class or meeting place, noting landmarks and streets. You may have to supply the street names. Note the major points of interest or landmarks with pictures or stick figures, and print the names of major streets on a sketch of the area to be mapped.

Then you might take a walk with your students, following the map and making corrections or additions as appropriate. The freedom and confidence a simple individualized neighborhood map provide will broaden your students' day-to-day life.

Use that same map as a visual aid, starting with listening comprehension techniques. You might say:

Point to the school.
Point to the supermarket.

Then ask for simple directions in English:

Where is the church?
Where is the library?

Continue with practical responses in English:

It's straight ahead.
Go one block and turn right, and then go two blocks and turn left.

Maps can also be made for taking public transportation. Venturing alone on a bus can be a big undertaking. Make a simple map, showing the number of blocks and where the bus turns. If it is appropriate, go with your students for the first time, pointing out landmarks.

If your students are unable to ask the bus driver for help, write a note to be carried along or teach these instructions:

Please tell me when the bus gets to Main and Elm Streets.

Using a world map, students can indicate where their countries are in relation to the United States. An enlarged map of their countries gives them opportunities to show you more specifically where they used to live. They may even want to talk about their friends and their families back home.

Family Trees

Respect for ancestors and elders is important in many cultures. Doing research together to find out about your students' forebears can be a rewarding project.

Your own family tree could be a model for your students' family trees, as you show and tell about your own parents, grandparents, and children.

Photocopy the family tree on the next page, and give each student a copy. Have each student write his or her name in the center box and gradually add names of other family members. Using some of the drills and strategies you've learned, you can add new vocabulary words to indicate relationships on the family tree (*mother, father, parents, son, daughter, sister, brother, children, grandmother, grandfather, cousin, aunt, uncle*) and, later, more general words (*siblings, peers, relatives, ancestors, heritage*).

The students are the experts on their families; you are not. Just say, *Tell me about your family,* and let them talk in English about their families and their homelands. Remember that their families may consist of more, fewer, or different individuals than yours. They may also have lost family members in a war or left some behind, so be sensitive to their reservations and emotions.

My Family Tree

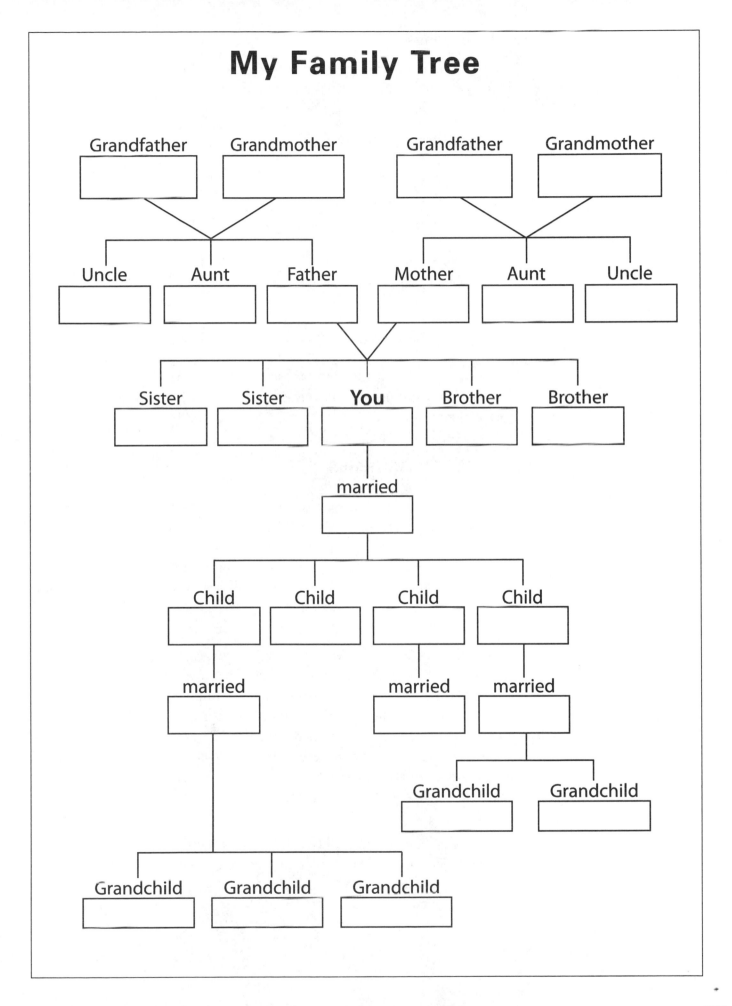

Simple Drawings

You may want to draw a picture to help teach a word or an action or a concept that can't wait for a more formal illustration. You can make your own stick-figure illustrations; you need not be an artist to do this.

You can easily illustrate a sentence.

The man is sitting and reading.

Or

A man is sitting in a chair reading.

The woman picked the flower from the garden.

Or

A girl is smelling a flower.

Note that the same picture can be used with either the present or the past tense, depending on the verb, as in this picture. It's fun; you will all laugh; you will have communicated.

BILINGUAL DICTIONARIES

A bilingual dictionary, with words from both English and the student's or students' language, can be a big help. Whenever possible, use real objects or pictures to communicate word meanings. Encourage the students to link English words directly with images, and avoid translations. Naturally, there are times when abstract words such as *beauty, challenge,* or *understanding* are difficult to explain through demonstration or pictures. In these cases, a bilingual dictionary may come in handy.

If your students can read in their native languages, look the difficult word up in a bilingual dictionary and have the students read that word in their own language. Many students want to make their own bilingual dictionaries, writing new words in both English and their native languages. An easy way to do this is to get an address book already labeled from *A* to *Z*. Students can easily add new words. A plain sheet of paper for each letter in the alphabet works well, too. If your students cannot read in their native languages, you can try to pronounce the word in a student's language using the phonetic symbols in the bilingual dictionary.

Bilingual dictionaries can be very helpful, but they should be used sparingly and carefully. Be sure you have the right part of speech, and if more than one definition is given, read the whole dictionary entry to see what other English meanings are given.

I was writing to my Spanish-speaking friend in Mexico. I wanted to begin the letter with the greeting that is traditional in American culture: Dear Lupe. *I looked up* dear *in the Spanish-English dictionary, where I found the Spanish words* caro, cara. *Confidently I wrote:* Cara Lupe.

It wasn't until months later that I learned that cara *means* costly *or* expensive, *and thus* dear. *The next time I wrote to my Spanish friend, I used the correct word:* querida.

Even if you happen to know a student's language, use English during lessons. Occasionally it can be helpful to explain something in the student's language when you have difficulty getting the meaning across in other ways. Use a bilingual dictionary only to translate the words you are having real trouble explaining.

TEXTBOOKS AND WORKBOOKS

Good ESOL textbooks and workbooks can provide a logical, incrementally difficult sequence for teaching vocabulary, grammar and usage, pronunciation, and comprehension. Since they progress gradually, such books can be used both with students who can read and write some English and with those who can't read or write at all. Some books are now available that have only pictures, no words. These are invaluable as basic tools for teaching conversational English because they stimulate drill substitution and vocabulary and phrase building with beginning-level students and more extensive dialogues with advanced students.

Use textbooks as guides, but don't depend on them totally. Be creative in how you use them, keeping in mind that they can help give continuity to your lessons. Look over several textbooks (see Appendix H, page 216, for guidelines on selecting them). You may feel more comfortable with a particular text and find it more appropriate for your students. If practical, ask your students to help select the text(s). After you have chosen a textbook or workbook, use it as a guide to follow up on or reinforce any part of your lesson. Textbooks necessarily have printed words. But if you read the foreword or teacher's guide, you'll discover that many authors suggest that lessons be introduced by listening/speaking, not by reading.

Some textbooks have simple placement tests that you may wish to use. Start your lessons at the point where your students falter or show little understanding. Students may have a fairly good vocabulary and may understand singular and plural, negatives and questions, and present tense. However, they may have problems with the past tense. Review quickly the earlier lessons in that text, and concentrate on the lessons where they need help. Don't be misled into thinking your students understand because they nod their heads. A nod is often a polite way to show appreciation for what you are doing and may cover the anxiety associated with not comprehending.

Some of the following points are stressed in good ESOL textbooks and are listed here as a reminder to take a comprehensive approach with any resource or material.

- Give a simple explanation of the purpose of the lesson, perhaps showing some of the pictures in the book.
- Read aloud the sentences or paragraphs, suggesting that the students not look at the book.
- Ask your students to tell in their own words what you read. They can ask questions, and you can ask questions to check comprehension.
- Read aloud any questions or exercises to be done at the end of the textbook lesson and ask students to respond verbally. You might want to read the questions aloud before reading the text, giving them an idea of what to look for.
- Give the students copies of the sentences or paragraphs you read aloud. Have the students read the same words, first silently, then aloud. This way you can check their pronunciation.
- Have the students read silently the questions or exercises at the end of the lesson, asking them to respond orally as well as in writing.
- Go over the written exercises to correct grammar, spelling, or punctuation.

Don't overlook children's books. Many of them have wonderful illustrations to stimulate conversation. Also, the children's section of the library contains books that concentrate on specific competencies, such as grammar. Some simply written books are all in the past tense; others are in the present or future tense. Books for adult basic education students are another invaluable resource; they're actually written for adults. Many are written by students themselves. Save copies of stories your students write to use as reading selections with later students or classes.

Be selective as you use textbooks and workbooks. Fit them into your own individualized lesson plans.

MORE ACTIVITIES

Role Playing/Skits

In planning your lessons, you and your students will want to think together about the everyday situations that your students face. With the use of a few props, you can act out ordinary situations with your students.

Ask your students what they need to say in English. Where do they use English? Many situations, including the following, will probably come to mind:

- Answering the telephone
- Asking directions

- Shopping in various kinds of stores
- Telling a doctor about pain or illness
- Ordering in a restaurant
- Visiting a friend
- Cashing a check at a bank
- Making a recommendation at work

Most people will find statements and questions involving food items of immediate use. Although students may know some of the words, they may be pronouncing them incorrectly. Bring in food ads with prices from local papers. Set up a demonstration with a few items, and act out a grocery shopping situation. Refer to the lists in the Performance-Based Curricula and Outcomes (MELT Project) in Appendix C, page 202, for more topics that incorporate real-life language skills that your students may need.

To use the lists most advantageously, look through them and compare the suggestions of topics and competency areas with your students' needs and skill levels. Choose activities that will introduce a topic and develop it so that it becomes part of your students' language skills. Note that each topic in a list progresses from the simplest required listening comprehension to more complex conversation production.

Planned dialogues in role-playing situations can prepare students for real experiences.

> *Can I help you?*
> *Yes, I'd like a hamburger and French fries.*
> *Anything to drink?*
> *Yes, a diet Coke.*
> *Thank you.*

Spontaneous conversations are easier when specific topics of conversation have been identified. Many of us are "hams" who enjoy acting and pretending. Try a little skit just for fun. You and your students might write a short skit with a specific part for each person, or you could look for existing skits. There are books containing short dramas that stress specific skills and are geared to ESOL students. Before you distribute copies, read aloud the entire play or skit, and act it out yourself. Check that the students understand first. Then have them read or role-play the parts.

The first skit one teacher used with a small group was "Fly Soup" (Hines, 1987), a two-page skit about a man in a restaurant who insisted that there was a fly in his soup. The skit has a surprise ending—the man had a box of flies in his pocket and was obviously getting free meals by dropping one into his food after he'd eaten most of it. The students loved it and got more dramatic each time they reread and re-acted the skit. Taping the third rehearsal gave them an opportunity to hear themselves and to laugh again. They didn't realize they were arguing, expressing curiosity, and using the present tense—all objectives of this little drama.

One group of young mothers was concerned about visiting a doctor with their children. They enacted a visit to the doctor, which included making an appointment, arriving and talking to the nurse, asking the doctor questions, and reprimanding the children when necessary. This activity made the mothers feel more comfortable going into a real-life situation.

Field Trips

You may wish to accompany your own students or make group trips to a grocery store, a restaurant, a museum, a park, or any other place relevant to the students. They will be given opportunities to hear other voices speaking English with you as support. Have them take notes, record other voices, make a personal word list, take pictures—all can lead to class discussion and writing.

Music

Music can create a wonderful bond between people. It is also an excellent tool for helping students to feel the rhythm of the new language and build vocabulary. Because songs rhyme and are usually repetitive, they can help develop pronunciation as well. Even if you can hardly carry a tune, you might want to try singing some well-known simple songs. For example, for beginning students, you could sing "Row, Row, Row Your Boat"; for intermediate students "Three Blind Mice" is fun; and for more advanced students, try singing old campfire songs. These will be good choices, especially for parents, since their children are likely to be learning songs like these in school. Have pictures available to help with comprehension. Sing the song through twice while the students listen. Then have the students hum along, tapping the rhythm with a pencil on the table or clapping their hands.

You could bring in sing-along recordings or CDs of some traditional American songs, such as "Yankee Doodle," "Jingle Bells," "America the Beautiful," or "This Land Is Your Land." Or bring recordings of songs from around the world that have been translated into English. Play a recording through and then together hum the melody along with it. Try inserting some of the words. You'll be surprised how many words the students can repeat. Do this several times, teaching the students the words as they go. Finally, give them a sheet with the words they have sung printed on it. Have them read the words and then sing them.

You can show the rhythm of English by having them say *la la la* to the tune even before they repeat the words. You can use this same exercise with nursery rhymes or even regular English sentences.

One tutor heard her Korean student humming "Amazing Grace" as she came to meet her. The tutor asked if she'd sing it for her in Korean. Quietly, in the corner of the local library, the student sang in Korean, and the tutor gradually joined along in English. The student said she wanted to learn to sing that song in English. There was no doubt where the rest of the lesson would be focused.

Several commercial books are available that show how to use music to teach English, or you can search "music ESL" on the Internet for suggestions. Some songs use rhyming words with a steady beat, and others use nonrhyming words with an irregular beat, typical of much current music. There are many songs from which to choose.

Holidays and Parties

You can always make an upcoming holiday the theme of several lessons, bringing in appropriate objects, pictures, decorations, and possibly songs. Consider:

New Year's Eve/Day	Fourth of July
Valentine's Day	Halloween
President's Day	Thanksgiving
Easter	Hanukkah
Memorial Day	Christmas
Canada Day (Canadian)	Boxing Day (Canadian)

Don't forget to have your students share holiday traditions from their native cultures. Here are a few—there are many more.

Carnival	Diwali
Chinese New Year	Ramadan
All Saints' Day	Eid ul-Fitr
Cinco de Mayo	Eid al-Adha
Independence Day	

Members of a small group were discussing Memorial Day, America's day to remember veterans who have died in battle. This reminded a woman from Japan of a Buddhist holiday. The group decided they would go to a cemetery to honor and show respect to their dead relatives—and celebrate by having a picnic afterwards.

When his class was discussing how Americans celebrate birthdays, a Vietnamese student said that birthdays are not celebrated in his country. Birthday festivities are strange and new to many. The student from Vietnam told how the Vietnamese commemorate days of death as well as days of birth. Celebrating and explaining an American birthday party could open up a popular American tradition to many newcomers.

Potluck dinners or lunches with ESOL students can open doors to sharing foods of different countries. Suggest that each student bring some food native to his or her country. You might want to focus on one country at a time. For example, you might have a Polish day, when a Polish student brings one item of native food and tells about a holiday in Poland. The student given the limelight that day can speak in English about something familiar. The other students then get to listen to English being spoken by someone other than the teacher. The student could also teach a few Polish words to the group or even share the recipe. This could be followed up by a written thank-you letter that the group sends to the student presenter.

Games

Both you and your students will be putting much effort into learning new skills, but be sure to allot time for fun and relaxation. Games are a natural way to learn and reinforce learning.

Listening Games

Games can be fun as the students practice listening skills. Make bingo sheets. Instead of using numbers in the boxes, use words or pictures depicting words of minimal pairs of contrasting sounds that need reinforcement. For instance, if you're working on the /th/ and /t/ sounds, you could use these words:

thorn	*torn*
thread	*tread*
three	*tree*
thug	*tug*

For the /i/ and /ee/ sounds, you could use words such as:

sit	*seat*
mitt	*meat*
fit	*feet*

You call out words, and the students cover those words on the bingo sheets. The winners are those who correctly identify the words they hear, in rows or columns or diagonally, just as in regular bingo. Later you can uncover the words on the bingo card, asking your students to read them.

Vocabulary Games

Use games to reinforce the skills taught in lessons. You can ask students to give the female or male counterparts of the following words:

boy - girl	*niece - nephew*
man - woman	*father - mother*
groom - bride	*brother - sister*
uncle - aunt	*son - daughter*
actor - actress	*waiter - waitress*

Or you might ask for plurals:

boy - boys	*girl - girls*
man - men	*woman - women*

You can use the same idea with opposites:

tall - short	*slow - fast*
up - down	*top - bottom*
old - young	*old - new*
fat - thin	*big - small*

Concentrate on regular patterns at first; the irregular ones can come later. Don't be surprised if the lesson doesn't go exactly as planned. One student gave *secondhand* as the opposite of *new*. This is, of course, a perfectly acceptable, and maybe even preferable, answer.

Here is another activity that reinforces listening comprehension and expands vocabulary. Decide on a specific topic for vocabulary building, such as kitchen items, garden plants, or parts of a car.

If your students want to know the vocabulary of kitchen items, you could try this. Make stick drawings of three kitchen items such as a table, a stove, and a refrigerator on small cards, or clip pictures from magazines, catalogues, etc. Create a 3 by 3 grid on a large sheet of paper.

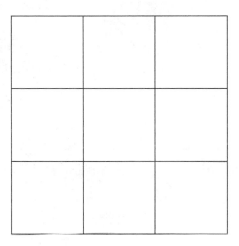

Ask the students to put the refrigerator in the upper left-hand corner of the grid, the stove in the lower right-hand corner, the table in front of the stove, etc. Make sure your students know the meaning of *upper, left-hand, corner,* etc.

Word bingo is always fun. Use a similar grid, with words your students want to learn. If they are studying food words, you might use columns headed with *fruits, vegetables, cereals, baked goods* and call out words such as *apple, tomato, wheat, bread* to fit under the appropriate column.

Another helpful activity for ESOL students is identifying the kinds of things they can buy at certain types of stores:

> *What do you buy at a . . . shoe store?*
>   *bakery?*
>   *post office?*
> *Where can you buy fruit?*
> *Where can you get stamps?*

After your students are familiar with the names for colors, use them in real situations:

> *The traffic signals have _____, _____, and _____ lights.*
> *Nurses wear _____ uniforms.*
> *The colors of the American flag are _____, _____, and _____.*
> *In traffic, a blinking _____ light means proceed with caution or go slowly.*

Sometimes it is easier to learn new vocabulary words that have something in common. They're called "group words." You can make your own group words by bringing items from one category for fun and learning. If your students are interested in gardening, you might bring garden tools: a watering can, pruning shears, a weeder, a sprinkler, garden gloves, and so on. Another time you might bring articles having to do with an office: pen, paper clips, three-hole paper punch, eraser, ruler, highlighter. Pictures often suggest natural groups of words.

Start the activity with a sentence describing how the articles are used or how they could be used in a sentence. One group was interested in cooking, and the teacher brought kitchen-related materials: knife, fork, spoon, bowl, cup, saucer, and several other basic kitchen items. It's reassuring if the teacher names and points to each item first. Then the teacher picks up the knife and says:

To make dinner, I need a knife.

The first student picks up the knife, repeating the teacher's sentence, adding a second item, picking it up, and naming it:

To make dinner, I need a knife and a bowl.

The students and the teacher continue until all the items have been named. Have the names of all the articles written down on 3" × 5" cards or on a piece of paper. The students can then read the new words and copy them for their own review.

For the next session, the teacher asks the students to bring their own kitchen items for identification, and the teacher brings more unusual kitchen tools: spatula, salt and pepper shakers, napkins, strainer, can opener. Some of the students know specific items and use them often but do not know the English words for them: *rolling pin, colander, double boiler, knife sharpener.* This is true collaboration: The students are participating in the lesson plans.

At one meeting, a Greek student brought in spanakopita. Everyone enjoyed eating it and wanted to know how she made it. This group adapted the group word game. Maria started by saying:

I made spanakopita. I used flour.

Maria listed the ingredients, and each student had to say their names.

Maria made spanakopita. She used flour and water.

They included other ingredients: *feta cheese, spinach, eggs, pepper, onions,* and *butter.* The students listened first and then spoke. Later the students read Maria's recipe and copied it for themselves.

Conversation Games

As you try to engage the students in free conversation, it's surprising how one thing leads right into another.

We were enjoying strawberry shortcake. I said we really could brag about Alicia's strawberry shortcake. I saw eyebrows rise as I said brag. *They had never heard the word and didn't know what it meant.*

I explained, giving examples, and then each one was to brag about someone or something. It was revealing to hear students brag about their husband's work, their children's activities, their own cooking, their achievements at the university—being modest yet proud.

There are hidden talents in every person and in every group. One student was a baker and invited his teacher to his home where he gave him a baking lesson. Another student showed how to quilt a pillow. Another planted a miniature garden. As these students showed their special skills, they talked. That's conversational English. Pictures can always be used to generate and focus conversation. Use whatever you can to encourage students to talk.

A good conversation game is Twenty Questions. One person mentally picks out an object in the room or a well-known place or person. The others take turns asking up to 20 questions that can be answered by *yes* or *no*, trying to identify the object, place, or person. The person who guesses correctly gets the opportunity to choose another object, place, or person.

You can add new vocabulary words by bringing in a special object from another country or something unique. Whatever it is, it becomes the focus of conversation. Have a variety of questions ready, and solicit discussion in English.

What do you think this is?
What's it made of?
What's it used for?
Where do you think it was made?
Do you have one?
Would you like one?

Once the students see how it is done, they are often willing to bring in objects from their countries. They then become the leaders and ask similar questions.

Be alert to ways you can use new words from the students' conversations, explaining them when necessary, and then let the students carry their ideas further. Once I was discussing with a small group of students how individuals felt when they first came to America. Johanna from Zaire in Central Africa had never seen snow or felt such cold when she arrived in Syracuse in midwinter. In her limited English, Johanna explained that she was confined to her small apartment. She said she was in a . . . She groped for the right word. With gestures, she made bars at the window. We understood. *Prison*, someone said. That opened the conversation to more vocabulary: *prisoner, thieves, judge, lawyer, fine,* and *speeding.*

Show and Tell gives individual students an opportunity to share. One student showed colored slides of her country. In her enthusiasm about sharing her country with us, she forgot her embarrassment about her poor English. Another brought objects from her country and described them and their uses. Putting a student in the limelight with a familiar subject helps build pride and confidence.

Communication Games

An information gap activity is a communication game in which some people know something that the others don't, and they must communicate in order to solve a problem or complete a puzzle. The following is a communication game that two people can play. Player A and Player B sit back-to-back. Similar small objects or pictures are in front of each, plus paper and pen. Player A tells Player B to draw something or to move one of the objects or pictures to a certain spot. Player A could say:

> *Put the paper between pages 23 and 24 of the book.*
> *Draw a circle at the bottom of the page.*
> *Fold the paper in half.*
> *Put the paper clip on page 12.*

After six or seven directives, have the players compare what they've done. If the results are the same, Player B understood Player A. Even if there are differences, they are likely to have had a good time and to have learned as well.

Another communication game can be played by several people. Place several objects or pictures in front of the group. One player describes one item. The other players try to identify the object or picture described. If some of the items are similar, the game is more difficult. The only restrictions are that the person describing the item must use English, and the identifier must listen and identify that item in English, not merely point to it.

Some ESOL students with traditional educational backgrounds may think games are only for children. It may be useful to point out to parents in the group that they can teach the new games they learn to their children. Of course, there are many adult games like Scrabble and Monopoly that your students may well enjoy. When introducing these games, be sensitive to your students' reactions. Some students may enjoy playing games; others may not.

Keep your eyes open for books that give suggestions for games and activities appropriate for English language learners. Remember that in working with ESOL students, hard-and-fast rules rarely apply. ESOL students come from all over the world and represent many different ages, educational and vocational backgrounds, and general life experiences. No two students will fit into the same mold, and you will want to adapt any game to the interests of your particular students.

SUMMARY

Once you've learned and practiced various techniques, strategies, and exercises for teaching English to speakers of other languages, it's rewarding and fun to apply them to the everyday needs of your students. The resources and activities described in this chapter are only the beginning. You'll encounter other activities in books, journals, and workshops. But don't hesitate to create your own resources and activities as well. Do share those that you find helpful and fun for your students with other tutors and teachers in your local program.

Importance of Students' Goals
Step-by-Step to Long-Term Goals

Planning Together
Learner-Centered Lessons
Problem Posing and Solving

Lesson Plans

Sample Lesson Plan
Warm-Up Reception
Homework Assignment Review
Last Session's Work Review
New Material
Home Assignment
Questions and Comments
Stories in English for Pleasure
Joint Summation

Specific Help Needs Chart

The First Lesson

Ongoing Lessons
If Things Don't Go as Planned
Portfolio Assessment

More on Lesson Plans

Summary

IMPORTANCE OF STUDENTS' GOALS

Every student has a goal in mind when asking for help to learn English. Sometimes these goals may take a long time to achieve. One ESOL student may wish to become a computer programmer. Another may want to pass a high school equivalency exam. Still another may want to gain confidence in listening and speaking in order to attend parent-teacher conferences or to participate in the school parent-teacher organization. Others want to get better jobs or enter college classes.

These are long-term goals. Such goals are desirable and should be encouraged. However, it is difficult to develop lessons on a daily or weekly basis with only long-term goals in mind. From these long-term goals, short-term goals can be identified with objectives that can be attained daily, weekly, or monthly.

A beginning student's first short-term goal may be to be able to understand and respond to simple greetings in English. Another student may want to learn enough survival vocabulary to do weekly grocery shopping or to make an appointment with a doctor. An advanced student might want to practice a dialogue for an upcoming job interview.

Some of your lesson planning should focus on the more immediate needs of your students, but you should also keep your students' longer-range goals and objectives in mind as you plan lessons. Both short-term and long-term goals may be revised as you and your students work together. As you make your lesson plans, keep in mind who your students are and how you can help them address their real-life concerns. Adapt techniques, exercises, and activities so they relate to the interests of your students.

Step-by-Step to Long-Term Goals

It is difficult for many students to divide long-term goals into smaller components. You might suggest that they think of a ladder where each step is a short-term doable goal that leads to that ultimate goal at the top of the ladder.

Write down the student's long-term goal as the top rung on the ladder; then think what must be done to get there, what barriers must be overcome, and eventually where to start and what to do first.

> Margarita, 22 years old, went to school for six years in El Salvador and then came to America three years ago as an immigrant. She can read and write in Spanish, but her English is limited, perhaps low-intermediate level. She has been working for a year as a housekeeper in a local hotel and enjoying her work, but she realizes that she cannot become a supervisor unless she learns to read and write in English. In addition, she is eager to become a U.S. citizen.

> Margarita's two long-term goals are to become a citizen and to become head of housekeeping in a hotel. She is confident that she can attain both goals, but she isn't sure how to do it. She discussed this with

her teacher, and they came up with two success ladders—one to get her U.S. citizenship and the other to prepare for a top job in housekeeping. They focused on specific skills she would need. After making her two long-term goal ladders, Margarita realized that she could work toward both goals through similar beginning paths.

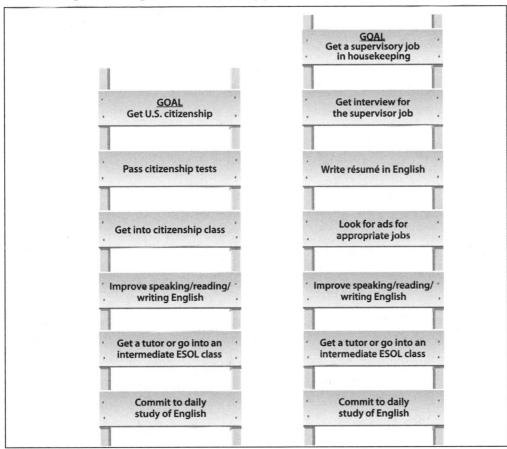

Students gain confidence from identifying and writing down long-term goals and listing doable short-term steps that will move them toward those goals. Achieving short-term success provides students with concrete evidence of progress and supports their hard work as they climb a ladder to a goal.

PLANNING TOGETHER

Planning for individual lessons is mainly your responsibility, but it should involve the students as much as possible.

As you plan, keep the following in mind:

1. **Assessment.** Find out:
   - where your students use English now with relative ease
   - where they have difficulty with English now
   - where they will need to use English in the future
   - what their strengths and weaknesses with English are
   - what their interests are

° what they want to accomplish

Review the results of the assessment tools suggested in this book as well as the continuing assessment done in individual students' portfolios.

2. **Teaching.** Incorporate listening, speaking, reading, and writing while maintaining a balanced communicative approach; vary the activities and resources you use as you focus on both authentic materials and real-life situations.

3. **Reinforcement.** Review and reteach; give suggestions for using the newly acquired skills outside of lesson time.

4. **Evaluation.** Answer the following questions with your students:

   ° Have we done what we set out to do?

   ° Are the students improving their English skills?

   ° Are the lessons focused on the students' needs?

   ° Are the students eager and contributing?

The first cycle of planning becomes complete when you and the students go back to assessment as you plan for continuing lessons.

Learner-Centered Lessons

As you teach listening, speaking, reading, and writing English, you will want to build lessons around your students' interests and concerns. How do you identify those interests and concerns so you can choose relevant subjects for your learner-centered lessons? You've learned techniques, strategies, and activities in this book, and as you get to know your students and earn their trust, you'll find other ways.

Communication is the key, and with students who know no English, this can be difficult. As you teach the listening skills, you, the teacher, will be mostly in control of the lessons, teaching basic skills using Total Physical Response (see page 74) and the colored paper exercise (see Appendix F, page 209).

As you and your students learn more about each other, you will want more input from them. Language Experience activities (used for teaching reading and writing; see page 119) can help you gather information about your students' interests and concerns, as can dialogues and journal writing. Ask questions. Use pictures. Encourage free discussions. Listen carefully as your students cautiously share their thoughts with you.

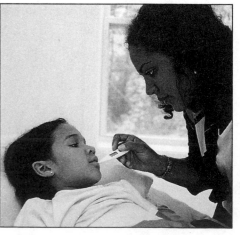

Problem Posing and Solving

As teachers and tutors, you're looking for specific areas where students want and need help. You want to identify their concerns so you can focus your lessons on those issues and help students to identify and solve their own problems. But before students will share their thoughts with you, they must trust you. To build that trust, you might want to show pictures of probable concerns—for instance, a picture of a mother with a child sick in bed. What should she do when a school-age child is sick and both parents have full-time jobs? In many countries, the grandparents look after such children. What should they do in America?

Other problem-posing images might include a picture of a person standing by a car with a flat tire, a picture of someone in a supermarket looking confused, or a picture of someone looking at an ad for refrigerators and questioning how to buy and pay for one. Pictures can allow your students to explore some of the problems they face without becoming personal. Such pictures open doors to discussion of sensitive topics, even for beginning students.

Jane Vella (2002) suggests using open-ended questions when showing pictures that pose problems to learners:

1. *What do you see happening here?* (description)
2. *Why do you think it is happening?* (analysis)
3. *When it happens in your situation, what problems does it cause?* (application)
4. *What can we do about it?* (implementation)

These and other similar questions will probably promote discussion and give you topics for upcoming lessons. In addition, such a discussion can provide an opportunity for students to think of possible alternative solutions. It encourages critical thinking.

Problem posing and solving can be an entrée into helping your students with real-life issues as you interweave these areas of interest and concern into your lessons. Encourage the students to bring in their own or imaginary problems with alternative suggestions for solving them. You, too, can bring in problems that you foresee could happen to them. Use oral/aural language initially—listening to the problem, then paraphrasing, and finally discussing possible solutions. Reading and writing can follow.

> *Victor was trained as a nurse in Russia, but he found that his Russian credentials were not accepted by American hospitals. He worked as a maintenance worker in a local hospital, and after observing the nursing procedures used there, he felt that his skills were more than adequate. He realized that he must improve his English first, but he was unsure what to do next.*

> *Victor shared his problem with the members of his small ESOL group. They listened attentively, thinking that eventually Victor should be given an opportunity to use his nursing skills in America. They wondered, "How can we help?"*

> *They suggested that Victor contact the admissions office of the local nursing school and submit his Russian credentials, giving evidence of his efforts to improve his English. They even worked as a group to draft a cover letter. Victor was elated and felt a real confidence boost. Ensuring Victor's success would now be a project for the entire class.*

The teacher and members of a small group or class are not expected to be counselors. They are not expected to solve all problems. However, they can listen well and be facilitators. With lessons focused on learner-centered subjects, the techniques, strategies, and activities suggested in this book will be meaningful in real-life situations. So adapt, mix, and match them as you plan your lessons.

LESSON PLANS

You may have prepared wonderful lesson plans, but you should always be ready to adapt them to students' immediate concerns. Lists of suggested topics for learner-centered curricula for each student level are included in the Performance-Based Curricula and Outcomes (MELT Project) list in Appendix C, page 202.

It is difficult to plan a lesson until you have specific students in mind and know about their abilities and interests. When you are actually working with students, you can tailor your lesson plans to their real needs and goals. Making realistic lesson plans is an important part of your teaching. Knowing what you are going to do and how you plan to do it will give you confidence, eliminating that *What will I do next?* feeling. Your confidence will spread to your students. That's one reason why preparation is so important. The more self-assured you are as a teacher, the more reassured your students will feel.

Planning allows you to be more flexible and more creative. It is better to plan more than you can use rather than not enough. Plan some easy activities and some more challenging ones. Plan some that are short, others that will take longer. Vary the pace in your lessons. Every lesson should be interesting and challenging but never frustrating.

Lesson plans can be as simple or as complex as you want. You can photocopy the Sample Lesson Plan or use a spiral or loose-leaf notebook, putting specific things to be done on the left page and using the right page for your own comments. Or you can simply draw a line down the center of a page, using the left half for your present lesson plan and the right half for the next session's lesson plan, extending what you did today.

SAMPLE LESSON PLAN

Date: _____ Student's name or group name: _____

Goal (simple statement of what you want to accomplish):

Objectives (simple statement of what you'll do to get there):

Materials needed:

Warm-up:

Review of homework:

Review of last lesson's work:

New material:

Assignment of homework:

Questions and comments:

Evaluation:

Comments:

The goal for a lesson could be *to be able to say and understand the vocabulary needed to buy a used car.* The objective could be as simple as *learn appropriate vocabulary; act out a dialogue for buying a used car.* In the lesson plan, list the specific exercises and activities you plan on doing. This will help alert you to materials you might need.

Warm-Up Reception

You can vary the way you open your lessons, but if your students know that you will start on time, they will usually make an effort to be on time. When working one-to-one, it might be a simple greeting. For a small group or a class, simple chain drills are fun. You might review greetings in English, varying the words by using different situations. Show a picture of two teenage friends meeting. Their greeting could be *Hi,* said while slapping each other's palms high-five fashion. Going into a doctor's office or a car salesroom would suggest a more formal greeting of *Good morning* or *Good afternoon.* Your students might suggest other situations where they would like to know how Americans greet each other.

For advanced students, you might do a chain drill. You start by saying, *I visited my mother yesterday. What did you do yesterday?* Each student tells what was done the day before in English, turning to the next student to ask the question.

Homework Assignment Review

Two or three hours a week of class work is only a part of language learning. Students must use English in order to learn it. Show that you really are interested in the assignments your students did.

If students completed written assignments, you might ask them to volunteer to read them aloud or just hand them in so that you can review their work later. If they were to listen to a specific news broadcast, you might want to discuss what they heard. Don't be surprised if, in spite of great intentions, some students don't have the time or the inclination to do the assigned homework. Remember, they are adults and usually have lots of responsibilities and full, active lives outside the teaching sessions. They are not neglectful if they don't do their home assignments. They are merely working at a pace that is comfortable for them. They are putting their language lessons in the context of their lives and priorities.

Last Session's Work Review

A review of successful work done during the last session helps build the students' confidence. A review of work accomplished prepares them for accepting the challenge of new work. It is especially important to review the last session's work if it relates to the current session.

New Material

How do you find and determine learner-centered topics to include in your lesson plans? There are several ways.

1. Language Experience (see page 119)
2. Problem posing and solving (see page 172)
3. *The Oxford Picture Dictionary* (see Bibliography, page 247)
4. Ideas for MELT (see Appendix C, page 202)
5. Ideas from Conversation Starters (see Appendix G, page 212)

When presenting new material, remember to balance the four language skills. You should first have the students listen to the new material; then have them speak, either repeating or paraphrasing what you said or read to them. Invite them to read the same selection, either to themselves or aloud. Then have them write. Sometimes you may want to vary this. Students might write something and then read it aloud so the group can discuss what they have heard. New material could be as simple as new words using colored paper exercises for beginners or free conversation on any given subject, depending on the competency level of your students and their goals and needs.

After you've agreed on specific topics for a series of lessons, check the Quick Reference Guides in Appendix N (page 241) and Appendix O (page 245). There, you'll find suggested lesson plans for five levels as well as useful techniques, strategies, and activities to use in those plans.

Introduce new material early in the lesson while the students are fresh. For instance, if the students want to learn the vocabulary necessary to buy a car, you will have prepared some suggested *group words*. They could include the brands of some of the cars your students express interest in buying, such as *Ford, Chevrolet, Honda*.

If you have ads for used cars, you will find many pertinent words: *lease, time plans, interest, color, interior, engine, mileage*. After you read the ads aloud to your students, ask them which words are new to them.

You might want to have them memorize a dialogue to make them more comfortable on a first shopping trip.

> **Salesperson:** Good afternoon. May I help you?
> **Student:** Yes, thank you. I'm looking for a used car. I don't have much money, so it must be inexpensive.
> **Salesperson:** Did you have something specific in mind?
> **Student:** Yes, I saw your ad for a 2008 Ford.

A lesson on buying a used car could be the main topic for several sessions. You might even want take the group to a used-car lot. A game could be included in this part of your lesson, or you could use a game later as reinforcement. Vary the activities, books, and pictures you use.

If you have not been given levels for individual students, you might find individual levels by checking the ESL Educational Functioning Levels (EFL) in Appendix B, page 197.

Home Assignment

You have watched the time, and you note that you have only five to ten minutes left. This is just enough time to give specific home assignments, get questions from your students, and end the lesson. When you meet with your students for the first time, it's important to discuss the importance of home study and encourage each to set aside specific times for study.

Ask them how much time they can devote to homework assignments. Don't give more than they can reasonably do in the amount of time they have available. Learning English is not a marathon. Go at the students' pace. If some students have more free time, give those students more to do at home.

Language skills must be practiced to be acquired and maintained. No one learns a language without practice, but it is the students who are in charge of how much they practice. Anyone who suggests that a new language can be learned during lesson time alone raises false hopes and wastes the time of both the teacher and the students. Students must practice every day.

You can always suggest reading and writing assignments. But how can beginning students practice their listening and speaking skills without the teacher present?

- Encourage your students to listen to spoken English—on TV and radio, in groups, in the family—even if they don't fully understand what they hear. Surrounding themselves with English will help them get a feel for the rhythm of the language.
- Record stories for your students to listen to if they have access to playback equipment.
- Give each student a folder, envelope, or notebook for study materials. Then students can repeat some of the activities alone or get English-speaking friends or members of their families to help. Such a folder might include the following:
  - Colored pieces of paper
  - Numbers and letters on index cards
  - Stick-figure cards
  - Pictures
  - Written words from the lesson
- Assign students a simple task to perform using only English:
  - Ask in English for the time.
  - Listen to a specific TV program, and report what you learned to the class.

- ° Speak English to a clerk or a doctor, and report what you said.
- ° Read road signs—STOP, YIELD, etc.
- ° Greet two people in English.
- ° Say aloud the parts of your body.
- ° Look around you and say the colors you see.
- ° Look for license numbers and say the numbers aloud.
- ° Answer the phone.
- Homework assignments for a more advanced student could include:
  - ° Participate in an English-speaking group, and speak even if you're not sure of your English.
  - ° Listen to a specific TV or radio broadcast, and be ready to discuss it at the next lesson.
  - ° Discuss a picture with a friend, or write a few sentences about it.
  - ° Practice a written dialogue from a lesson.
  - ° Repeat recorded sentences.
  - ° Review a recorded story.
  - ° Perform a special task (e.g., call directory assistance for a certain number; ask someone in a store or on the street for directions).
  - ° Read a story and write your version of it.

Questions and Comments

Near the end of each session, both you and your students can start to wind down. The work part of the lesson is over, and home assignments have been given. Encourage your students to ask questions, to give feedback on what they felt was especially useful and where they would like more help. Taking time for this assures the students that their feelings and input are important. Note their comments on your lesson plan sheet.

Stories in English for Pleasure

The last few minutes of your lesson should be spent relaxing. Learning new material in a new language can be very tiring, and it's important to end the session with something that is fun. If you have beginning students, you might want to share family or magazine pictures.

As soon as you know that your students understand some English, tell in your own words or read aloud to them a short story in English. Show the pictures from the book first, telling them what the story will be about. You might want to talk or read more slowly than normal for beginning students, but read at a normal pace for more advanced students. Let them enjoy the story. Don't ask for their input. This is purely for their relaxation and enjoyment; language learning doesn't always have to be work. They will be hearing the flow of English and picking up new vocabulary as well.

Joint Summation

You might end a session by suggesting that your students write a few sentences in their journals. Some will remain to do so, but others will probably have other commitments and may prefer to write in their journals later. You can use that time to write as well. Sum up the day's lesson. Note what the students have learned and what still needs to be worked on. Then start planning the next session.

SPECIFIC HELP NEEDS CHART

Mistakes occur naturally when one is learning a new language, and beginning students often are hesitant to speak, knowing they'll make errors. Don't focus on errors at first; focus on communication. Often students will self-correct if you give them time. Errors are actually steps in the learning process.

Most students do want to know when they make errors, but it's not important for beginning ESOL students to know rules about language—that can come later. It is important that they use the English they know and learn to hear what sounds right.

A Specific Help Needs Chart can be of real help in lesson planning. Rather than interrupting the lesson constantly to correct your students, jot down special problems to return to later. You may notice a pattern of pronunciation, grammar, or spelling problems. Sometimes you will want to help your students immediately by modeling correctly, but often you may prefer to work on errors in future lessons.

SPECIFIC HELP NEEDS CHART		
Error	**Needs Help**	**Completed**
Says *shocks* for *socks, shun* for *sun*	Work on /s/ sound	
Confuses *bit* and *beet*	Work on words that sound alike (minimal pair exercises)	
Doesn't understand difference between *hospital* and *clinic*	Work on difference between hospitals and clinics	

THE FIRST LESSON

The first lesson will be a get-acquainted meeting. You and your students have been notified of when and where to meet. You probably have information about your students—names, native countries, education, family information, etc.

Your students probably have been tested, and you'll know their approximate levels of understanding, speaking, reading, and writing in English, and perhaps their goals and interests. You may even be a bit nervous. But remember, your students know nothing about you and are probably hesitant and uncertain, too. Your job is to make them feel comfortable and welcome. You are setting the climate for future meetings.

You might want to keep your "teaching tools" in a tote bag or big folder:

- Information about your students: names, telephone numbers, native countries, levels of education, etc.
- *I Speak English* and other ESL books
- Notebooks, pens, colored post-its, portfolio folders, name tags
- Bilingual dictionary
- Pictures/picture dictionary
- Simple books, including some from other countries and cultures

Display the pictures and simple books on a table for your students to review if they wish.

As each student enters, speak distinctly as you introduce yourself, saying simply,

> *Hello, my name is. . .*

Some students may respond with *Hello* and give their names. To the student who merely smiles, you could ask,

> *What's your name?*

If there is still no response, you know that the student probably doesn't understand any English and cannot even respond with his or her name. If you are tutoring and have one student, you'll know his or her name. Start right there. Point to the student, and say his or her name. Point to yourself as you say your own name. Repeat this procedure to make sure the student understands. Then point to yourself and say,

> *My name is. . .*

Then point to the student, inserting his or her name, and say,

> *My name is. . . ,*

and gesture for the student to repeat. You say *my* when saying your student's name because your student will be repeating your exact words. In practice, this procedure is not confusing. Most students will catch on quickly. If you have more than one student and they don't respond with their names, then look over your list, say the names, and they'll probably respond by raising their hands. Generally the students will want to be able to introduce themselves and will welcome the chance to learn how to say the introductions correctly.

This first get-acquainted meeting is a time to begin to learn what the language needs of your students are. Your students will be looking you over and wondering how these teaching sessions will work out. You will be assessing your students' abilities—strengths and weaknesses—and striving to build up the confidence you both need. As you make plans for your next meeting, be sure to write down the date and time. You might make copies of pages of a calendar, jotting down the date and time of the next lesson. If any students cannot read, you can suggest that perhaps a friend or family member will help. Write your name and telephone number on a 3 × 5 card or on a student's notebook with the dates of the next lessons.

A friendly *Hello* and *Good-bye* in English can begin and end each session, but you might want to learn the greetings in your students' languages. You would then have a taste of new languages and would certainly put your students at ease by sharing an interest in their languages, too.

If you have more than one student, you might want to try the introductory chain drill, learning each other's names and perhaps native countries. The first time:

> *Hi, I'm _____, and I'm from _____.*

Later, they might introduce each other:

> *Hi, this is _____, and he's from _____.*

And you might, even at that first meeting, introduce a simple greeting dialogue:

> **A.** *Hello. My name is _____. What's your name?*
>
> **B.** *My name is _____.*
>
> **A.** *Pleased to meet you.*
>
> **B.** *Thank you.*

Even after just your initial meeting, you will have a basic assessment of the level of your students, and you can start your planning. Know that assessment will be ongoing. You may want to give each student a folder or envelope in which to organize and keep his or her own work. You should also have your own folder or portfolio for each student, always available for quick assessment.

If you know that your students understand some English, you might read a short story in English at the end of the lesson. End the lesson promptly or even a few minutes early. Ask if there are any questions. Remind them of the next meeting, and give a simple way to say *Good-bye*. It could be as simple as:

> *Good-bye. I'll see you on Thursday.*

Encourage them to repeat the words. Next session, you can build on that.

After you end the session, stay just a few minutes longer so you can jot down what you did and what you learned about each student. Put those comments in your individual student portfolios. It is easier to do this immediately after the lesson when things are fresh in your mind. From those notes, you can quickly make a new lesson plan for the next session.

Once you are in the habit of making lesson plans immediately after each session, you can quickly pull together the material you need—pictures, audio recorder, textbooks, etc. You then have no worries about *What will I do?* because you have your plans ready.

ONGOING LESSONS

Lessons now can be focused on *your* students' interests and needs. You might want to read again the earlier pages of this chapter that suggest how to identify subjects for lessons and what techniques or strategies you'll want to consider given the level of your students.

If your students speak and understand no English, you can start with beginning techniques and strategies. However, if your students speak and understand some English, you need to ask them what they want to learn and to tell them a bit of what you expect to do together.

It is crucial that each student learn at least one needed thing, even in the first lessons. It might be learning to say their addresses and phone numbers in English, or learning common English greetings, or finding out how to ask for help when they're lost, or learning how to read a bus schedule.

By the second or third meeting, you'll know your students' English levels, interests, and goals, so you can plan your lessons accordingly. If the students know absolutely no English, you might try the colored paper exercises (Appendix F, page 209). If they are more advanced, you'll want to get them to talk so you can learn about their interests. You might start with a Language Experience activity and then expand into more discussion through pictures within their interest area (use *The Oxford Picture Dictionary* or any pictures you have). You might introduce a dialogue.

If Things Don't Go as Planned

Even the best-laid plans can't always be adhered to, so you must be adaptable. If you have had good training and rely on this book as a constant companion, you should have no troubles.

Your students will understand—in fact, they may feel more confident if they know that you aren't perfect. So when things don't go exactly as planned, just relax, laugh, and explain that you, too, will have to do more homework to adjust to new situations. The more experience you gain as a teacher, the more answers you will have to questions and new situations that come up.

If you are a volunteer tutor, you can always call your program office for help and suggestions. There are probably in-service training sessions you can attend. Join as many "help" groups as you can. Life is indeed a series of learning experiences, and this training and your new teaching experience can be valuable ones.

Portfolio Assessment

As you add to each student's portfolio, keep in mind that you will want to set times to review portfolios with individual students. It is helpful to set at least a half-hour aside for each student perhaps once every eight to ten weeks. This will help you and your students to actually see the progress they are making. You could refer together to the ESL Educational Functioning Levels grid in Appendix B, page 197, and let them see for themselves their undeniable progress.

Advanced English learners may want to learn more about American history and why and how things are done in America. *American Ways* (Datesman, Crandall, & Kearny, 2005) gives excellent exercises and stories that help students identify main ideas, discuss details, build vocabulary, and review for context clues. It also provides opportunities to write about the subjects discussed, such as volunteerism, government and politics, ethnic and racial diversity. For each subject, it suggests exercises, websites, books to read, and even movies to see, as well as vocabulary for the more advanced students.

As you progress in your own teaching, you might want to learn more about how you can help your students. In *Practical English Language Teaching,* Nunan (2003) selected experts in a variety of fields to write chapters on their specialties—listening, speaking, reading, writing, pronunciation, vocabulary, grammar, etc. Once you're dedicated to teaching, it's lifelong learning.

MORE ON LESSON PLANS

You will save yourself a great deal of time and do a much better job if you jot down your comments and suggestions immediately after each lesson while the completed lesson is fresh in your mind. With your materials at hand, you can plan quickly and easily. If you need additional new materials, write a note to yourself and attend to it immediately. The habit of planning the next lesson immediately pays big dividends.

Although you will want to vary the lessons, do not neglect repetition. The importance of repetition in learning a new language cannot be overstressed. Since learning requires unconscious assimilation before it becomes natural, students need to hear and say words, phrases, and sentences many times and in many contexts before they can use them automatically.

Integrate new material immediately, and begin to expand its context. For example, if you are teaching or reviewing numbers in English, your students can progress from simple arithmetic to reading prices, telling time, and giving change in American money. You might even go with them to a nearby store where they can actually find prices, purchase something, pay for it, and count their change to be sure it's correct. Help your students realize that what they are learning has many practical applications. Using material in many different ways gives you an opportunity for repetition and review.

To encourage your students to think in English, get them personally invested in activities: Have them follow directions or add a sentence to a story you have started. Such activities, if done with few pauses, allow no time for translation from the students' native languages to English. The object is to get the students to think in English, so don't stop to correct errors. Make notes about errors for later lessons in your Specific Help Needs Chart.

When you are working with one student, lesson plans seem to come easily because you get to know your student well. You know the student's capabilities and needs and can project them into lesson plans. Working together is a dialogue when there is one tutor and one student. However, when you work with several students in a small group or a class, keep in mind that you want to include all the students in activities. Realize that your plans should include the following:

- Some activities where the entire group works together, even repeating or speaking chorally as a group
- Some activities where students work in pairs, practicing techniques and exercises, working on a joint project, or perhaps just talking together
- Some times when the group watches a movie or listens to a recording, a student presenter, or the teacher
- Some quiet times when students work on writing activities

A balanced lesson that includes everyone is a satisfying lesson. Knowing techniques and exercises thoroughly will help you adapt to individual students' needs whether you have one student, a small group, or a class.

SUMMARY

Your goal is to help your students reach their long-term goals by climbing the goal ladder one short-term goal at a time. By making lesson plans ahead of time, you'll help your students reach those goals more quickly. While you can always be flexible and adapt, it's a comfortable feeling to know that you have that plan in front of you. Both you and your students will relax and enjoy the lessons more.

TECHNOLOGY

Audio Recording, CDs, TV, and Radio

Computers, Smartphones, and Tablets

Assessment Tools on the Internet

Surfing the Internet

Summary

The continuing explosion of technology has opened doors to knowledge that was unimaginable a few years ago. Surfing the Internet, using computers, texting, listening to iPods, using smartphones—these have become a way of life for younger students, and they can be ways for tutors and teachers to learn as well. It's lifelong learning, and we must embrace technology and take advantage of all it makes available to us.

AUDIO RECORDING, CDs, TV, AND RADIO

Encourage your students to record whatever parts of lessons they want to review. They can then go over the lesson as many times as they wish at home, using you as a model for both pronunciation and rhythm.

It usually takes playing a new recording several times for most ESOL students to really understand its content well enough to paraphrase it. As your students progress, longer and longer audio segments may be used.

First playing Ask simple *yes* and *no* questions as you check for comprehension.

Second playing Ask open-ended questions (*why, when, who, what, where,* and *how*), challenging the students to respond in their own words.

Third playing Suggest that the students put in their own words what they heard.

You can always follow up by having them write what they heard.

Listening to the TV and radio to get the news, sports, or weather reports gives excellent practice in developing listening skills. You might suggest you all listen to the same broadcast, perhaps the 6 o'clock news or weather, and discuss it at the next lesson. Providing a brief chart to fill out can help students with comprehension.

For example:

	TODAY	TOMORROW	DAY AFTER TOMORROW
High Temperature (degrees)	82°	85°	77°
Low Temperature	65°	62°	60°
Weather (cloudy, rainy, etc.)	sunshine	cloudy	rain

Many international students come to the United States for advanced degrees. They can read and write well in their chosen fields, but they often have trouble understanding American lecturers in classrooms. Suggest that they record a lecture and play it back later in small chunks. Encourage them to replay the recording as often as needed. You can play back portions of it in your sessions.

Libraries have many recorded books. Match unabridged recordings to books so that students can read along—hearing, seeing, and saying. Even advanced students who want to improve their listening skills can benefit from listening to different voices on recordings, stopping and replaying them when necessary.

COMPUTERS, SMARTPHONES, AND TABLETS

Because tutors and teachers are always looking for new teaching ideas, and because more and more of these have become available on the Internet or through iTunes, we've added Appendix M, page 236: Useful Websites and Free Apps. Links often change or become unusable, so check with your library if you have trouble opening one.

Most libraries have computers. Tutors often work with students in libraries and can take advantage of the computers available there. Some teachers have computers available where they teach. As soon as students have learned to read and write their names and addresses, they can type that personal information into a computer and print it out. Beginning students are often embarrassed by their poor handwriting, but they can key in whatever they want on a computer. They can even use a spell checker to be assured of correct spelling. This opens new doors to them and gives them tools for learning that they can use on their own. Software that asks questions to check comprehension is available even for beginning readers.

Computers are being used more and more to support individual, small group, or class work in teaching reading and writing, as are iPods and Smartphones. Devices with audio capabilities enable students to hear words while they see corresponding words or pictures on the screen.

Smartphones and tablets are easy for a tutor to transport to a tutoring session. In addition, many students seem to own these devices now. Free applications (apps) such as dictionaries are available to help in your lessons, and some apps are available for students to use independently. See Appendix M, page 236, for a list of free apps.

ASSESSMENT TOOLS ON THE INTERNET

In Chapter 6, Assessment, we referred you to ESL Educational Functioning Levels (EFL), included in Appendix B, page 197. These descriptors tell what learners at each level—low and high beginning, low and high intermediate, and advanced—should be able to do when they start. You can get suggested daily living themes and topics as well as lists of abilities expected upon completion of each level at http://www.adultedcontentstandards.org/ReferenceFiles/PALanguage.htm.

SURFING THE INTERNET

Second-language learning has been affected by the explosion in computer-based technology. Many interactive teaching materials are now available. New ideas and new theories as well as creative ways to teach ESL are coming out all the time on the Internet. Although the subject itself hasn't changed much, the way it is taught has evolved.

You can supplement your lessons by exploring electronic resources and encouraging your students to learn from them. See Appendix M for suggestions. Do check these, whether to find help for yourself as tutor or teacher or to suggest websites to your students.

SUMMARY

Technology is important, but nothing replaces face-to-face teaching and learning. Students process learning in diverse ways, so it's critical to blend face-to-face teaching with support from websites. Find ways to integrate technology as you plan your lessons, but keep a reasonable balance. Remember, you're touching and changing lives as you teach and interact with your students.

While technology is valuable, how you use it is equally important. You, the tutor or teacher, are the vital link between the students and their learning of English. Knowing you can get extra help and support right from the Internet can be a big help to you as teacher or tutor, but use this resource wisely.

NATIVE LANGUAGE LITERACY AS A FIRST STEP TO ENGLISH

Native Language Literacy

Spanish Literacy as a First Step to English

Summary

NATIVE LANGUAGE LITERACY

Research and experience suggest that those with little or no reading and writing skill in their native languages find it most difficult to learn a second language. Adult English language learners who have better-developed first language skills together with more years of formal schooling in their first languages will tend to acquire English more quickly than those with weaker skills and less experience in formal schooling.

If lack of native language literacy is a barrier to helping students learn English, why not teach English by first teaching basic native language literacy? First language literacy is a great foundation for acquiring second-language literacy.

There are bonuses, too, for learning to read and write in their spoken tongues. Most immigrants gather into communities where signs, food items, and newspapers are in their local languages. Those who can read and write in their native language can read these signs and papers. Writing letters and emails to families and friends left behind means they are not forgotten. It is important to keep each language and culture alive, to record stories and traditions to pass on to future generations.

Over the years, many children of immigrants have retained their native languages and cultures, giving them the advantage of being bilingual and bicultural. But because many children of immigrants do not pass the native language down to their children, the grandchildren of immigrants do not speak the language of their ancestors (Datesman, Crandall, & Kearny, 2005). Some newer immigrants to America are so anxious to learn English and become Americanized that they forget the importance of keeping native languages and cultures alive, even as they learn English. They have the opportunity to give their children the advantage of being bilingual and bicultural, a worthy effort.

It's impossible to have basic literacy classes or materials available for the many languages adult learners speak but cannot read or write. Look around your community—there just might be a basic literacy class in a student's native language. Encourage your students to attend such classes. Let them know that this will not only be a good foundation for learning English but will also give them the added bonus of being able to read and write in their native tongues.

SPANISH LITERACY AS A FIRST STEP TO ENGLISH

More than 25 million people in the United States (9 percent of the population over age five) have limited English proficiency (LEP). From 1990 to 2010, this number grew by 80 percent. And 66 percent of the LEP population speaks Spanish (Migration Policy Institute, 2011).

Many in the Spanish-speaking LEP group cannot read or write in Spanish. They have found it difficult to fit into and keep up in traditional English classes. If you have any Spanish speakers who cannot read or write in Spanish and want to learn English, you might want to look at *Lectura y Escritura en Español: Para los Estudiantes,* and the teacher's guide in both English and Spanish, *Lectura y Escritura en Español: Guía del Maestro* (Colvin, 2011).*

Basic Spanish literacy is taught in the first five chapters. The Spanish lessons continue in the rest of the book, but there is a gradual transition to teaching English as well. The directions are simply written in both English and Spanish so that even those with limited Spanish themselves can become effective teachers.

Language Experience stories are used throughout the lessons. Students dictate their thoughts in Spanish, and the teacher writes those words in Spanish, teaching the students their own words. Learning to read and write in their spoken tongue gives students both self-confidence and the ability to read and write letters to loved ones in their native language.

Because Spanish is phonetically regular, it is practical to teach decoding skills through syllables and key words. Key words are generated through discussion, with teacher and learners working collaboratively and focusing on a chapter's illustrations and the key words that describe them. The subjects and illustrations are noncontroversial and are focused on Hispanic lives and interests—greetings, family, a family tree, markets, clinics and health, schools and education, visits to a rural farm and to a big city, and a surprise ending.

Each chapter begins with a discussion of the illustration for that chapter. Key words, the sounds of the five vowels in Spanish (*a, e, i, o, u*), and syllables using those vowels follow. Students write and read words out of context and then read words in a story (students read aloud words they've learned as the teacher reads the new words). And finally, students answer comprehension questions.

Beginning lessons in English are introduced after Chapter 5 and are patterned after those suggested in this book. Because the learners have been successful in beginning to read and write in Spanish, they have overcome that first barrier, illiteracy in Spanish, and are usually much more confident starting English. Half of the continuing lessons are in Spanish and half in English in the remainder of the book.

SUMMARY

Students are given a certificate when they complete the book, and how excited they are that they *can* read and write in Spanish after all! Their self-confidence is obvious, and they already have the beginnings of English. They can continue with the rest of the book in English, or the students are free to go on to an English-only class.

*Colvin's similar books for Haitian Creole and Somali Bantu (2007) are also available from ProLiteracy, but the Teacher's Guides are only in English for these two languages.

EPILOGUE: OPENING A NEW WORLD

To have peace in this world, we must be able to communicate with each other. For commerce, for safety, for happy individual and family lives, we must be able to communicate, and English has become an important link language.

It will be exciting to watch your students grow as they develop new skills in English. A whole new world will be opened to you as you learn more about your students' countries and cultures and as you develop confidence in your ability to teach English to speakers of other languages. Both you and your students will be enriched.

We sometimes forget that most of us are immigrants or descendants of immigrants. What better way to pay homage to our own immigrant ancestors than to reach out a helping hand to the newcomers who have come to live in or visit our land? When we open channels of communication with people of different cultures, our own insights are sharpened, and we can truly conceive of the peoples of the world as brothers and sisters.

We don't choose our native language and customs. We inherit them. But we can share them with others, and we can learn about our students' languages and customs, too. Both students and teachers have something to give and something to gain. The teachers give new skills in English and friendship. The students give the gift of insight into another culture. May the exchange prove worth the effort. Everyone smiles in the same language, so let's smile as we work and learn together.

APPENDICES

A. Glossary of Terms Used in the ESOL Field

B. National Reporting System (NRS) Outcome Measures Definitions: Educational Functioning Level (EFL) Descriptors for English as a Second Language (ESL)

C. Performance-Based Curricula and Outcomes: The Mainstream English Language Training Project (MELT) Updated for the 1990s and Beyond

D. Sample Student Intake Form

E. Manuscript and Cursive Alphabets

F. Colored Paper Exercises

G. Conversation Starters for Learning About International Students

H. Guidelines for Selecting ESOL Textbooks

I. Citizenship Information

J. Suggested Key Words for Teaching Phonics

K. Word Patterns

L. Three Hundred Most Frequently Used Words

M. Useful Websites and Free Apps

N. Quick Reference Guide—Suggested Lesson Plans for Five Levels

O. Quick Reference Guide—Techniques, Strategies, and Activities

APPENDIX A: GLOSSARY OF TERMS USED IN THE ESOL FIELD

ABE: Adult basic education

ACE: Adult continuing education

ACTFL: American Council on the Teaching of Foreign Languages

ALM: Audiolingual method. A behaviorist approach to teaching languages that relies heavily on oral repetition and drills

APL: Adult Performance Level

BEST Literacy: Basic English Skills Test (for reading and writing)

BEST Plus: Basic English Skills Test (for listening and speaking)

BICS: Basic Interpersonal Communication Skills (social language)

Bilingual: Proficient to some degree in two languages

CAL: Center for Applied Linguistics

CALP: Cognitive Academic Language Proficiency (academic language)

CASAS: Comprehensive Adult Student Assessment Systems

CBI: Content-based instruction

CBE: Competency-based English

CELT: Comprehensive English Language Test

CLD: Culturally and linguistically diverse

Conversational English: Listening comprehension and speaking skills in English

EFL: Educational Functioning Levels

EL: English learner

ELL: English language learner

ELPS: English Language Proficiency Standards

ESL: English as a second language

ESLOA: *English as a Second Language Oral Assessment* (an assessment of oral skills, written by Joye Coy Shaffer and Teresa McLean)

ESOL: English for speakers of other languages

ESP: English for specific purposes

Functionally illiterate: Unable to read or write well enough in a language to meet daily needs

GED® tests: Subject tests created by the American Council on Education and GED Testing Service (people passing the GED tests earn a credential approximately equivalent to a high school diploma)

Grammar translation: Method of teaching languages by learning grammar rules and translating into and from any native language

Illiterate: Unable to read or write

L1: First or home language

L2: Second or additional language

LEA: Language Experience Approach

LEP: Limited English proficiency

LESLLA: Low Educated Second Language and Literacy Acquisition

Linguistics: Science that systematically analyzes and describes languages as used by native speakers

LVA: Literacy Volunteers of America

Monolingual: Proficient in only one language

MTELP: Michigan Test of English Language Proficiency

Natural approach: Learning of a foreign language intuitively by using it in natural or real situations

NFE: Non-formal education

NLL: Native language learning

NNEST: Non-Native English Speaking Teachers

NRS: National Reporting System

Primary language: Language learned as a child, generally used for communication

READ: Reading Evaluation—Adult Diagnosis

Secondary language: Language learned after a primary language, generally the language used for daily communication.

TABE: Tests of Adult Basic Education

TEAL: Teaching English as an Additional Language (used in Canada)

TEFL: Teaching English as a Foreign Language

TESL: Teaching English as a Second Language (used in Canada)

TESOL: Teachers of English to Speakers of Other Languages (the professional organization of ESOL teachers)

TOEFL: Test of English as a Foreign Language

TPR: Total Physical Response

VESL: Vocational English as a Second Language

Educational Functioning Level (EFL) Descriptors for English as a Second Language (ESL)

Adapted from U.S. Department of Education, Division of Adult Education and Literacy (2011). *Implementation Guidelines: Measures and Methods for the National Reporting System for Adult Education.* Washington, DC: Author (pp. 19–21). Retrieved from http://www.nrsweb.org/docs/ImplementationGuidelines.pdf

Literacy Level	Listening and Speaking	Basic Reading and Writing	Functional and Workplace Skills
Low Beginning ESL *Test benchmark:* *CASAS scale scores* Reading: 181–190 Listening: 181–190 Writing: 136–145 BEST Plus: 401–417 (SPL 2) BEST Literacy: 21–52 (SPL 2) *TABE CLAS E scale scores:** Total Reading and Writing: 395–441 Total Listening and Speaking: 408–449	Individual can understand basic greetings, simple phrases, and commands. Can understand simple questions related to personal information, spoken slowly and with repetition. Understands a limited number of words related to immediate needs and can respond with simple learned phrases to some common questions related to routine survival situations. Speaks slowly and with difficulty. Demonstrates little or no control over grammar.	Individual can read numbers and letters and some common sight words. May be able to sound out simple words. Can read and write some familiar words and phrases, but has a limited understanding of connected prose in English. Can write basic personal information (e.g., name, address, telephone number) and can complete simple forms that elicit this information.	Individual functions with difficulty in social situations and in situations related to immediate needs. Can provide limited personal information on simple forms, and can read very simple common forms of print found in the home and environment, such as product names. Can handle routine entry-level jobs that require very simple written or oral English communication and in which job tasks can be demonstrated. May have limited knowledge and experience with computers.

Literacy Level	Listening and Speaking	Basic Reading and Writing	Functional and Workplace Skills
High Beginning ESL *Test benchmark:* *CASAS scale scores* Reading: 191–200 Listening: 191–200 Writing: 146–200 BEST Plus: 418–438 (SPL 3) BEST Literacy: 36–46 (SPL 3) *TABE CLAS-E scale scores:** Total Reading and Writing: 442–482 Total Listening and Speaking: 450–485	Individual can understand common words, simple phrases, and sentences containing familiar vocabulary, spoken slowly with some repetition. Individual can respond to simple questions about personal everyday activities, and can express immediate needs, using simple learned phrases or short sentences. Shows limited control of grammar.	Individual can read most sight words and many other common words. Can read familiar phrases and simple sentences, but has a limited understanding of connected prose and may need frequent rereading. Individual can write some simple sentences with limited vocabulary. Meaning may be unclear. Writing shows very little control of basic grammar, capitalization, and punctuation and has many spelling errors.	Individual can function in some situations related to immediate needs and in familiar social situations. Can provide basic personal information on simple forms, and recognizes simple common forms of print found in the home, workplace, and community. Can handle routine entry-level jobs requiring basic written or oral English communication and in which job tasks can be demonstrated. May have limited knowledge or experience using computers.

Literacy Level	Listening and Speaking	Basic Reading and Writing	Functional and Workplace Skills
Low Intermediate ESL *Test benchmark:* *CASAS scale scores* Reading: 201–210 Listening: 201–210 Writing: 201–225 BEST Plus: 439–472 (SPL 4) BEST Literacy: 47–53 (SPL 4) *TABE CLAS-E scale scores:** Total Reading and Writing: 483–514 Total Listening and Speaking: 486–525	Individual can understand simple learned phrases and limited new phrases containing familiar vocabulary spoken slowly with frequent repetition; can ask and respond to questions using such phrases; can express basic survival needs and participate in some routine social conversations, although with some difficulty; and has some control of basic grammar.	Individual can read simple material on familiar subjects and comprehend simple and compound sentences in single or linked paragraphs containing a familiar vocabulary; can write simple notes and messages on familiar situations, but lacks clarity and focus. Sentence structure lacks variety, but shows some control of basic grammar (e.g., present and past tense) and consistent use of punctuation (e.g., periods, capitalization).	Individual can interpret simple directions and schedules, signs, and maps; can fill out simple forms, but needs support on some documents that are not simplified; and can handle routine entry-level jobs that involve some written or oral English communication but in which job tasks can be demonstrated. Individual can use simple computer programs and can perform a sequence of routine tasks given directions using technology (e.g., fax machine, computer).

Literacy Level	Listening and Speaking	Basic Reading and Writing	Functional and Workplace Skills
High Intermediate ESL *Test benchmark:* *CASAS scale scores* Reading: 211–220 Listening: 211–220 Writing: 226–242 BEST Plus: 473–506 (SPL 5) BEST Literacy: 54–65 (SPL 5-6) *TABE CLAS-E scale scores:** Total Reading and Writing: 515–556 Total Listening and Speaking: 526–558	Individual can understand learned phrases and short new phrases containing familiar vocabulary spoken slowly and with some repetition; can communicate basic survival needs with some help; can participate in conversation in limited social situations and use new phrases with hesitation; and relies on description and concrete terms. There is inconsistent control of more complex grammar.	Individual can read text on familiar subjects that have a simple and clear underlying structure (e.g., clear main idea, chronological order); can use context to determine meaning; can interpret actions required in specific written directions; can write simple paragraphs with main idea and supporting details on familiar topics (e.g., daily activities, personal issues) by recombining learned vocabulary and structures; and can self- and peer-edit for spelling and punctuation errors.	Individual can meet basic survival and social needs, can follow some simple oral and written instruction, and has some ability to communicate on the telephone on familiar subjects; can write messages and notes related to basic needs; can complete basic medical forms and job applications; and can handle jobs that involve basic oral instructions and written communication in tasks that can be clarified orally. Individual can work with or learn basic computer software, such as word processing, and can follow simple instructions for using technology.

Literacy Level	Listening and Speaking	Basic Reading and Writing	Functional and Workplace Skills
Advanced ESL ***Test benchmark:*** *CASAS scale scores* Reading: 221–235 Listening: 221–235 Writing: 243–260 BEST Plus: 507–540 (SPL 6) BEST Literacy: 66 and above (SPL 7)** *TABE CLAS-E scale scores:** Total Reading and Writing: 557–600 Total Listening and Speaking: 599–600	Individual can understand and communicate in a variety of contexts related to daily life and work. Can understand and participate in conversation on a variety of everyday subjects, including some unfamiliar vocabulary, but may need repetition or rewording. Can clarify own or others' meaning by rewording. Can understand the main points of simple discussions and informational communication in familiar contexts. Shows some ability to go beyond learned patterns and construct new sentences. Shows control of basic grammar, but has difficulty using more complex structures. Has some basic fluency of speech.	Individual can read moderately complex text related to life roles and descriptions and narratives from authentic materials on familiar subjects. Uses context and word analysis skills to understand vocabulary, and uses multiple strategies to understand unfamiliar texts. Can make inferences, predictions, and compare and contrast information in familiar texts. Individual can write multiparagraph text (e.g., organizes and develops ideas with clear introduction, body, and conclusion), using some complex grammar and a variety of sentence structures. Makes some grammar and spelling errors. Uses a range of vocabulary.	Individual can function independently to meet most survival needs and to use English in routine social and work situations. Can communicate on the telephone on familiar subjects. Understands radio and television on familiar topics. Can interpret routine charts, tables, and graphs and can complete forms and handle work demands that require nontechnical oral and written instructions and routine interaction with the public. Individual can use common software, learn new basic applications, and select the correct basic technology in familiar situations.

Note: The descriptors are *entry-level* descriptors and are illustrative of what a typical student functioning at that level should be able to do. They are not a full description of skills for the level.

CASAS: Comprehensive Adult Student Assessment System
BEST: Basic English Skills Test
TABE CLAS-E: Tests of Adult Basic Education Complete Language Assessment System—English

* Refer to the TABE CLAS-E Technical Manual for score ranges for individual reading, writing, listening, and speaking tests. Table shows only total scores.

** Students can be placed in advanced ESL using BEST Literacy, but the test does not assess skills beyond this level so students cannot exit Advanced ESL with this test. Retesting of students who enter this level with another assessment is recommended.

The Mainstream English Language Training Project (MELT) Updated for the 1990s and Beyond

Sponsored by the Office of Refugee Resettlement, U.S. Department of Health and Human Services, 370 L'Enfant Promenade, SW, 6th Floor/East, Washington, DC 20447. Adapted from Grognet, A. G. (1997).

Pre- and Non-Literate (Student Performance Levels 0–1)

Basic Language

- Give personal information orally, and copy onto simple forms (name, address, phone, country of origin, ID/Social Security number, etc.).
- Spell, read, and print own name, indicating which is first, last, and middle.
- Use appropriate greetings/farewells (Hello, Good-bye).
- Introduce oneself.
- Read clock time on the hour, half-hour, and quarter hour.
- Read days of the week.
- Express a lack of understanding.
- Ask for repetition.
- Ask simple yes or no questions.
- Respond to what and where questions.

Community Services

- Read and interpret emergency words (e.g., FIRE, POLICE, POISON).
- Read, say, and dial telephone numbers for emergency services.
- Using the telephone, spell name and address and report an emergency in simple terms.
- Identify basic community facilities and services (post office, school, etc.).
- Ask for stamps at a post office.

Consumer Economics

- Identify basic consumer economic services (bank, market, clothing store, etc.).
- Cash a check or money order, endorse it, and provide proper ID.
- State basic food and clothing needs.
- Identify names of U.S. coins and bills, and read simple money amounts.
- Pay the total amount requested orally or in writing.

Employment

- Identify common entry-level jobs.
- Read common warning or safety signs at work.
- State previous employment and own job skills in simple terms.
- State current job status.
- Print or sign own name on time sheet.
- Ask if a task was done correctly.
- Ask a supervisor or coworker for help.
- Respond to simple questions about work progress and completion of tasks.
- Respond to simple oral warnings or basic safety commands.
- Give simple excuses for lateness or absence.
- Follow one-step instructions.

Health

- Identify medical facilities, workers, and signs.
- State a need for medical help (*I'm sick; my _____ hurts*).
- Identify major body parts, illnesses, or injuries.
- State a need for an interpreter.

Housing

- Identify common household rooms and furniture.
- Identify basic types of available housing.
- Read EXIT signs in housing.

Transportation and Directions

- Ask for the location of a place.
- Follow simple oral directions to a place.
- Orally give streets and landmarks near residence.
- Read a limited number of symbols or transportation/pedestrian signs.

Beginning (Student Performance Levels 2–3)

All of the above plus the following:

Basic Language

- Write personal information (name, address, phone, Social Security number, country of origin, etc.).
- Ask *what, where,* and *when* questions.
- Ask for clarification.

- Use appropriate social language to introduce self and others.
- Recognize days, months, times.
- Write dates.

Community Services

- Read emergency words.
- Address an envelope/package, including return address.
- Call 911 (or local equivalent).

Consumer Economics

- Ask for and read the price of food, clothing, or other items in a store.
- Differentiate size by reading tags, and request size and color for an item in simple terms.
- Ask for information and follow directions for buying food, clothing, and household items.
- Read and ask about store signs, aisle numbers, and store hours.
- Locate and read expiration dates on food items.
- Ask for food using common weights and measures.
- Read abbreviations for weights and measures.
- Order and pay for food at a restaurant.
- Respond to requests for change.
- Buy and fill out a money order.
- Identify total amounts due on monthly bills.

Employment

- Enumerate job skills.
- Fill out simple application forms.
- Respond to simple direct questions about work.
- Report on work progress and completion of tasks.
- Read alphanumeric codes.
- State a need for frequently used material.
- Locate common materials and facilities at the work site.
- Follow two-step instructions.

Health

- Follow simple instructions during a health visit.
- Make a doctor's appointment in person.
- Read the time and date on an appointment card.
- Ask for nonprescription medication at a drugstore.

- Read generic names of common nonprescription medicines.
- Ask about and follow simple instructions for using medicine.
- Read and follow simple directions on medicine labels.
- Read and report body temperature as indicated by a thermometer.
- Ask for a patient's room number in a hospital.
- Identify oneself, appointment time, and doctor's name upon arrival at a doctor's office.

Housing

- Answer simple questions about basic housing needs.
- Ask about rent.
- Read common housing signs (FIRE ESCAPE, FOR RENT, etc.).
- Report basic household problems.
- Request repairs in simple terms.

Transportation and Directions

- Ask for bus, train, or plane destinations.
- Read signs indicating bus or train destinations and street numbers.
- Use a simple map to locate a place.

Intermediate (Student Performance Levels 4–5)

All of the above plus the following:

Basic Language

- Clarify by spelling or writing.
- Repeat instructions for verification.
- Ask about the meaning or pronunciation of a word.
- Ask and respond to *how* and *why* questions.

Community Services

- Report an emergency outside of home.
- Answer questions about a child, and fill out simple school enrollment form.
- Read and respond appropriately to simple written communications from school.
- Respond appropriately to recorded messages and instructions from school.
- Ask about correct postage for mailing.
- Fill out a change-of-address form.
- Locate telephone numbers in a telephone book or yellow pages.

Consumer Economics

- Write a check.
- Fill out a deposit/withdrawal slip.
- Use and report problems in using coin-operated machines.
- Read unit price labels to compare products for value.
- State reasons for returning an item to the store.
- Respond to a cashier's questions concerning means of payment.
- Interpret clothing care labels.

Employment

- Ask and answer questions at a job interview (qualifications, experience, preferences, long-term goals, benefits, etc.).
- Fill out a standard job application.
- Read want ads, and identify skills needed for a job.
- Modify a task based on changes in instructions.
- Respond to a supervisor's comments about quality of work (including mistakes, speed, incomplete work).
- Initiate and respond to social language from coworkers.
- Report specific problems encountered in completing a work task.
- Read warnings, storage directions, and emergency instructions.
- Write a note to explain absence from work.

Health

- Identify common symptoms, illnesses, and health problems.
- Change or cancel a doctor's appointment.
- Make or change a doctor's appointment by telephone.
- Follow oral instructions during a medical exam or about treatment.
- Fill out a simple insurance form (with assistance).

Housing

- Question errors on bills.
- Ask about and follow instructions for using and maintaining household equipment.
- Ask for information about location, rooms, rent, deposit, utilities.

Transportation and Directions

- Identify major streets and landmarks on a map.
- Use a map to find a place.
- Read about and get a driver's license (with help).
- Give and follow simple oral or written directions to a place.

APPENDIX D: SAMPLE STUDENT INTAKE FORM

Each program will require different information about the students it serves. Adapt this sample intake form to the information you need for your program and for reports to your funders.

STUDENT INTAKE FORM

Student's Name _____ Date _____ Reviewer _____

Address _____ Telephone _____ Email _____

STATUS: ☐ U.S. citizen ☐ Permanent resident ☐ Refugee

NATIVE LANGUAGE: ☐ English ☐ Other _____
☐ Speak ☐ Read ☐ Write

ETHNICITY: ☐ American Indian ☐ Asian ☐ African American ☐ Caucasian
☐ Hispanic/Latino ☐ Other _____

GENDER: ☐ Male ☐ Female

MARITAL STATUS: ☐ Married ☐ Single ☐ Divorced ☐ Widowed _____ Number of children

EDUCATION: ☐ 0–4 years ☐ 5–8 years ☐ 9–12 years ☐ GED/high school graduate
☐ 2 years college ☐ 4 years college ☐ Advanced degree(s)
☐ In English ☐ In other language _____

EMPLOYMENT STATUS: ☐ Employed full-time ($_____/hour) ☐ Homemaker
☐ Employed part-time ($_____/hour) ☐ Retired
☐ Unemployed, looking for work ☐ Disabled
☐ Unemployed, not looking for work ☐ On public assistance

Do you need help with understanding/speaking English at work? ☐ Yes ☐ No
Do you need help with reading/writing English at work? ☐ Yes ☐ No

HEALTH: Hearing _____ Vision _____
Other (that might affect student's attendance/learning) _____

ASSESSMENT SCORES:

Date	Testing tool	Score

STUDENT'S GOALS: _____

STUDENT'S TIMES AVAILABLE: _____

SUGGESTED LOCATIONS FOR LESSONS: _____

WRITING SAMPLE: If student can, ask him or her to write name, address, telephone, and a simple sentence (e.g., something he/she did this week).

STUDENT WAIVER

I give permission to _____ to share this information with my tutor/teacher and to use the information for data gathering, research, and evaluation purposes. I have been assured that the information will not be made public.

Student signature _____ Date _____

D'NEALIAN™ MANUSCRIPT ALPHABET

a b c d e f g h i j k l m

n o p q r s t u v w x y z

A B C D E F G H I J K L M

N O P Q R S T U V W X Y Z

D'NEALIAN™ CURSIVE ALPHABET

a b c d e f g h i j k l m

n o p q r s t u v w x y z

A B C D E F G H I

J K L M N O P Q

R S T U V W X Y Z

D'NEALIAN™ NUMBERS

0 1 2 3 4 5 6 7 8 9

From *D'Nealian Handwriting* by Donald N. Thurber. Copyright © 1981 by Scott, Foreman and Company. Reprinted by permission.

APPENDIX F: COLORED PAPER EXERCISES

Adapted from C. Gattegno, 1972.

Using colored strips of paper as props, you can set up an excellent and entertaining exercise, especially for students who understand or speak very limited or no English. You will be teaching simple sentences, and you can add new vocabulary as quickly or as slowly as students respond.

Have on hand the following materials:

> Slips of colored paper—blue, red, black, yellow, etc.,
> sizes l" × 6", l" × 5", l" × 3" for each color

The vocabulary used will be controlled and limited to the following words during this part of the lesson:

Lesson 1   *a, paper, blue, red, pick, up, put, on, the, table*

Lesson 2   *give, me, point, to, black, yellow, take*

Lesson 3   *touch, it, him, her, one, two, three*

Lesson 4   *white, green, down*

Lesson 5   *on, under, between, more colors*

Lesson 6   *big, bigger, biggest, small, smaller, smallest*

Lesson 7   *next, here, there*

Lesson 8   *right, left, hand, quickly, slowly*

Lesson 9   other useful words

For the first lesson, use three blue and three red pieces of paper of varied sizes. The new vocabulary will include only basic words that go along with your actions. Your students do not see these words written but hear you say them when you demonstrate with the pieces of paper. At first, your students may try to repeat what you say. Discourage this by gesturing that the students should listen only.

Pick up any slip of paper, either color, any size, and say, *A paper,* at a normal speed. Repeat this with each piece of paper. Repetition gives students confidence that they understood you. Then pick up a blue piece of paper, any size, and say, *A blue paper,* repeating for each blue piece of paper. Repeat this action with the red papers. Next, pick up a blue paper and say, *Pick up a blue paper.* Repeat this with all the blue and red papers. Next, put each paper on the table as you say, *Put a blue (red) paper on the table.*

When you feel your students have understood your demonstration, push the six pieces of paper to one student and tell the student, *Pick up a red paper.* If your student hesitates and doesn't understand, you can help by motioning him to pick up the red paper. After the student has picked up all the papers, say, *Put a red (blue) paper on the table.* Give help as needed. This exercise should be repeated for each student.

Next, gesture for your students to *repeat,* and go through the entire exercise again, starting with a *paper,* demonstrating while you speak and your students repeat.

Finally, suggest that the students give the commands, asking you or other students to demonstrate with appropriate papers. This demonstrates that they understand and can give the commands.

Now it is time for you to write all the words in the same order as you gave them, reading them together and suggesting that the students write the words.

Then they can practice at home all four skills: listening, speaking, reading, and writing.

> *A paper.*
>
> *A red (blue) paper.*
>
> *Pick up a red (blue) paper.*
>
> *Put a red (blue) paper on the table.*

If beginning students have never written before or use non-Roman characters in their native languages, reading and writing even the words they have understood and said may be difficult. Having the words they've just learned written on cards may be helpful. If they read and write in their own language, they may want to write the words phonetically in their own language to help them remember the correct pronunciation.

When starting a new lesson, always review the skills learned in the previous lesson. Then go on to new vocabulary.

> *Give me a blue (red, black, yellow) paper.*
>
> *Point to a blue (red, black, yellow) paper.*
>
> *Touch a blue (red, black, yellow) paper.*

Continue manipulating these patterns until you are sure your students understand all the words. Your students may be concentrating so hard on following directions that they confuse the colors. Be patient. Go only as fast as is comfortable for the students. Reassure the students with verbal praise and a warm smile. During this exercise, they've learned colors, some commands and directions, and some reading and writing. This is an excellent icebreaker for students who can speak no English at all. Confidence can be built up quickly because the exercise requires active response rather than passive listening.

But what about more advanced students? You can use colored paper exercises with students at any level by including more complex commands for them to follow. The following commands can be quite complicated:

> *Pick up three green papers, and put down two red papers.*
>
> *Put two blue papers in the box, give me four red papers, and keep one red paper yourself.*

Hold all the red papers in your left hand, but pick up the yellow papers with your right hand. Put a red paper between a blue and yellow paper, and put a black paper under them all.

You can teach the concepts of size (longer, shorter, larger, smaller), position (on, under, next to, etc.), or distance (e.g., two steps, across the room) through listening tasks. Later, encourage students to speak the sentences they've heard and understood, followed by reading and writing. Much practice will be needed. You might want to use colored pencils or crayons instead of papers, or pieces of colored yarn or string, or even colored toothpicks. Whatever medium you use, know that you can teach concepts in English with any readily available material, using controlled vocabulary at first and expanding it as needed. Although exercises like these are useful for reinforcing certain skills, most of the lesson time should focus on real communication needs.

APPENDIX G: CONVERSATION STARTERS FOR LEARNING ABOUT INTERNATIONAL STUDENTS

Food

1. How many meals a day do people usually eat in your country?
2. What would you eat and drink at each of these meals?
3. Where do you get most of your food?
4. What would you say is the favorite vegetable? Meat? Fish? Dessert?
5. What food would you serve a favorite guest?
6. Is your country famous for a special crop?
7. Please explain how to make one of your favorite meals.

Shelter

1. Please describe what a typical home looks like in your country.
2. How many rooms does the average apartment or home have?
3. What furniture is inside a typical house in your country?
4. Are any homes air-conditioned or heated?
5. Are the walls painted, or is wallpaper used?

Clothing

1. What do young children wear to school in your country?
2. What kinds of clothes do men and women wear to work?
3. What kinds of clothes do men and women wear to a party?
4. Is there special clothing to sleep in?
5. Do fashions change frequently?

Transportation

1. Do many people walk to work or school, or do they use bicycles or other forms of transportation?
2. Do many people own automobiles?
3. How much money does a taxicab driver charge in your country? What are the tipping customs?

Cultural Values

1. Is certain behavior allowed at home but not in public?
2. How are people punished for disobeying the law?
3. What's considered the most serious crime a person can commit?
4. Do high school students have religious education at school?
5. What is the attitude in your country toward the death penalty?

Schools

1. Do you have a special preparatory school for university in your country?
2. How many classes a week do high school students have?
3. Is it difficult for high school graduates to find a job?
4. What status do college students have in the society?
5. Are there any differences in the quality of education between a public and a private school?

Attitudes Toward Animals

1. Do families keep dogs or cats as pets in their homes?
2. Would you see an aquarium in some homes?
3. What is done for sick animals?
4. What wild animals are in your country?
5. What animals are useful?

Social Structure

1. What is the size of an average family?
2. Do grandparents live in the same house?
3. What are the responsibilities of each member of the family?
4. Do married women work outside the home?
5. Who takes care of the children?
6. Is it customary for the family to gather around the dinner table and talk?
7. Do the children often fight among themselves?
8. How do people feel about divorce?
9. What is the acceptable way of meeting someone to marry?
10. When does a child leave home to be on his or her own?

Children

1. How do parents decide on a name for their baby?
2. Do children have a certain share in work at home?
3. Do children start school at an early age?
4. Do boys and girls have the same education? Do they go to the same schools?
5. Where do children play?
6. Do children have a favorite game they like to play?
7. How are children expected to behave with adults?
8. Are parents strict in disciplining their children?
9. Who punishes children—the mother or father or both?
10. Please tell me a favorite story children know.
11. What songs did you learn at an early age?

Social Groups

1. Do people of different social groups live in different neighborhoods?
2. How is prejudice against minority groups shown in your country?
3. How strong are class distinctions?
4. Do people speak different languages in different parts of your country?
5. Do women often visit local beauty salons?
6. Do children wear uniforms in your schools?
7. What is the most common religion in your country?
8. Do people discuss religion a lot?

Leisure-Time Activities

1. Do you like American films? Which ones?
2. What types of movies do you like?
3. Who are your favorite actors or actresses?
4. What movies have you seen in your country?
5. What kind of music do you listen to?
6. Do you like American music?
7. Do you have a radio? A TV? Do you play music recordings?
8. Do most cities have libraries? Are they free?
9. What kinds of books do you read?
10. Do special community centers provide sports activities?
11. Are volunteer activities available? What are some common forms of charity?
12. What do university students do in their leisure time?
13. Do families share activities outside the home? What are these activities?
14. Are there many museums open to the public?

Language Formulas and Gestures

1. How would you introduce me to your family?
2. Would I be expected to shake hands?
3. What would be the polite way for me to leave after a social evening at your home?
4. Would I be expected to bring a gift?
5. What do people say and do after they are introduced?
6. What do you say to another person when you see him or her in the morning? Evening?

Holidays and Celebrations

1. Is one day a week set aside as a day of rest in your country?
2. What special holidays do you celebrate in your country?
3. How do you celebrate them?
4. Describe a marriage ceremony in your country. Describe a funeral.

Community Units

1. Do most of the people in your country live in cities, small towns, or farms? Describe them.
2. Are there many factories in the cities?
3. What products are produced?

This list came originally from Dr. V. F. Allen, Temple University, Philadelphia, PA. You can adapt it to fit your students.

APPENDIX H: GUIDELINES FOR SELECTING ESOL TEXTBOOKS

Ask yourself these questions as you look for an appropriate text for your ESOL students.

Method

1. Is the approach consistent with your teaching method?
2. Is the approach student-centered?
3. Is the approach varied?

Subject Matter

4. Is the subject matter of current interest?
5. Is cultural and other information up-to-date and accurate?
6. Is the subject matter varied and appropriate to the interests of adult students?

Use

7. Is the text easy to use?
8. Is the text flexible enough to be used in a variety of ways?
9. Is there a teacher's manual or preface that explains how the text can best be used?

Format

10. Does the text provide plenty of review of newly introduced material in subsequent lessons?
11. Are exercises and activities usable with one student or a small group rather than requiring a larger group of students to be effective?
12. Do the exercises require the students to engage in a variety of activities?
13. Are there exercises that allow the students to engage in meaningful communication?

Appearance

14. Are the illustrations lifeless or realistic?
15. Is the print adequate or too small?
16. Is the layout cluttered or easy to look at?

Cultural Stability

17. Does the text avoid giving the impression that all Americans are white Anglo-Saxon?

18. Does the text avoid racist and sexist stereotypes, and is ethnic stereotyping avoided?

Illustrations

19. Are there clear illustrations that aim to help students understand new vocabulary and structure?

20. Do the illustrations show individuals of both sexes and different racial and ethnic groups?

Bibliography

Daoud, A. M., & Celce-Murcia, M. (1979). Selecting and evaluating a textbook, in M. Celce-Murcia and Lois McIntosh (Eds.), *Teaching English as a second or foreign language*. Rowley, MA: Newbury House. pp. 302–307.

Donoghue, M. R., & Kunkle, J. F. (1979). *Second languages in primary education*. Rowley, MA: Newbury House. pp, 119–120.

Most ESL tutors and teachers will have students whose ultimate aim is attaining U.S. or Canadian citizenship. Most cities have citizenship classes either in the public schools or run by community groups, and you should encourage such students to enter those classes. Your role as an English teacher is important because many students don't have the self-confidence to pursue this goal alone.

The U.S. citizenship test is pegged to the "high beginning" NRS Educational Functioning Level for ESL (see Appendix B, page 197). A substantial part of your teaching session should be spent on the material to be covered in the Naturalization Examination. *Citizenship: Passing the Test* from New Readers Press is an excellent resource to help you with this work (Weintraub, 2009, 2012). It is written for beginning-level ESL students.

You will find detailed U.S. citizenship information on the U.S. Citizenship and Immigration Services (USCIS) website, **http://www.uscis.gov/citizenship**.

U.S. Citizenship Eligibility Requirements

To be eligible for U.S. citizenship, an applicant must:

- be at least 18 years old at the time of filing Form N-400, Application for Naturalization
- be a permanent resident (have a "green card") for at least 5 years
- have lived within the state or USCIS district with jurisdiction over your place of residence for at least 3 months prior to the date of filing Form N-400
- have continuous residence in the United States as a lawful permanent resident for at least 5 years immediately preceding the date of filing Form N-400
- be physically present in the United States for at least 30 months out of the 5 years immediately preceding the date of filing Form N-400
- be able to read, write, and speak basic English
- have a basic understanding of U.S. history and government (civics)
- be a person of good moral character
- demonstrate an attachment to the principles and ideals of the U.S. Constitution

About the U.S. Citizenship Test

The U.S. naturalization interview, commonly called the citizenship test, has four components: speaking, reading, writing, and civics (U.S. history and government). Applicants demonstrate English-speaking ability by answering oral questions about their N-400 applications in the normal course of an interview. To demonstrate knowledge of civics, applicants are asked 10 questions from a study list of 100 questions and must (orally) answer at least 6 of them correctly.

The reading and writing components, referred to in combination as the literacy test, are also administered in the course of the naturalization interview. In the reading component, applicants are given a printed question and asked to read it aloud. Note that they do not need to provide an answer to the question. Applicants are offered three chances at this task, so inability to read the first or second question offered does not automatically result in a failure. To test writing ability, the examiner dictates a sentence for the applicant to write. This sentence will turn out to be the answer to the question that the applicant has just read aloud in the reading test. Again, applicants are offered three chances at this dictation, so inability to write the first and second sentences will not necessarily result in a failure.

After the citizenship test has been administered, the applicant is given a checklist showing the test results. An applicant who fails any component of the test will be scheduled for another interview appointment to retake the test a few months later. Applicants are retested only on components that they failed the first time. For example, if at the initial interview the applicant passed the civics, speaking, and reading tests but failed the writing test, only the writing test will be administered at the "second chance" interview. If a student returns from an interview and has failed but doesn't know the reason for the failure, ask to see the results checklist. Then you can help the student review skills related to the particular test component(s) indicated.

Keep in mind, however, that passing the speaking interview and the civics and literacy tests will not automatically qualify an applicant for citizenship. Applicants must also demonstrate that they meet all of the other requirements for citizenship, such as continuous residence in the United States and good moral character. For more information on citizenship requirements, see the USCIS publication "A Guide to Naturalization" (Form M-476), available as a free download from **http://www.uscis.gov**.

Adapted from *Citizenship: Passing the Test Teacher's Guide* (2009) by Lynne Weintraub, p. 1. Available from New Readers Press.

APPENDIX J: SUGGESTED KEY WORDS—PHONICS

For use when teaching initial consonant sounds

As you use phonics, keep these three items in mind:

- Teach only the letter-sound relationships each individual student needs—those identified in the student's assessment.

- Suggest as possible key words those the students can best relate to. Ask the students to pick the key word.

- Remember that English is not a phonetically regular language. Some consonants have more than one sound or may behave irregularly. For example, the letter *c* has the /k/ sound (e.g. *corn, camera*) but it also has the /s/ sound (e.g. *ceiling, city*). Also, the letter *k* has no sound (e.g. *knife, know,* etc.).

B	bus, baby, ball, bed, banana, bag, bird
C	cat, cup, can, cake, comb, coffee **/** cigar, city, cent, celery
D	dog, dish, doll, desk, doughnut
F	fish, fan, fire, feet, feather
G	gas, girl, game, gate, garage **/** gem, gentleman, giraffe
H	hand, hat, house, ham, horn, hi-fi
J	jar, jacket, jet, jug, jeep
K	key, kite, king, kerchief
L	leg, lamp, lock, leaf, ladder, leather
M	man, motor, money, milk, mother
N	name, nose, nail, needle
P	pot, pan, pig, pants, pipe, pumpkin, pen
Q(QU)	quarter, queen, quilt, quick
R	rat, radio, rocket, rope, river, red
S	sun, sink, socks, sandwich
T	telephone, towel, table, tub, turkey, tea
V	valentine, valley, violin, vacuum, van
W	window, wing, wig, watch, wagon, water
X*	wax, fix, box, tux
Y	yellow, yarn, yo-yo, yardstick
Z	zipper, zebra, zoo

I SPEAK ENGLISH, 5TH EDITION

DIGRAPHS

CH	church, chair, children **/** cholesterol, chemical, choir
CH	chute, chauffeur
PH	phone, photo, pharmacy
SH	shoe, ship, shower, shovel
TH	this, the, them, these **/** thumb, thank, theater
WH	wheel, whale, white

*There are no words in English that begin with x as it makes the /ks/ sound.

SHORT A SOUNDS

-ab	-ack	-ad	-ag	-am	-amp	-an	-and	-ang	-ank
cab	back	ad	bag	am	camp	an	and	bang	bank
dab	hack	bad	gag	ham	damp	ban	band	fang	rank
gab	jack	cad	hag	jam	lamp	can	hand	gang	sank
jab	pack	dad	lag	clam	champ	fan	land	hang	tank
lab	rack	fad	nag	slam	clamp	man	sand	rang	yank
nab	sack	had	rag	swam	cramp	pan	gland	sang	blank
tab	tack	lad	sag		stamp	ran	grand	tang	clank
blab	black	mad	tag		tramp	tan	stand	clang	plank
flab	slack	pad	wag			van		slang	crank
slab	crack	sad	brag			clan			drank
crab	track	clad	drag			plan			frank
drab	shack	glad	flag			scan			spank
grab	whack	shad	shag			span			thank
scab	smack		snag			than			
stab	snack		stag						
	stack								

-ap	-ash	-asp	-ass	-ast	-at	-atch	-ath	-ax
cap	ash	asp	ass	cast	at	catch	bath	ax
gap	bash	gasp	bass	fast	bat	hatch	path	wax
lap	cash	hasp	lass	last	cat	latch	wrath	flax
map	dash	rasp	mass	mast	fat	match		
nap	gash	clasp	pass	past	hat	patch		
rap	hash		brass	vast	mat	thatch		
sap	lash		grass	blast	pat			
tap	mash		class		rat			
chap	rash		glass		sat			
clap	sash				vat			
flap	clash				brat			
slap	crash				chat			
snap	smash				flat			
trap	stash				slat			
	trash				scat			
					that			

SHORT E SOUNDS

-eck	-ed	-eg	-elf	-ell	-elp	-elt	-em	-en	-end
deck	bed	beg	elf	bell	help	belt	hem	den	end
heck	fed	egg	self	dell	yelp	felt	them	hen	bend
neck	led	keg	shelf	fell		melt	stem	men	lend
peck	red	leg		hell				pen	mend
check	wed	peg		sell				ten	send
speck	bled			tell				glen	blend
	fled			well				then	spend
	sled			yell				when	trend
	shed			quell					
	sped			shell					
				smell					
				spell					
				swell					

-ent	-ept	-ess	-est	-et
bent	kept	less	best	bet
dent	wept	mess	nest	get
lent		bless	pest	jet
rent		chess	rest	let
sent		dress	test	met
tent			vest	net
went			west	pet
spent			chest	set
			crest	wet
			quest	yet
				fret

SHORT I SOUNDS

-ib	-ick	-id	-ift	-ig	-ilk	-ill	-im	-in	-inch	-ing
bib	kick	bid	gift	big	bilk	bill	dim	in	inch	bing
fib	lick	did	lift	dig	milk	fill	him	bin	cinch	ring
rib	nick	hid	rift	fig	silk	gill	rim	din	pinch	sing
crib	pick	kid	sift	jig		hill	skim	fin	clinch	wing
	sick	lid	drift	pig		kill	slim	kin		bring
	tick	rid	shift	rig		mill	swim	pin		fling
	wick	grid	swift	wig		pill	trim	sin		sling
	brick	skid		brig		rill	whim	tin		sting
	trick	slid		swig		sill		win		swing
	chick					till		chin		thing
	thick					will		shin		
	click					chill		thin		
	flick					drill		grin		
	slick					grill		skin		
	quick					quill		spin		
	stick					skill		twin		
						spill				
						still				

-ink	-int	-ip	-ish	-iss	-ist	-it	-itch	-ive	-ix
ink	hint	dip	dish	hiss	fist	it	itch	give	fix
pink	mint	hip	fish	kiss	list	bit	ditch	live	mix
sink	tint	lip	wish	miss	mist	fit	pitch		six
wink	flint	nip	swish	bliss	twist	hit	witch		
blink		rip				kit	stitch		
slink		sip				lit	switch		
stink		tip				pit			
think		yip				sit			
		zip				wit			
		chip				grit			
		ship				mitt			
		whip				quit			
		flip				skit			
		slip				slit			
		grip				spit			
		trip				twit			
		quip							
		skip							
		snip							

SHORT O SOUNDS

-ob	-ock	-od	-og	-oll	-on	-ond	-ong	-ot	-ox
cob	cock	cod	bog	doll	on	bond	bong	cot	ox
fob	dock	god	cog	loll	don	fond	gong	dot	box
gob	hock	hod	dog	moll	non	pond	long	got	fox
job	lock	nod	fog		yon		song	hot	
mob	mock	pod	hog				tong	not	
rob	pock	rod	jog				wrong	pot	
sob	rock	sod	log				strong	rot	
blob	sock	clod	clog					blot	
slob	tock	plod	frog					clot	
snob	clock	shod	smog					plot	
	flock							slot	
	crock							shot	
	frock							spot	
	shock							trot	
	smock								
	stock								

SHORT U SOUNDS

-ub	-uck	-ud	-uff	-ug	-ull	-um	-ump	-un	-unch
cub	buck	bud	buff	bug	cull	bum	bump	bun	bunch
dub	duck	cud	cuff	dug	dull	gum	dump	fun	lunch
hub	luck	mud	huff	hug	gull	hum	hump	gun	punch
nub	muck	stud	muff	jug	hull	mum	jump	nun	brunch
pub	puck	thud	puff	lug	lull	rum	lump	pun	crunch
rub	suck		bluff	mug	mull	sum	pump	run	
sub	tuck		gruff	pug	null	glum	clump	sun	
tub	chuck		stuff	rug	skull	slum	plump	shun	
club	shuck			tug		drum	slump	spun	
grub	cluck			chug		scum	stump	stun	
stub	pluck			thug		chum	thump		
	stuck			plug					
				slug					
				smug					

-ung	-unk	-up	-us	-ush	-usk	-ust	-ut	-uzz
dung	bunk	up	us	gush	dusk	bust	but	buzz
hung	dunk	cup	bus	hush	husk	dust	cut	fuzz
lung	hunk	pup	plus	lush	tusk	just	gut	
rung	junk	sup	thus	mush		lust	hut	
sung	sunk			rush		must	jut	
clung	chunk			blush		rust	nut	
flung	drunk			flush		crust	rut	
stung	flunk			plush			shut	
swung	skunk			slush			brush	
							crush	
							shush	

LONG A SOUNDS

-ace	-ade	-age	-aid	-ail	-aim	-ain	-aint	-ait	-ale
ace	fade	age	aid	ail	aim	gain	faint	bait	ale
face	jade	cage	laid	bail	maim	main	paint	gait	dale
lace	made	page	maid	fail		pain	saint	wait	gale
mace	wade	rage	paid	hail		rain	quaint	trait	hale
pace	blade	sage	raid	jail		vain			kale
race	glade	wage	braid	mail		brain			male
brace	grade	stage		nail		drain			pale
place	shade			pail		grain			sale
space	spade			rail		train			tale
	trade			sail		chain			vale
				tail		plain			scale
				wail		slain			shale
				frail		stain			stale
				quail					whale
				snail					
				trail					

-ame	-ane	-ape	-ase	-aste	-ate	-ave	-ay	-aze	-eigh
came	cane	ape	base	baste	ate	cave	bay	daze	eight
dame	lane	cape	case	haste	date	gave	day	faze	sleigh
fame	mane	gape		paste	fate	nave	gay	gaze	weigh
game	pane	nape		taste	gate	pave	hay	haze	
lame	sane	rape		waste	hate	rave	jay	maze	
name	vane	tape		chaste	late	save	lay	raze	
same	wane	drape			mate	wave	may	blaze	
tame	crane	grape			rate	brave	nay	glaze	
blame		shape			sate	crave	pay	graze	
flame					crate	grave	ray		
frame					grate	shave	say		
shame					plate	slave	way		
					skate		clay		
					slate		play		
					state		fray		
							gray		
							tray		
							stay		
							sway		

LONG E SOUNDS

-e	-ea	-each	-ead	-eak	-eal	-eam	-ean	-eap	-east	-eat	-eech
be	pea	each	bead	beak	deal	beam	bean	heap	east	eat	beech
he	sea	beach	lead	leak	heal	ream	dean	leap	beast	beat	leech
me	tea	peach	read	peak	meal	seam	lean	reap	feast	feat	
we	flea	reach	plead	weak	peal	team	mean	cheap	least	heat	
she	plea	teach		bleak	real	cream	wean			meat	
		bleach		freak	seal	dream	clean			neat	
				speak	veal	gleam	glean			peat	
					zeal					seat	
					steal					cheat	
										cleat	
										pleat	
										treat	
										wheat	

-eed	-ee	-eef	-eek	-eel	-eem	-een	-eep	-eet	-ief	-y
deed	bee	beef	leek	eel	deem	keen	beep	beet	brief	carry
feed	fee	reef	meek	feel	seem	seen	deep	feet	chief	marry
heed	see		peek	heel	teem	teen	jeep	meet	grief	bunny
need	tee		reek	keel		green	keep	fleet	thief	funny
seed	wee		seek	peel		queen	peep	greet		sunny
weed	free		week	reel		sheen	seep	sheet		
bleed	tree		cheek				weep	sleet		
breed	glee		creek				creep	sweet		
creed	thee		sleek				sheep	tweet		
freed	three						sleep			
greed							steep			
speed							sweep			
steed										
tweed										

LONG I SOUNDS

-ice	-ide	-ie	-ife	-igh	-ight	-ike	-ild	-ile	-ime
lice	bide	die	life	high	fight	bike	mild	file	dime
mice	hide	lie	rife	nigh	light	dike	wild	mile	lime
nice	ride	pie	wife	sigh	might	hike	child	pile	time
rice	side	tie		thigh	night	like		rile	chime
vice	tide	vie			right	mike		tile	crime
slice	wide				sight	pike		vile	grime
spice	bride				tight	spike		smile	slime
twice	glide				bright			while	
	slide				fright				
					flight				
					plight				
					slight				

-ind	-ine	-ipe	-ire	-ise	-ite	-ive	-y	-ye
bind	dine	pipe	ire	rise	bite	dive	by	dye
find	fine	ripe	dire	wise	kite	five	my	eye
hind	line	wipe	fire		mite	hive	cry	lye
kind	mine	gripe	hire		site	live	dry	rye
mind	nine	swipe	mire		quite	chive	fly	
rind	pine		sire		spite	drive	ply	
wind	tine		tire		white		fry	
blind	vine		wire				shy	
grind	wine						sky	
	shine						sly	
	spine						spy	
	swine						sty	
	thine						thy	
	twine						try	
	whine							

LONG O SOUND

-o	-oach	-oad	-oal	-oam	-oan	-oast	-oat	-obe	-ode	-oe	-oke
go	coach	goad	coal	foam	loan	boast	oat	lobe	ode	doe	coke
no	poach	load	goal	loam	moan	coast	boat	robe	bode	foe	joke
so	roach	road		roam	roan	roast	coat	globe	code	hoe	poke
		toad			groan	toast	goat		mode	toe	woke
							moat		rode	woe	yoke
							bloat				bloke
							float				choke
							gloat				smoke
											spoke

-old	-ole	-olt	-ome	-one	-ope	-ose	-ost	-ote	-ove	-ow
old	dole	bolt	dome	bone	cope	hose	host	note	cove	bow
bold	hole	colt	home	cone	dope	nose	most	rote	dove	low
cold	mole	dolt	Nome	lone	hope	pose	post	tote	rove	mow
gold	pole	jolt		pone	mope	rose		vote	wove	row
hold	role	volt		tone	rope	chose		quote		sow
mold	stole			zone	scope	those				tow
sold				shone	slope	close				blow
told				stone						flow
										glow
										slow
										crow
										grow
										show
										snow

LONG U SOUND

-ew	-ule	-use	-ute
few	mule	use	cute
hew	yule	fuse	mute
blew		muse	flute
flew			
slew			
chew			
crew			
drew			
grew			
stew			

OTHER SOUNDS IN WORD PATTERNS

-all	-alk	-ar	-arch	-arge	-ark	-arm	-arn	-arp	-arsh
all	talk	bar	march	barge	bark	farm	barn	carp	harsh
ball	walk	car	parch	large	dark	harm	darn	harp	marsh
call	chalk	far	starch	charge	hark	charm	yarn	sharp	
fall	stalk	jar			lark				
gall		par			mark				
hall		tar			park				
mall		scar			shark				
tall		star			spark				
wall					stark				
small									
stall									

-aught	-aul	-aunch	-aunt	-ause	-aw	-awl
caught	haul	haunch	gaunt	cause	caw	awl
naught	maul	launch	haunt	pause	jaw	bawl
taught		paunch	jaunt	clause	law	brawl
		staunch	taunt		maw	crawl
			vaunt		raw	shawl
					saw	
					chaw	
					claw	
					flaw	
					draw	

-en	-er	-ern
brighten	either	fern
dampen	fatter	stern
darken	matter	
freshen	poorer	
hasten	richer	
lengthen	scatter	
shorten		
silken		

-ew	-ird	-irl	-irt	-oard	-oice	-oil	-oin	-oint	-oise
dew	bird	girl	dirt	board	voice	oil	coin	joint	noise
Jew	gird	swirl	shirt	hoard	choice	boil	loin	point	poise
new	third	twirl	skirt			coil			
brew		whirl	squirt			foil			
crew						soil			
drew						toil			
grew						broil			
chew						spoil			
flew									
slew									
stew									

-oist	-oo	-ood	-ook	-ool	-oom	-oon	-oop	-oost	-oot
foist	boo	food	book	cool	boom	boon	coop	boost	boot
hoist	coo	mood	cook	fool	doom	coon	hoop	roost	hoot
joist	moo	brood	hook	pool	loom	goon	loop		loot
moist	too		look	drool	room	loon	droop		root
	zoo		nook	spool	zoom	moon	troop		toot
	shoo		took	stool	gloom	noon	scoop		scoot
			brook		groom	soon	stoop		shoot
			crook			spoon	swoop		
			shook			swoon			

-ooth	-or	-ord	-ore	-ork	-orm	-orn	-ort	-orth	-ouch
booth	or	cord	ore	cork	form	born	fort	forth	ouch
tooth	for	ford	wore	fork	norm	corn	sort	north	couch
	nor	lord	chore	pork	storm	horn	tort		pouch
			score	York		morn			vouch
			swore	stork		torn			
						worn			

-ought	-ould	-ound	-our	-ouse	-out	-outh	-ow	-owl
ought	could	bound	four	house	out	mouth	bow	owl
bought	would	found	pour	louse	bout	south	cow	cowl
fought	should	hound		mouse	gout		how	fowl
sought		mound			pout		now	howl
brought		pound			shout		vow	jowl
thought		round			spout		wow	yowl
		sound			stout		plow	
		wound			trout			
		ground						

-own	-sion	-tion	-ude	-ue	-uke	-ull	-une
down	collision	action	dude	rue	duke	bull	dune
gown	decision	attention	nude	sue	Luke	full	June
town	division	fraction	rude	blue		pull	tune
brown	occasion	mention	crude	clue			
crown	television	motion		glue			
clown		nation		true			
frown							

-ush	-ute
bush	lute
push	flute

APPENDIX L: THREE HUNDRED MOST FREQUENTLY USED WORDS

1. the	38. your	75. see	112. me
2. of	39. can	76. number	113. back
3. and	40. said	77. no	114. give
4. a	41. there	78. way	115. most
5. to	42. use	79. could	116. very
6. in	43. an	80. people	117. after
7. is	44. each	81. my	118. thing
8. you	45. which	82. than	119. our
9. that	46. she	83. first	120. just
10. it	47. do	84. water	121. name
11. he	48. how	85. been	122. good
12. was	49. their	86. call	123. sentence
13. for	50. if	87. who	124. man
14. on	51. will	88. oil	125. think
15. are	52. up	89. its	126. say
16. as	53. other	90. now	127. great
17. with	54. about	91. find	128. where
18. his	55. out	92. long	129. help
19. they	56. many	93. down	130. through
20. I	57. then	94. day	131. much
21. at	58. them	95. did	132. before
22. be	59. these	96. get	133. line
23. this	60. so	97. come	134. right
24. have	61. some	98. made	135. too
25. from	62. her	99. may	136. mean
26. or	63. would	100. part	137. old
27. one	64. make	101. over	138. any
28. had	65. like	102. new	139. same
29. by	66. him	103. sound	140. tell
30. word	67. into	104. take	141. boy
31. but	68. time	105. only	142. follow
32. not	69. has	106. little	143. came
33. what	70. look	107. work	144. want
34. all	71. two	108. know	145. show
35. were	72. more	109. place	146. also
36. we	73. write	110. year	147. around
37. when	74. go	111. live	148. form

I SPEAK ENGLISH, 5TH EDITION

149. three	187. animal	225. story	263. grow
150. small	188. house	226. saw	264. took
151. set	189. point	227. left	265. river
152. put	190. page	228. don't	266. four
153. end	191. letter	229. few	267. carry
154. does	192. mother	230. while	268. state
155. another	193. answer	231. along	269. once
156. well	194. found	232. might	270. book
157. large	195. study	233. close	271. hear
158. must	196. still	234. something	272. stop
159. big	197. learn	235. seem	273. without
160. even	198. should	236. next	274. second
161. such	199. America	237. hard	275. later
162. because	200. world	238. open	276. miss
163. turn	201. high	239. example	277. idea
164. here	202. every	240. begin	278. enough
165. why	203. near	241. life	279. eat
166. ask	204. add	242. always	280. face
167. went	205. food	243. those	281. watch
168. men	206. between	244. both	282. far
169. read	207. own	245. paper	283. Indian
170. need	208. below	246. together	284. really
171. land	209. country	247. got	285. almost
172. different	210. plant	248. group	286. let
173. home	211. last	249. often	287. above
174. us	212. school	250. run	288. girl
175. move	213. father	251. important	289. sometimes
176. try	214. keep	252. until	290. mountain
177. kind	215. tree	253. children	291. cut
178. hand	216. never	254. side	292. young
179. picture	217. start	255. feet	293. talk
180. again	218. city	256. car	294. soon
181. change	219. earth	257. mile	295. list
182. off	220. eye	258. night	296. song
183. play	221. light	259. walk	297. being
184. spell	222. thought	260. white	298. leave
185. air	223. head	261. sea	299. family
186. away	224. under	262. began	300. it's

Fry, E. B., Kress, J. E., & Fountoukidis, D. L. (1993). *The reading teacher's book of lists* (3rd Ed.). Paramus, NJ: Prentice Hall.

APPENDIX M: USEFUL WEBSITES AND FREE APPS

Suggested by Amy Thorna, from the Onondaga County Public Library in Syracuse, and Todd Evans, ProLiteracy's program administration and credentialing manager, with Ruth Colvin.

You, as tutors and teachers, can supplement your lessons and add to your own knowledge of teaching ESOL to adults by exploring electronic resources. You can also encourage your students to learn from them. We've included suggested websites and apps that might be helpful, but be aware that links change. Consult your librarian, or use Google or another search engine to locate web-based information that has moved.

Use the websites whenever you need additional help, but remember that face-to-face teaching is most important. You'll note that some suggested websites are duplicated because they're relevant for both tutors/teachers and adult learners.

Websites for Teachers /Tutors

Dave's ESL Café

http://eslcafe.com

The Idea Cookbook has lesson ideas on many different topics including pronunciation, listening, writing, and math.

About.com

http://www.about.com

Click Explore Topics and then on English as 2nd Language. Teachers can access printable quizzes, lesson plans, and information on best practices and training.

English-zone.com

http://english-zone.com/index.php

In addition to many activities for students, the site also has a teacher's zone with worksheets, games, and other teaching ideas.

OWL Purdue Online Writing Lab

http://owl.english.purdue.edu

The OWL site has an ESL section. In it, teacher resources include information on professional organizations, scholarship and policy resources, and links to teaching tools.

The First 100 Most Common Words in English

http://www.duboislc.org/EducationWatch/First100Words.html

From this site, you can get to the second hundred, third hundred, etc., up to 1,000.

Although the **Internet TESL Journal** is no longer published, the journal's archives hold many useful materials for teachers.
http://iteslj.org/t

Government funding requires standardized assessments. You can review websites for the **BEST Literacy/BEST Plus** and **CASAS** tests.
http://www.cal.org/aea
http://www.casas.org

I SPEAK ENGLISH, 5TH EDITION

Translations can be helpful for lessons with beginning students and for instant translation of a text or individual words. Try these three sites:

http://www.microsofttranslator.com
http://www.freetranslation.com
http://www.appliedlanguage.com/free-tools

ProLiteracy Education Network (EdNet)

http://www.proliteracyednet.org

Free online courses, lesson plans, activities, techniques, and strategies for adult education instructors.

Web English Teacher

http://www.webenglishteacher.com/esl.html

Provides links to a wealth of materials for teaching ESL students. The target audience is K–12 learners, but much of the content could be adapted for adults.

Adult Learning Activities

http://www.cdlponline.org

This site is a product of the California Distance Learning Project. It has stories on many topics with audio or video support as well as follow-up activities and games.

Bloom's Taxonomy

http://edorigami.wikispaces.com/Bloom's+Digital+Taxonomy

In 1956, a group of educational psychologists developed a classification of levels of intellectual behavior important in learning—Bloom's Taxonomy. It was updated in the 1990s. Andrew Churches (2009) has adapted the revised taxonomy to the digital environment. You can read about his version at this website.

Search Google for "**International Gesture Body Language**" to find many sites that describe specific gestures and their international meanings.

Websites for Students (Adult Learners)

Dave's ESL Café

http://eslcafe.com

For students, there are lessons in grammar, idioms, phrasal verbs, and slang; quizzes for testing skills; and forums on many different topics that allow English language learners to communicate with each other.

About.com

http://www.about.com

Click Explore Topics and then on English as 2nd Language. Student courses for beginning English, a word of the day, grammar, and vocabulary. Learners can take quizzes and practice speaking.

English-zone.com

http://english-zone.com/index.php

Activities for learners to study grammar, idioms, pronunciation, and reading.

OWL Purdue Online Writing Lab

http://owl.english.purdue.edu

Handouts covering grammar rules and exercises for practicing them. Also resources for studying writing skills and business writing skills.

Randall's ESL Cyber Listening Lab
http://www.esl-lab.com

Gives students practice listening to real people speaking in conversational voices. General listening quizzes are organized into easy, medium, and difficult lessons. Each listening quiz includes a pre-listening exercise, listening exercise, vocabulary activities, and post-listening exercises. Also includes basic listening quizzes and 20-minute vocabulary lessons.

Activities for ESL students
http://a4esl.org

Over 1,000 self-study quizzes on grammar, homonyms, idioms, and vocabulary. Also bilingual quizzes in 49 languages, podcasts, videos, and crossword puzzles.

USA Learns
http://www.usalearns.org

Great site for comprehensive instruction in beginning to intermediate English. Animated instruction gives students practice in listening, speaking, reading, and writing.

Merriam-Webster's Learner's Dictionary
http://www.learnersdictionary.com

Type in any English word to get a definition, examples of use, and pronunciation. Includes a word of the day that learners can subscribe to and have emailed to them. *My Learner's Dictionary* lets users build a personal dictionary of meaningful vocabulary, provides a list of the 3,000 most common English words, and includes audio pronunciation exercises.

Merriam-Webster's Visual Dictionary Online
http://visual.merriam-webster.com

Great tool for learners who are able to visually choose topics and vocabulary such as clothing, house, earth, society, and sports. Labeled diagrams help learners make sense of a wide range of English words.

GCF Learn Free
http://www.gcflearnfree.org

Reading lessons can be personalized for learners. Learners can brush up on math skills, using tutorials for addition and subtraction, multiplication and division, fractions, decimals, and percents. Study basic computer skills.

The Everyday Life Project
http://www.gcflearnfree.org/EVERYDAYLIFE

Life is filled with chaos, and we have to learn how to work and solve problems in the midst of it every day. These interactive lessons give students the opportunity to experience these daily challenges without real-world consequences.

News for You
http://www.newsforyouonline.com

This easy-to-read weekly news source for adult ESL and ABE students is now available online and in an app for iPhones and iPads. Students can listen to seven news stories each week, either sentence by sentence or in full as they read along. They can write comments on those stories, too. Online exercises and puzzles are included. Contact New Readers Press if you would like to learn more about subscribing.

Websites for Professional Development

ProLiteracy Education Network (EdNet)
http://www.proliteracyednet.org (formerly Thinkfinity)

Self-paced courses for instructors include online courses and webinars. Detailed lesson plans and best practices will help tutors improve their teaching techniques.

National Center for Family Literacy
http://www.famlit.org

Details about initiatives, research and statistics on family literacy, a newsletter, projects, an FAQ, press releases, and links to community programs.

Minnesota Literacy Council
http://www.themlc.org

Resources for tutors including instructions on lesson planning, tutoring tips, and lessons that accompany their *Reading for Life* Curriculum. Online courses, some of which are free, and some of which offer continuing education credits. Educational website search.

National English Language Learning Development
http://www.ell-u.org

Free professional development portal for adult ESOL educators where teachers can learn more about the latest thinking in the field.

Websites for Specific Subjects

English Club
http://www.EnglishClub.com

Lessons, games, quizzes, forums, chat rooms, lesson plans, and more for ESL learners and teachers.

Dave's ESL Café
http://www.eslcafe.com

Information on employment overseas as well as helps on resources, games, etc.

Azar Grammar
http://www.azargrammar.com

Go to Classroom materials. There you can download free "Fun with Grammar" for beginners, intermediates, or advanced learners. Includes worksheets and activities.

Math—Changemaker
http://www.funbrain.com/cashreg/index.html

Targets school-age students, but adult students can practice making change in easy, medium, and hard levels.

Math.com
http://math.com

This site is geared to school-age learners, but games are applicable to adults. Free instruction is offered on many different math topics, with unlimited practice exercises.

Guide to Grammar and Writing
http://grammar.ccc.commnet.edu/grammar

Many resources are available for both tutors and learners at a higher level, as are multiple grammar rules handouts. Students can test their knowledge with online graded tests.

ESL Games
http://www.eslgamesworld.com

It is directed toward children, but beginning adults can have fun with grammar games and other activities. Teachers can download activities for lessons.

ManyThings.org
http://www.manythings.org

Quizzes, word games, word puzzles, proverbs, slang expressions, anagrams, a random-sentence generator, songs, and other computer-assisted language learning activities for English language learners.

Healthy Roads Media
http://www.healthyroadsmedia.org/index.htm

Health information in many languages. Some of it is in audio or video as well as print form. The information in English is written in simplified language.

Free Apps for English Language Learners (Smartphones and Tablets)

Johnny ESL by Johnny Evtimovski

This is an ESL book app especially for students who study business English. They can study grammar, idioms, reading, and pronunciation.

ESL Express: Words Frequently Confused Lite by Yorgos Avgoustidis

This app covers difficulties that occur because of similarities in the sounds of two different words.

Grammar Up: Free Edition by Eknath Kadam

This app is designed to replicate questions with a business focus commonly found in the TOEIC test. Helps learners improve grammar and vocabulary.

Grammar Express: Tenses Lite by Eknath Kadam

This app helps learners master English grammatical tenses.

Pronunciation Power by English Computerized Learning

This app is an easy way to learn the 52 sounds of the English language. Includes side- and front-view animations of the mouth, jaw, and tongue; sample words for each sound; and comparative words.

American Idioms Challenge by iWillSpeak

This app includes quizzes on many different American idioms.

GCF Vocabulary Videos by Goodwill Community Foundation

This vocabulary dictionary uses short video clips to explore the most common words in the English language.

Merriam-Webster Dictionary by Merriam-Webster, Inc.

The dictionary gives definitions from the *Merriam-Webster Collegiate Dictionary* as well as voice search, audio pronunciation, an integrated thesaurus, and a word of the day.

Examples of Lessons in Each of Five Levels

In all lessons, it is useful to include elements of the four communication skills—listening, speaking, reading, and writing. The specifics will differ depending on the level of your students, what they want to learn, and what types of material you use. The following examples take you through one general content objective at five different language levels to show the associated progression in complexity. These are not lesson plans in the strict sense, with timed sequences for instructional activities. Rather, they illustrate how to integrate language skills for a given topic and show the developmental complexity of the lessons. They are based on a student's language level. Use the sample lessons as a model or a framework as you begin planning with and for your own students.

How do you find and determine learner-centered subjects to be included in your lesson plans? There are several ways.

- Language Experience (page 119)
- Problem posing and solving (page 172)
- Ideas from MELT (Appendix C, page 202)
- Ideas from conversation starters (Appendix G, page 212)

In the following examples, assume that you and your students have identified "shopping for food" as a topic of interest.

Beginning Learners Who Know NO English

Content Objective: Build self-confidence and teach very basic listening/speaking skills

- Teach a simple greeting so that students can say and respond to their names in a greeting.
- Use colored paper exercises (Appendix F, page 209). Bring colored paper in different colors and sizes.
- Use Total Physical Response (page 74), again stressing comprehension.
- Bring a basket of fruit and/or vegetables (real or artificial), and/or pictures of food, or *The Oxford Picture Dictionary,* and use the same techniques as used in the colored paper exercises, substituting the words for fruits and vegetables as you identify those items.
- Add more exercises using the words they've learned: substitution drill, response drill, transformation drill (pages 90–95).
- Start teaching the sounds of consonants. Use words the students have learned (e.g., teach the sound of /f/ using *food* or *fruit* as a key word) (page 125).
- Teach a simple dialogue in an area of interest to students (page 105).

- When students can understand and speak even a little, try having them tell *you* whatever they want using Language Experience (page 119).

Beginning Learners
Content objective: Shopping at the market for food

- Work with actual food items (real or artificial), with pictures of food items, or work from *The Oxford Picture Dictionary*.

- Have students make a shopping list from the pictures. Limit it to a few items. Adapt the Language Experience process.

- Practice listening comprehension by showing the pictures and saying the names of the food, and continue as you did using the colored paper exercises.

- Make flashcards of the words ahead of time, and ask the students to read them. Ask students to write the words on the backs of the pictures.

- Practice the substitution drill (*I want to buy some _____*) and other simple drills (page 90).

- Teach simple grammar lessons such as when to use *a* or *an* (*a banana, a pear, a red apple; an apple, an orange*).

- If possible, make plans to go to the market with the students at a later date, or suggest that they go individually. When they are there, ask them to identify the names of important food items.

- Point out the differences in prices of different brands.

Low-Intermediate Learners
Content objective: Shopping at the market for food

- Work with actual or artificial food items or with pictures of food items from *The Oxford Picture Dictionary*. Use dialogue, role playing, vocabulary building. Ask questions as suggested in conversation starters (Appendix G, page 212). Practice listening comprehension activities.

- Have students make a shopping list from the pictures. Group the list items according to food type.

- Ask students to make flashcards of food items and note on the back the food type to which each item belongs.

- Ask students to cut pictures of foods out of newspaper food ads you have brought, and have them sort the pictures by food category and item.

- Read and discuss with students the contents of the ads.

- Practice simple and complex substitution drills (e.g., *Harold bought lettuce, tomatoes, and carrots to make a salad. Martha bought wine, steak, potatoes, and French bread to prepare a special meal.*) Create more complex drills using food items as the basis.

- Grammar lesson: sounds of -ed at end of words (*tasted, reached, pictured,* etc.) (page 89).

- If possible, make plans to go to the market with the students later, or suggest they go individually. Point out names of food items, compare prices of different brands, and figure out the final prices after using coupons.

High-Intermediate Learners

Content objective: Shopping at the market for food

- Discuss with students what they need help with in shopping for food. Possible topics may include "stretching" dollars, doing comparison shopping, or assessing nutritional value of food items.

- In preparation for a major shopping trip, have students make a list of essential and nonessential items that they would purchase.

- Have students cut out coupons in the newspaper in preparation for the trip. Discuss the potential value of the coupons, and make sure that your students understand all the fine-print details. Add new vocabulary, using patterned words.

- Bring in canned or boxed food items of varying sizes, and discuss nutritional information with your students.

- Bring in a general text on nutrition to help students make appropriate food choices. Read it to your students to stimulate discussion. Have them paraphrase the message of the text and then write up their own version (Language Experience).

- Discuss and plan possible meal selections for the week that would help them organize shopping. Discuss the amounts of money required. Ask your students to create a meal list for the week.

- If possible, go to the market together, or suggest they go individually. Work with the list, budget, and coupons. Do comparison shopping, noting differences in prices among various brands and sizes of food items.

- Grammar lesson: contractions (*isn't = is not, won't = will not,* etc.).

- Discuss with your students how the trip went, problems they encountered (if any) and possible solutions, and plans for going to the market next time. For homework, have them write up their experiences (adaptation of Language Experience).

Advanced Learners

Content objective: Shopping at the market for food

- Discuss with students what they may need or want help with in shopping for food.

- Make sure that they have sufficient knowledge of comparison shopping, budgeting, coupon usage, and nutrition (see High-Intermediate section). Include a shopping trip and debriefing (in groups or individually).

- Identify and discuss newspaper articles from food sections or from various texts on nutrition, cooking, or meal customs from around the world.

- Ask your students to write out favorite recipes, including amounts of ingredients, for personal reference and possible sharing with others. Discuss as a possible project the idea of developing a collaborative cookbook that would have cultural information as well as recipes.

- Have your students identify and share names and locations of various specialty grocery stores or markets in the area.

- Have your students write inquiry or complaint letters or make phone calls to store owners. This would be a good opportunity to check grammar needs.

- Have your students prepare nutritional information for their children or their families or friends.

APPENDIX O: QUICK REFERENCE GUIDE—TECHNIQUES, STRATEGIES, AND ACTIVITIES

Most techniques, strategies, and activities can be adapted to all levels. (B=Beginner, I=Intermediate, A=Advanced)

LISTENING ACTIVITIES/STRATEGIES

- Colored paper exercises (B) pp. 76, 209
- Comprehension checks (all levels) p. 77
- Total Physical Response (B) p. 74
- Audio recordings (A) pp. 63, 74, 83, 187
- Telephone exercise (all levels) pp. 77, 152

SPEAKING ACTIVITIES/STRATEGIES

- Modeling English (B) p. 82
- Stress, rhythm, intonation patterns (I) p. 83
- Pronunciation (all levels)
  ○ Contractions p. 88
  ○ Homographs and homophones p. 89
  ○ Individual sounds p. 85
  ○ Linking p. 87
  ○ Minimal pairs p. 86
  ○ Pausing p. 88
  ○ Prefixes/suffixes p. 89
- Oral exercises
  ○ Backward buildup (B, I) p. 97
  ○ Chain drill (B, I) p. 99
  ○ Completion drill (I) p. 103
  ○ Continuing story (A) p. 104
  ○ Conversation starters (all levels), Appendix G, p. 212
  ○ Dialogue (all levels) p. 105
  ○ Idioms (A) p. 109
  ○ Response drill (B) p. 93
  ○ Restatement (B) p. 102
  ○ Sentence combining (B) p. 101
  ○ Sentence structure/grammar (I, A) p. 110
  ○ Substitution drill (B) p. 90
  ○ Transformation drill (B) p. 95
  ○ Vocabulary expansion (all levels) p. 112

READING TECHNIQUES/STRATEGIES/ACTIVITIES

- Cloze procedure (B, I) p. 132
- Comprehension (all levels) p. 131
- Consonants (B, I) p. 125
- Fluency (B, I) p. 130
- Language Experience (all levels) p. 119
- Phonics/letter-sound relationships (B, I) p. 125
- Sight words/context clues (all levels) p. 123
- Vocabulary expansion (I, A) pp. 112, 164–167
- Word patterns (all levels) pp. 127, 222

WRITING TECHNIQUES/STRATEGIES/ACTIVITIES

- Continuing stories (I, A) p. 104
- Grammar/sentence structure (all levels) p. 137
- Journals/letters (I, A) p. 137
- Manuscript/cursive (B) p. 133
- Note taking in lectures (A) p. 140
- Process writing (I, A) p. 134
- Spelling/punctuation (I) p. 139

GENERAL TECHNIQUES/STRATEGIES/ACTIVITIES

- Dictionaries—picture/bilingual (B, I) pp. 148, 158
- Games: listening/vocabulary/conversation/communication (all levels) p. 164
- Language structures (all levels) pp. 51, 110, 137
- Maps/directions (B, I) p. 155
- Music (all levels) p. 162
- Numbers/money (B, I) p. 152
- Problem posing/solving (all levels) p. 172
- Progressive picture stories (I) p. 150
- Role playing (I, A) p. 160
- Telephones/cell phones (B, I) p. 152
- Clocks/time (B, I) p. 151

BIBLIOGRAPHY

Adelson-Goldstein, J. (2008). *The Oxford picture dictionary: Monolingual English.* New York, NY: Oxford University Press (USA).

Auerbach, E. R. (1995). From deficit to strength: Changing perspectives on family literacy. In G. Weinstein-Shr & E. Quintero (Eds.), *Immigrant learners and their families* (pp. 63–76). McHenry, IL: Center for Applied Linguistics and Delta.

Auerbach, E. R. (1992). *Making meaning, making change: Participatory curriculum development for adult ESL literacy.* McHenry, IL: Center for Applied Linguistics and Delta.

August, D., & Shanahan, T. (Eds.) (2006). *Developing literacy in second-language learners: Report of the National Literacy Panel on language-minority children and youth.* Mahwah, NJ: Lawrence Erlbaum.

Baker, A., & Goldstein, S. (2008). *Pronunciation pairs: An introduction to the sounds of English* (2nd ed.). New York, NY: Cambridge University Press.

Bonham, L. A. (1988). Learning style instruments: Let the buyer beware. *Lifelong Learning, 11*(6), 12–16.

Burke, V., & Greenberg, D. (2010). Determining readability: How to select and apply easy-to-use readability formulas to assess the difficulty of adult literacy materials. *Adult Basic Education and Literacy Journal, 4*(1), 34–42.

Byrne, D. (1967). *Progressive picture compositions.* Harlow, England: Longman Group United Kingdom.

Churches, A. (2009). *Bloom's Digital Taxonomy.* Retrieved from http://edorigami .wikispaces.com

Colvin, R. J. (2011). *Lectura y escritura en Español* (D. Shoudy, Trans.) (3rd ed.). Syracuse, NY: Author. Available from ProLiteracy.

Colvin, R. J. (2009). *TUTOR 8* (8th ed.). Syracuse, NY: New Readers Press.

Colvin, R. J., & Root, J. H. (1999). *READ: Reading Evaluation—Adult Diagnosis* (5th ed.). Syracuse, NY: New Readers Press.

Crandall, J. A., & Peyton, J. K. (1993). *Approaches to adult ESL literacy instruction.* McHenry, IL: Center for Applied Linguistics and Delta.

CultureGrams Online. Retrieved from http://www.culturegrams.com

Daoud, A. M., & Celce-Murcia, M. (1979). Selecting and evaluating a textbook. In M. Celce-Murcia & Lois McIntosh (Eds.), *Teaching English as a second or foreign language* (pp. 302–307). Rowley, MA: Newbury House.

Datesman, M., Crandall, J., & Kearny, N. (2005). *American ways: An introduction to American culture* (3rd ed.). White Plains, NY: Pearson.

Donoghue, M. R., & Kunkle, J. F. (1979). *Second languages in primary education*. Rowley, MA: Newbury House.

Flavier, J. (1970). *Doctor to the barrios*. Quezon City, Philippines: New Day.

Freire, P. (2000). *Pedagogy of the oppressed: 30th anniversary edition*. New York, NY: Continuum.

Gardner, H. (2006). *Multiple intelligences*. New York, NY: Basic Books.

Gattegno, C. (1972). *Teaching foreign languages in schools the silent way* (2nd ed.). New York, NY: Educational Solutions. Retrieved from http://calebgattegno.org/teaching-languages.html.

Gramer, M. F. (2002). *The basic Oxford picture dictionary: Monolingual English* (2nd ed.). New York, NY: Oxford University Press.

Grognet, A. G. (1997). *Performance-based curricula and outcomes: The mainstream English language training project (MELT) updated for the 1990's and beyond*. Denver, CO: Spring Institute for International Studies. Retrieved from http://eric.ed.gov (ED416719).

Guzmán, B. (2001). *The Hispanic population: Census 2000 brief*. Washington, DC: U.S. Census Bureau.

Hadley, A. O. (2000). *Teaching language in context* (3rd ed.). Boston, MA: Heinle & Heinle.

Hall, E. T. (1966). *The hidden dimension*. Garden City, NY: Doubleday.

Hines, M. E. (1987). *Skits in English*. New York, NY: Prentice Hall College Division.

Ligon, F., & Tannenbaum, E. (1990). *Picture stories: Language and literacy activities for beginners*. White Plains, NY: Longman.

Marshall, B. (2002). *Preparing for success: A guide for teaching adult English language learners*. McHenry, IL: Delta.

Migration Policy Institute (2011). *LEP data brief*. Washington, DC: National Center on Immigrant Integration Policy. Retrieved from http://www.migrationinformation.org/integration/LEPdatabrief.pdf

Morley, J. (1991a). Listening comprehension in second/foreign language instruction. In M. Celce-Murcia (Ed.), *Teaching English as a second or foreign language* (2nd ed.) (pp. 81–106). Boston, MA: Heinle ELT.

Morley, J. (1991b). The pronunciation component in teaching English to speakers of other languages. *TESOL Quarterly 25,* 481–520.

Mydans, S. (2007, May 14). Across cultures, English is the word. *New York Times*. Retrieved from http://www.nytimes.com

Nash, A., Cason, A., Rhum, M., McGrail, L., & Gomez-Sanford, R. (1992). *Talking shop: A curriculum sourcebook for participatory adult ESL*. Washington, DC: National Clearinghouse on Literacy Education, Center for Applied Linguistics. Retrieved from http://eric.ed.gov (ED356687).

Nation, P. (Ed.) (1995). *New ways of teaching vocabulary*. Alexandria, VA: TESOL.

Nation, I. S. P. (2001). *Learning vocabulary in another language*. Cambridge, England: Cambridge University Press.

Nilsen, D. L. F., & Nilsen, A. P. (2010). *Pronunciation contrasts in English* (2nd ed.). Long Grove, IL: Waveland.

Nunan, D. (2003). *Practical English language teaching*. New York, NY: McGraw-Hill.

Parrish, B. (2004). *Teaching adult ESL: A practical introduction*. New York, NY: McGraw-Hill.

Peyton, J. K. (2000). *Dialog journals: Interactive writing to develop language and literacy*. Washington, DC: Center for Applied Linguistics. Retrieved from http://www.cal .org/caela/esl_resources/digests/Dialogue_Journals.html

Schmidley, A. D. (2001). *Profile of the foreign-born population in the United States*. Current Population Reports, Series P23-206. Washington, DC: U.S. Census Bureau.

Shaffer, J. C., & McLean, T. (1996). *English as a second language oral assessment (ESLOA)* (3rd ed.). Syracuse, NY: ProLiteracy Worldwide.

Smith, C. R. (2003). *Learning disabilities: The interaction of students and their environments* (5th ed.). Boston, MA: Allyn & Bacon (Pearson).

Tuckman, B. W., & Jensen, M. A. C. (1977). Stages of small-group development revisited. *Group & Organizational Studies, 2*(4), 419–427.

U.S. Census Bureau (2011). *Current population survey: Annual social and economic supplement 2010* (Tables 3.1 and 3.5). Retrieved from http://www.census.gov/population/ foreign/files/cps2010/T3.2010.pdf

U.S. Government Accountability Office (2009, July 29). *English language learning: Diverse federal and state efforts to support adult English language learning could benefit from more coordination*. Report GAO-09-575. Washington, DC: Author. Retrieved from http://www.gao.gov/products/GAO-09-575

Vella, J. (2002). *Learning to listen, learning to teach* (rev. ed.). San Francisco, CA: Jossey-Bass.

Weintraub, L. (2012, 2009). *Citizenship: Passing the test*. Syracuse, NY: New Readers Press. (This series includes student books titled *Civics and Literacy* and *Literacy Skills,* both at the literacy to low-beginning level, and *Ready for the Interview,* at the high-beginning to intermediate level. There is also a *Teacher's Guide* for the whole set.)

Wrigley, H. S. (2003). A conversation with FOB: What works for adult ESL students. *Focus on Basics, 6*(C), 14–17. Retrieved from http://www.ncsall.net/?id=189